3/17

THE
LOCKERBIE
BOMBING

THE LOCKERBIE BOMBING

THE SEARCH FOR JUSTICE

KENNY MacASKILL

Biteback Publishing

First published in Great Britain in 2016 by
Biteback Publishing Ltd
Westminster Tower
3 Albert Embankment
London SE1 7SP

ISBN 978-1-78590-072-3

10 9 8 7 6 5 4 3 2 1

A CIP catalogue record for this book is available from the British Library.

Set in Minion Pro and Brandon Grotesque by Adrian McLaughlin

Printed and bound in Great Britain by
CPI Group (UK) Ltd, Croydon CR0 4YY

To Linda Hamilton, Linda Pollock, Ian Inglis and Karen Newton,
who stood with me where others feared to tread.

CONTENTS

INTRODUCTION

On the cold winter's night of Wednesday 21 December 1988, a jumbo jet departed from London bound for New York. It hadn't taken off from Scotland, nor was ever scheduled to land there. Yet its impact on this country was to be momentous; its span international in reach and its consequences set to linger for years to come, if not for ever. It was to be the site of a terrorist atrocity that killed all aboard and many more in the small Scottish town below. It unleashed grief and heartache that reverberated around the world. It also marked the start of one of the biggest criminal investigations ever seen and the launch of one of the greatest whodunnits of all time.

As with so many transatlantic flights between northern Europe and North America, this flight would follow the great north circle route, heading up towards Scotland after take-off. Aviation, being steered by the curvature of the earth rather than a straight line, sees most flights head north towards Iceland and Greenland, before often making landfall in eastern Canada.

On a clear night in Scotland many planes can be seen high in the sky following that route, but the journey time over this small country will be short and often the land will go unnoticed by those aboard, obscured by darkness or hidden below the clouds. At most, it may be visible only by the lights of towns and cities sprinkled below. That Wednesday in December 1988 was also the winter equinox and the shortest day of the year. Darkness had already closed in on Scotland as it prepared for the longest night.

Down in London, the airport was a microcosm of what was happening all over the country and in many other lands. With Christmas fast approaching, business was being concluded, universities and schools had broken up for recess and people were heading home to be with family or friends. Many travellers were joyful and in a holiday mood as they did their last-minute Christmas shopping at duty-free, whilst others were more subdued or frenetic with the stress that comes with every such occasion. For the majority, take-off would be a brief lull before the festive storm.

London Heathrow, like many other airports around the world, was busy that evening, with literally thousands of flights arriving from around the globe. Pan Am flight 103 was one of hundreds of commercial flights to depart from London Heathrow that day, and it was bound for New York JFK airport. The plane, a Boeing 747-121, was named *Clipper Maid of the Seas*. There was nothing unusual or untoward about it. It had been in service for eighteen years but had undergone a major overhaul the year before. Maintenance work had been carried out with regularity but there were never any doubts expressed about the plane's safety from either flight or ground crews. The pilot, Captain Jim MacQuarrie, fifty-five years old and from New Hampshire in the United States, had many years' experience and flight time. His first officer, Ray Wagner, aged fifty-two, and flight engineer, Jerry Don Avritt, aged forty-six, were likewise seasoned flyers. They were based at JFK and on that fateful day in December were returning home. The cabin crew, a complement of two pursers (cabin managers) and eleven flight attendants, were based at Heathrow. They encompassed a range of nationalities; though many lived in the London area to suit their work schedule, some had applied for US citizenship to make matters smoother with regard to their employment with Pan Am. They, too, were experienced, in the main, with service periods ranging from eight months to twenty-eight years with Pan Am, and in age from twenty to fifty-one years. Doubtless, they were hoping for an uneventful flight and a speedy return in time for Christmas.

The flight was bookable from Frankfurt, Germany, through London Heathrow and New York JFK, onto Detroit, US. A different plane had brought the passengers booked through from Germany into London. Upon arrival at Heathrow, they then embarked, along with unaccompanied luggage from the Frankfurt flight, with the London-booked travellers upon the Boeing 747 for the transatlantic leg of the journey. The 243 passengers came from twenty-one different countries and five continents. Thirty-one were from the UK. Most, though, were American, with 178 coming from the US, many of them from the states of New Jersey and New York.

One prominent traveller was Bernt Carlsson, the United Nations Commissioner for Namibia, who was heading to the UN headquarters for a signing ceremony the following day. Volkswagen America had both their CEO and their Marketing Director on the flight,

returning from a meeting in Germany. Four US government officials were also on board, including Matthew Gannon, the CIA's
Deputy Station Chief, and Major Chuck McKee with the Defense
Intelligence Service, both based in Beirut, Lebanon. Two special
agents accompanied them as security guards. Thirty-five passengers
were students from Syracuse University in upstate New York. They were
going home for Christmas from the university's London campus
where they'd been since the autumn. Musicians, poets, writers, actors
and scientists were also on board. Most, though, were just ordinary
folk travelling to be with their families, looking forward, along with
the crew, to the upcoming festivities.

There were some who had been booked onto the flight but
did not board the plane. One such individual was an Indian car
mechanic who had been in Belfast for a family wedding and was
returning to New York where he lived and worked. He had checked
in but, delayed by friends and relatives in the bar eager to say
goodbye, had missed the flight. His luggage made it but not him.
(Suggestions were later made about a link to Sikh terrorism or
even, given the wedding venue, Northern Ireland, but all were
without foundation.)

Some celebrities were also amongst those scheduled to fly. The
Sex Pistols' Johnny Rotten had booked but missed the flight due to
other commitments. The same happened to a band called the Four
Tops. They'd been on a European tour and were heading back to
the US for Christmas, but a delayed recording session and oversleep
meant they never even made it to the airport. For once, their hec-
tic schedules worked in their favour. The Swedish tennis star Mats

Wilander and American actress Kim Cattrall had made earlier reservations but did not proceed further.

For those on board the plane, as well as those on the ground, there was nothing untoward on that cold and dark December night. All was peaceful as the plane left the terminal gate just after six o'clock. The jet queued for runway take-off before becoming airborne at 18.25 – a slightly later departure than scheduled. It approached the Solway Firth, one of the natural borders that separates England from Scotland, at 19.01, crossing it shortly after.

The Solway forms one of the larger firths (the Scottish word for a large bay of estuary, of which, given its significant coastline and island communities, Scotland has many) and for centuries it has had strategic importance, providing a natural barrier for the Scots from their larger and more powerful southern neighbour. It afforded protection from invasion as well as sanctuary for those 'border reivers' who raided south then retreated north with their booty. No such protection, it would turn out, could be provided from the skies above.

The Treaty of Union signed between Scotland and England in 1707 ensured a distinct civic identity for the Scots through separate and distinctive church, law and education systems. Since that night in 1988, a Scottish Parliament has been re-established and, in 2014, an unsuccessful referendum on independence has taken place. But, crossing the firth both then and now takes you into a different nation as well as legal jurisdiction. Few on board, though, would have known or cared about the historical events or legal niceties of the firth. In any event, it is crossed by a modern jet plane in a matter of seconds.

Radio contact was made with Air Traffic Control at 18.58 and the plane crossed the Solway coast at 19.02. It was cleared for its transatlantic crossing a matter of seconds thereafter. The crew, doubtless happy to have taken off without any issues, and with their route confirmed, could set course for New York. That message from Shanwick Oceanic Area Control, logged at 19.02.44, received no response from the flight crew. The cockpit voice recorder, once it was located, disclosed a loud sound at 19.02.50. It was at this moment that a bomb, later revealed to have been placed in the hold, exploded with catastrophic effect. It literally punched a hole in the plane. Within three seconds of detonation, the nose of the aircraft was separated from the main section and the plane hurtled to the ground in pieces across a wide expanse of land below. The flight recognition display disappeared from the radar screen. Instead, ominously, the operator at Shanwick could see five radar echoes fanning out where before there had been just a single one.

Such was the speed and effect of the explosion that there was no time for the crew to react with either distress calls or emergency action; no time, perhaps thankfully, for them or anyone on board to understand what was to be their fate. Subsequent investigation disclosed that, a mere eight seconds after the explosion, the wreckage had a spread of one nautical mile. Shortly thereafter, a pilot flying a shuttle flight between Glasgow and London reported to Air Traffic Control that he could see a huge fire on the ground below. Pan Am flight 103 was no more. What turned out to be a terrorist atrocity had destroyed it and all aboard.

And so began the investigation, and one of the biggest manhunts of the twentieth century. Only one man has ever been convicted in connection with the attack, yet even those who declare they are certain of his guilt are aware he didn't act alone. The pursuit of alleged accomplices, some known and others not, continues. Some profess his innocence and proclaim a miscarriage of justice. The case provokes debate and deeply divides opinion to this day. There are conspiracy theories and flights of fancy; some credible, others entirely incredible: was it state-sponsored terrorism, a terrorist group or even Western security services who were responsible? There have been trials and appeals and reviews.

There are court records and documents available, yet, a generation on, many of those involved, with some knowledge of the truth, are now dead or have gone to ground, taking their secrets with them. Libya has seen Gaddafi isolated, fêted, then toppled and has gone from military dictatorship to being on the brink of becoming a failed state. Presidents, Prime Ministers and law officers have come and gone in other countries, yet still the mystery remains.

I was neither involved with the disaster nor the investigation that followed. Yet, twenty years later, as Justice Secretary for Scotland, I found myself having to deal with consequences of those events in a significant and life-changing way. During that time I dealt with police, politicians and prosecutors, judges and the judged, victims and perpetrators, both Libyan and American.

I was required to consider the application for release on compassionate grounds made by Abdelbaset al-Megrahi, the sole man convicted for the Lockerbie bombing. I chose to free him for reasons I will detail, and I did so following the laws and adhering to the values I believe we hold in Scotland. The decision was made in the face of enormous pressure to deny the request and without any commercial gain for me or my country. Given my role, I was at the centre of a huge media and political storm that followed and in many ways the judgment now defines me, for better or ill, and I live with the consequences of it still.

It was always assumed that much larger and more powerful forces than Scotland were at play where the bombing was concerned, and that the bombing itself only one part of a broader international intrigue. Most of that intrigue was unknown at the time of my decision. They show that the tragedy did not happen in isolation, but was a consequence of years of action and reaction, terrorism and counter-terrorism.

This book is, therefore, a reprise of those tragic events and the investigations that followed. Moreover, it shows that the trial and the subsequent legal wranglings were in some ways a side issue to major international, commercial and security deals, from which Scotland and I were entirely excluded. I knew at the time that Scotland was just a small cog in a big wheel, but what I did not realise then was just *how* small and *how* big. Powerful corporations and security organisations were as much involved as nation states or individuals, and this book brings them all together.

* * *

The plane had been travelling at a speed of 499 mph, flying 31,000 feet above the small Scottish market town of Lockerbie. Situated in Dumfries and Galloway, in south-west Scotland, 75 miles south of Glasgow and just 20 miles from the border with England, Lockerbie then, as now, had a population of roughly 4,000. There had been a community there for over 1,000 years, though a town of significant size only since the eighteenth century. Land plots were made available by the Johnstone family, who owned it in 1730, and a pretty market town began to develop. Transport has always played a major role in its history. Firstly, it functioned as a staging post for the Glasgow to London carriage and then the great architect Thomas Telford's Carlisle to Glasgow road was built to run through it. The construction of railways followed and it remains a railway halt on the main West Coast Main Line between Glasgow and London to this day. The main highway between Scotland and England, the M74, also runs adjacent to it. Travelling by train or car between London and Glasgow, therefore, the town of Lockerbie is impossible to miss.

Although an important transport link, it was as a market town that Lockerbie principally developed. Indeed, livestock remains an important industry, its lamb market catering for well beyond its natural catchment area. It was Gretna Green, however, only a few miles further south, with its blacksmith forge for marriage runaways, that was better known around the world. Though significantly smaller, the town had a romance attached to it that resonated south of the border, if not well beyond the UK, whilst Lockerbie was virtually unknown outside of Scotland. That, though, was about to change for ever.

The town faced economic challenges in the 1980s, as did many communities at that time. As with many rural areas it suffered from the loss of so many of its young people leaving for higher education or employment. However, it's a town with good schools and a fine community spirit, with a pretty town centre filled with attractive red sandstone buildings. Located in a particularly scenic part of the world, it is a great place to live and bring up a family.

A few major disasters had afflicted the south-west of Scotland but not the town of Lockerbie directly, and, in any case, they were from times long gone by; tragedies to be remembered, never expected to be repeated. The Quintinshill rail disaster of 1915, a crash that killed 226 and injured 246, occurred just a few miles further south on the line that runs through Lockerbie and remains the record for the largest loss of life in any rail disaster in the UK to this day. A troop train taking soldiers from Leith in Edinburgh to Liverpool for embarkation for the front in Gallipoli was involved initially in a collision with a local passenger train and then with a Glasgow-bound express train. A fire engulfed all three passenger trains as well as two goods trains nearby. Most on board were young soldiers destined not to fall in the slaughter on the beaches of Gallipoli but die tragically in their native land. However, few were locals.

Then, in the winter of 1953, another tragedy struck the area, though this time it occurred not on land but out at sea. On 31 January, the MV *Princess Victoria* sank in the North Channel between Scotland and Northern Ireland during a scheduled trip between Stranraer and Larne. 133 lives were lost when the ship went down in stormy seas and rescue vessels struggled in vain to reach despairing passengers and crew. It was a tragedy for the families who lost loved ones, as well as the coastal communities that suffered damage as a result of the storm that became known as the Great North Sea Flood of 1953. The town of Lockerbie was inland, however, and insulated from any damage.

* * *

Following the explosion, the fuselage of the plane initially and eerily kept going under its own momentum, until at 19,000 feet it began plummeting earthwards like a stone and onto the unsuspecting town below. The aircraft then fractured, with one section attached to the wings landing in Sherwood Crescent, where the jet fuel inside exploded into a fireball, destroying several houses and incinerating those within. A huge crater, over 150 feet long, lay where homes and families had once been. Sherwood Crescent is adjacent to the M74 and the fireball crossed the land between it and the highway, scorching cars heading south. Another section of the fuselage landed in Park Place, over a mile away. Burning bits of debris careered up roads. The impact was so strong that it registered 1.6 on the Richter scale and the fireball so bright that some thought the nearby nuclear power station at Chapelcross had exploded. In terms of damage, it was as if a bomb had landed on the town of Lockerbie – in a way, one had.

Given the altitude at which it had been flying and the power of the explosion, the debris from the plane and the bodies of many of the victims were scattered far and wide. They went well beyond the town of Lockerbie, onto surrounding fields and moorland for miles. The nose section of the aircraft ended up near the church in the village of Tundergarth, some three miles south-east of the town. The captain and his flight crew, along with a flight attendant and some first-class passengers, were located still strapped in their seats. The flight attendant was found alive by a local resident in a farmer's field but died before medical aid could be administered. Though, given the shock and trauma in descending from such a height and in those circumstances, it's doubtless that they were a witness to merely the last flicker of life and no medical care could have assisted.

The distance over which items were scattered was vast. Two plastic bags of debris were later handed into police near Morpeth, Northumberland, hundreds of miles away in north-east England, by a lady who found them spread over fields near her home. Other farmers and locals in this area, having heard of the disaster, started picking up items strewn in adjacent fields as well. They included fragments of what would later be identified as a Toshiba radio cassette recorder and an item of great significance in the investigation that followed. Another vital piece of evidence, a portion of a shirt, was found in Newcastleton in the Scottish Borders, but still some considerable distance from Lockerbie.

All 243 passengers and sixteen crew members that were aboard Pan Am flight 103 were killed, as were eleven Lockerbie residents on the ground. It remains both the worst terrorist atrocity ever perpetrated in Britain and the largest loss of life in an air disaster in the UK. Not only the community, but the entire world was stunned. Lockerbie and, indeed, Dumfries and Galloway were quiet, rural areas with very little crime. Scotland was not a place where people lived in fear of their lives or endured terrorist atrocities.

One hundred and seventy-eight of the passengers and eleven of the crew were US citizens. Though more lives had been lost in the bombing of the US Marine corps in Beirut in 1983, this was an attack upon American civilians, ordinary people going about their daily business. The atrocity sent shockwaves across the US and seared deep in the American soul as terror hit home. They would not forget and would seek justice and retribution.

Thirty-one passengers and one crew member were UK nationals. Britain had never seen any attack on this scale before, and nothing equivalent in terms of a terrorist atrocity had ever occurred in Scotland. Only the devastation caused by German air raids during the Second World War bears any comparison.

The Irish Troubles had seen bombings and slaughter in Ulster and sometimes even on mainland UK. TV screens had shown car bombings and other atrocities on a regular basis. There had even been the attempt by the Provisional IRA to blow up Margaret Thatcher and her Cabinet in the Brighton bombing in 1984. Viewers were used to it, but not at this level of carnage. Life had changed in some ways in the preceding years, with security heightened at bus and rail stations as well as airports. Left luggage became a thing of the past. But still it remained primarily an issue for Northern Ireland, with the occasional incident elsewhere that was seen on the TV screens or read about in the newspapers. Terrorism happened, but not in Scotland, or so it had been assumed.

The town of Lockerbie itself lost eleven of its community as the fuselage and other parts of the plane smashed into it with catastrophic effect – a huge number for such a small community.

Like most Scots, I can recall exactly where I was when I first heard the tragedy begin to unfold. I was at home in the flat that my wife and I had in the south side of Edinburgh. She was out at the time, though hadn't gone far as she was four months pregnant with our second child. I was at home looking after our son, then thirteen months old. I vividly recall having settled him down and putting on the television. I'd missed earlier news broadcasts so switched on

Channel 4 News. It was just before 8 p.m., and the programme was about to finish. Suddenly, right at the end, the announcer indicated that news had come in that a plane had gone missing over south-west Scotland. The name of the town wasn't mentioned, nor was the cause of the incident. No other information was given or was doubt-less available, but no viewer could have missed the concern in the announcer's tone. Something was obviously seriously amiss.

I recall mentioning the news to my wife when she returned. Whilst Scotland had experienced aviation tragedies, for a plane to go missing was unheard of and I like many others had a sense of foreboding. By the time the later evening news bulletins came on, information of the tragedy was being revealed. News crews and journalists were heading for Lockerbie and the world was soon being shown the devastation caused by the downing of the aeroplane. Information was still unclear, however, and reports were scattered. The cause of the crash wasn't yet known; the focus understandably being on the crash scene and the impact on the town. I also remember the heart-breaking footage of families waiting forlornly for loved ones, never to arrive, in New York.

By the following morning, news reports were beginning to nar-rate the catastrophe and photographs and film displayed the true extent of the horror. The images were raw and harrowing. Broad-casters reported stories of huge sections of engine firing down the street in Lockerbie. These were not small pieces of debris or shrap-nel but huge engine parts and even a wing of the aircraft. It was not slight but serious damage that the town had sustained. The town was in a state of shock and the embers from fires seemed to be still burning in many parts.

The local people interviewed were explaining that they had no knowledge initially of what had happened, just that it was cataclysmic. The disorientation and bewilderment was understandable; and their consternation and concern evident. It was clear that it was a catastrophic incident and that no one would have survived from the plane crash.

Panoramic camera sweeps taken from the air by helicopter showed the town and surrounding area. The wreckage lay lonely on the moorland and the bleakness of the landscape at that time of year only added to the solemnity of the picture. Entire sections of the plane were clearly evident and seats could be seen embedded in the turf. Sadder still was the flotsam and jetsam, what had been people's personal possessions, simply lying about or blowing in the wind. Clothing and cases, papers and bags; matters of little consequence to others but each signifying a life that had once been. A picture, they say, is worth a thousand words, and so it was on this occasion. A bombsite was the best description for Sherwood Crescent, the epicentre for much of the destruction in the town. A giant crater now existed where once had been homes and families. No. 13 had been the home to Maurice and Dora Henry. Next door, in No. 15, lived the Somervilles: Jack and Rosalind and their children, Paul and Lyndsey, aged thirteen and ten. No. 16 was the home of the Flannigans: Thomas and Kathleen and their daughter, Joanne. Their son Steven, aged just fourteen at the time, survived, in one of those twists of fate, having gone to a neighbour's to have his sister's bike repaired.

He, however, had to not only witness it unfolding before his eyes, but had to live with it until his untimely death in 2000. Whether his tragic death was related to the events of Lockerbie can only be speculated on but his life thereafter cannot have been easy. His elder brother David was also away from home. He had moved out following a family argument and gone to stay in England but was due back on Boxing Day for a family reunion. That reunion sadly never took place. But he hurried home to Lockerbie on hearing the news. The following day when he visited the site, a neighbour told how he returned with a small plastic watering can – all he could recover from what had once been his family's home. He took the tragedy badly and seemed unable to come to terms with his grief; dying in Thailand in 1993. They are just a few of many sad and sorry tales that befell the town and its people.

The timing of the event added to the solemnity of the occasion. What was meant to be the season of good cheer seemed hollow when so many lives had been lost and such devastation had occurred. The news footage of grieving families in the US forlornly awaiting a loved one's arrival and leaving in tears and anguish was also shown around the globe. Thirty-five of the passengers were students from Syracuse University studying at their campus in London. Families were pictured seeking information about their children and struggling to cope with the cruelty of their loss. What had been meant to be a joyful reunion had become a wake. Bright and talented youngsters with the world at their feet had been blown from the skies and lost for ever.

It's often that a single black and white photograph can be more evocative in many ways than colour. There was a photograph and image in many papers of the nose cone standing on the bleak hillside. It was a haunting image of the tragedy. A Scottish Police officer in his coat to protect against the wind and weather, standing in front of the giant nose cone of a jumbo jet severed from the rest of the plane; and lying with debris from the flight strewn all around. It summed up both the loneliness of the occasion and the solemnity of the disaster.

Nothing could have prepared the community, county or country for what befell them on 21 December 1988. Emergency services reacted heroically and the local community responded likewise, displaying humanity that was to endear them to those that lost loved ones. The first calls emergency calls went to Dumfries and Galloway Constabulary and Dumfries and Galloway Fire Service. They may have been the smallest of the services in Scotland but they rose to the challenges that they and their community faced. Aid and assistance was soon to come from across the country. But, initially it fell to those few on duty and the citizens of the town and villages to do what they could to bring the situation under control.

Recollections from police early on the scene speak of both shock and disbelief. There were reports that a plane had crashed upon the town and surrounding countryside, though there was still no indication that terrorism had been the cause. The priority for them was to save any survivors, treat the injured and bring order and safety to the town.

Michael Stryjewski, a police officer who had watched the scene unfold from his home just outside Lockerbie, described the debris to the *Baltimore Sun* as running 'like a carpet across the countryside, a trail of devastation and bodies'. He'd heard jet engines and had then seen an orange glow in the sky from his window 'growing larger and coming downward'. He then 'saw shapes falling to the ground somewhere in Lockerbie ... There was a horrendous noise, an explosion, like a miniature atomic bomb, and a mushroom of cloud and flame went upward', reaching almost 1,000 feet. A colleague, Sergeant Ian McDowell, who'd been off duty but was soon at the scene, like others initially thought it may have been an explosion at the nearby nuclear power station at Chapelcross, or even a collision between two RAF planes from a base in the local area. He recalled that 'when people came out of their homes and found bodies lying about in their yard, they realised it had been a commercial flight. People were fainting in their yards.'[1] A local woman who was working in a garage forecourt that night recalled:

> It was a low rumble, like thunder, [that] came first, then the whole sky lit up. I was absolutely petrified. Suddenly everything started falling down – lumps of plane, bits of seatbelts, packets of sugar, bits of bodies. There were burning bits all over the forecourt. It seemed to shower for ages, but it was only about five minutes.[2]

One eyewitness who had a similarly lucky escape saw the fireball engulf Sherwood Crescent, and was within seconds enveloped in debris and deafening noise. The next thing he knew, an engine was careering towards him, screeching as it scraped along and dug into the road. It only came to rest in a parking lot, in front of houses, just two streets away from him.

---

1   *Atlanta Journal*, 24 August 1997
2   G. Sheridan and T. Kenning, *Survivors* (London: Pan Books, 1993)

Ella Ramsden, who lived at Rosebank Crescent, had been watching television when her dog suddenly became agitated. Seconds later, looking out of the window, the town was shrouded in an orange glow and the noise all-encompassing. Seeing an explosion at Sherwood Crescent, she picked up her dog and rushed to leave by her back door just as all the lights went out and then found she couldn't open the door. After that it wasn't noise but dust and plaster that cascaded down upon her. She survived, but her house had taken a direct impact from a part of the plane and was entirely wrecked. Her neighbour, Bunty Galloway, was also watching TV and ran to the front of her house when she heard the screaming noise. The sight that she beheld was gruesome indeed:

> There were spoons, underwear, headsquares, everything on the ground. A boy was lying at the bottom of the steps on the road. A young laddie with brown socks and blue trousers on. Later that evening my son-in-law asked for a blanket to cover him. I didn't know he was dead. I gave him a lambswool travelling rug thinking I'd keep him warm. Two more girls were lying dead across the road, one of them bent over garden railings. It was just as though they were sleeping.[3]

The body was to lie there for several days before being moved.

Constable McDowell remembered not just two engines coming to rest between two houses in Park Place, but a young girl who

---

3   Ibid.

was found hanging from a rooftop and still in her seat. Another house had almost twenty bodies in its garden alone. And it wasn't just the houses in the community that were hosting the dead – the golf course was to be an interim resting place for a total of sixty bodies.

That evening, in the aftermath of the crash, it was very dark, though fires still burned and embers smouldered. The weather was cold and wet and in some parts snow still lay. For those coming in even after midnight, flames were still visible. Tiles were torn off roofs, holes lay in others, and debris and carnage was both on the streets and in the rafters. On the roads and in gardens and hedgerows lay bits of aircraft seats as well as more sombrely broken bits of humanity. Human flesh and bodies littered the town and neighbouring countryside. Officers called in from other parts of the country recall driving through the town and approaching what they assumed to be a roundabout, only to discover that it was actually one of the engines of the aircraft.

Some people were walking about, looking anxiously for friends and relatives, whilst others huddled outside their shattered homes trying to come to terms with what had happened. An eerie silence seemed to prevail. Many recall the overpowering smell of aviation fuel – understandable, given that the town had been literally sprayed with it. A jersey caught in a tree and hanging forlornly and just blowing in the wind. An American passport partially obscured by an in-flight meal tray and all lying across a footpath of an ordinary home in an ordinary town in south-west Scotland. Those images remain in the memory of those who viewed them to this day.

It lay near to many homes and it was fortunate indeed that even more of the town had not been destroyed and more lives lost. However, even within the mayhem and shock some remember some light relief such as a wee boy showing a slight cut to his head and stating he'd been hit by a plane. In the main, though, it was a sight of death and carnage that prevailed. Some bodies seemed relatively intact in their seats, others had been smashed to smithereens whilst yet others were a strange concoction of parts intact and other bits warped and mangled. A gruesome scene for anyone, even those trained and expected to cope with such emergencies.

In the twenty-first century, where tragedies have become more common, emergency plans and computer systems immediately kick in when disasters such as these occur. Police and other emergency services action plans did exist in 1988, though nothing like this had ever been experienced in real life. Moreover, the technology, never mind the systems, was vastly different, if not archaic in comparison to that of today. Mobile phones had been invented but were not in common usage. Landline telephones were still the primary means of communication, not the plethora of social media that now exists. Similarly, word-processing was slowly making its way into the policing arena, but manual records remained the norm.

The situation was too big for any one force, however, and certainly for the smallest in Scotland. They couldn't be expected to deal with it on their own. Additional support was immediately offered by neighbouring constabularies. Strathclyde, as the largest and closest, as well as Lothian and Borders, prepared to despatch support. This, though, was going to stretch not just the local constabulary, but the entire police service the length and breadth of Scotland. Upon hearing news of the situation, officers around the country began to discuss their likely role, many leaving Christmas parties and gatherings early, conscious that they'd no doubt be heading to Lockerbie very soon.

It wasn't just the police and fire services who mobilised and arrived at the scene. Ambulance crews and health workers invoked their disaster plans and rushed to the site. However, after some initial treatment of the wounded, it soon became apparent that there was little for them to do. They hung around with their emergency vehicles, but their undoubted skills and desire to help were of no use. It was death, not injury, that confronted them. Crews from Strathclyde and Cumbria as well as Dumfries and Galloway just stood around, frustrated at their impotence. A journalist Andrew Cassel recalled:

> I knew within seconds of arriving in Lockerbie that there had been no survivors [from the crash]. The ambulances gave it away. They were strung out before me – two, three, four abreast – all along one of the country roads leading into the town. Their doors were splayed open in hopeful readiness, their flashing lights casting a flickering blue tinge to the Christmas decorations above them. But there was little sign of activity – no paramedics urgently preparing equipment, no police officers in sight, no drivers now running engines.[4]

---

4   BBC, 17 December 1998

The military were also quickly mobilised as existing plans to assist the civil power of police and local authority were instigated. The Royal Air Force was on the scene very early on, some not even in their uniform but simply in suits. Helicopters began to arrive not in ones or twos, but in squadrons. Chinooks, Sea Kings and every kind imaginable flew in. A police officer recalls knocking at a farmer's door and asking him to move his sheep as they had identified his field as a preferred landing site. The army followed, though a few military personnel had arrived soon after the crash. With the troubles in Northern Ireland still ongoing, the number of soldiers was significantly greater then than now. A regiment was quickly despatched down to Lockerbie to assist.

Soon after the arrival of the emergency services, the establishment of rudimentary incident and command rooms began. Lockerbie Academy, the town's high school, was opened up and became the location for the main site. The town hall was another, its first floor also serving as a makeshift mortuary. Everything was still chaotic as even the professionals struggled to cope, never mind comprehend. A teacher's desk in the main assembly hall of the school served as a very primitive, preliminary command space. Its technical room, usually used for teaching youngsters rudimentary skills in trades, was taken over by those in charge of communication and coordinating the emergency response. A temporary telephone exchange was soon obtained from British Telecom, who had fortunately been readying one already for the Open Golf Tournament, set to be held at Royal Troon the following summer, not far up the road. Officers responsible for noting down all the incoming information were quickly told to do so on paper that could be copied so that records could easily be checked later on. Records were simply kept in trays on the desk.

To try to create order amongst the chaos, a Superintendent was appointed to fulfil the duties of quartermaster – a role usually confined to the armed forces – to obtain paper and other essential supplies. Those involved recall simply trying to generally make do. One local Inspector asked for his own officers to be deployed on the streets of Lockerbie to provide reassurance to residents. On his makeshift desk, according to officers present, were two piles of paper, one labelled 'In', the other 'Out', that contained requests from members of the community and the constabulary. These were many and varied; from enquiries from officers as to whether leave that had been granted for a wedding would still be possible, to calls from members of the public who had human flesh on their carpet. Such was the scope and extent of the tragedy those involved in trying to create some order faced.

Still, things were haphazard, despite the best efforts of all to organise. Officers remember coming back to find that American TV stations had also established themselves in rooms in the school. Meanwhile, residents and others just strolled about almost at will it seemed. In due course order was imposed, though TV crews were still in the building, albeit away from the now-restricted area. Equally secure zones within the restricted area began to be established as the security services, along with the Air Accident Investigation Branch and the members of the Foreign Office, arrived.

Whilst those organisations inside the makeshift incident and command room made do and cooperated as best they could, the ordinary people of the town and surrounding area were also responding magnificently. The school's dinner ladies turned up for work to provide for those now installed in place of the usual children, locals arrived bearing bags of messages to support those working away within; and some even remember, rather humorously, that the school tuck shop was opened and its sweets made available for all.

Despite the initial disorganisation, bit by bit, order began to be imposed amidst the chaos that still reigned outside. It wasn't until the second day that major resources began to really arrive in the town. The Chief Constable of Dumfries and Galloway, John Boyd, gave a major briefing in the late morning the following day, many remembering the dignity he displayed whilst delivering it. Meanwhile, more officers continued to pour in to assist in the investigation, whilst some of those who had arrived on the scene earlier headed back for some brief rest. Notwithstanding the impressive performance of the local Chief Constable, discussions were ongoing in government, police and other circles as to who was going to lead the investigation. After all, Dumfries and Galloway was Scotland's smallest force and its staff and resources were limited. The Chief had himself previously been a Strathclyde officer, but the experience of the force's other senior officers in major incidents was quite limited.

It wasn't simply a case of which officer should be in charge, but also which jurisdiction. As the plane had taken off from London Heathrow, the Metropolitan Police had already established an Operation Avon into the plane crash. Given their experience with terrorism, but seemingly forgetting that Scotland was not in their jurisdiction, they had also sent officers to be on the ground in Lockerbie and assumed they'd be in the lead of the investigation. The Lord Advocate Lord Cameron of Lochbroom, Scotland's most senior law officer and prosecutor at the time, then made it clear that, since this atrocity had occurred on Scottish soil, it would be dealt with by Scottish Police and under Scottish Law. To be fair to them, the Metropolitan Police accepted this and quickly began to harmonise the investigations. In addition, Scottish officers were also despatched to London to liaise with the Met and link up with other national and international agencies. Many were to be there for quite some time.

There was never any likelihood of the Scottish officers being edged out. Initially there was a certain amount of awe amongst the ranks with regard to the high-profile events they found themselves involved with and the agencies that now surrounded them, whether the FBI, CIA, security services or whoever. Despite this, however, they were confident in their own abilities and never ceded their judicial responsibilities. All the Scottish officers, whether from Dumfries and Galloway or other constabularies, acted honourably and appropriately during the investigation and their role has rightly been acknowledged and honoured by other jurisdictions and law enforcement agencies since. It wasn't just in the early stages that the officers involved began to mix in elevated circles; in due course, they came into contact not only with British security services and the FBI, but many others, including the KGB and Mossad.

This, however, was an investigation like no other. The usual rules and procedures for those experienced in detective work were based more often than not upon a single locus, one victim, one suspect, with only the odd additional complication. Officers involved in the Lockerbie bombing instead faced a crime scene that extended over 846 square miles. Fragments and debris from the crash had landed not just in the town, but in the Solway Firth as well as the Keilder Forest, which extends for over 250 square miles in the north of England. The victims were multiple, their remains seldom complete and often unrecognisable as a human body, so extensive was the damage inflicted upon them. Of course, the highly sensitive task of recovering bodies brought challenges. The makeshift mortuary on the first floor of the Town Hall very quickly began to fill up. The historic old building that had hosted many vibrant community events now held growing rows of bodies. They were in vastly different states; some preserved and undamaged, others literally destroyed, smashed to smithereens. One old lady, whose home was entirely obliterated, was identified only by her artificial knee cap, which the doctor who had implanted it was able to confirm. That was all that remained of a human life.

The modern science and technology routinely available to police and forensic scientists now was in many instances not even invented then. DNA and software systems for data collection were at very early stages of development. Moreover, officers and pathologists had dealt with crash scenes and tragedies, but never on this scale or with this amount of trauma. Officers recall an initial, rather macabre discussion about what constituted a body for tagging as opposed to a piece of human remains for evidence. In the past mass searches of areas might have brutally been described as a 'bag and tag' of what you located. But here there were pieces of human life scattered everywhere and in every possible shape and size. Just what did you tag as a body and what was to be recorded as human remains? Whilst gruesome, it was necessary to make a distinction in order to make an assessment of the tragedy and ultimately issue victim numbers. There were also the families of the victims to consider; specifically, their basic human need for a body to grieve over and bury. Eventually a rudimentary criteria was established that said that a head would clearly justify identification, but legs, from the knee down, did not. So many bodies were in parts that such crude and tragic definitions were necessary.

Challenges such as this were considerable and also distressing for those involved. The preservation of the crash site alone was a huge test, given its scale, and this was only compounded by the sensitivities that go hand in hand with such a vast loss of life. The geography also posed difficulties. A local farmer warned police officers that unrecovered body parts would eventually come under threat from foxes, and though this sent shivers down the spines of many a hardened officer, a solution was impossible to devise given the sheer enormity of the area that had to be searched. Those in charge had to just work as quickly as they could without compromising the level of thoroughness that the search required. Though it is the case that the longer you faced it the more you became inured to it, there would always be sights that stood out as touching or particularly painful no matter how long you worked. One officer recalls walking through the makeshift mortuary and seeing a pair of lovely pristine feet and yet the body above was totally gone.

Pathologists recall bodies being located, still strapped into their aircraft seats, and yet embedded metres into the soft moorland on the outskirts of the town. As many a police officer has recounted after road traffic accidents, the bodies were seemingly untouched and gave the impression that the individual was simply serenely sleeping. Quite incredible given the trauma and drop but offering easy identification and a distinct human body for loved ones to grieve over. Trial and error also applied in some ways as officers and pathologists learned on the job – sometimes the hard way. Initially some victims had been coated in embalming fluid but when an RAF pathologist arrived and indicated that the bodies couldn't be properly X-rayed as a consequence, a young female officer was tasked to scrub them clean of it. A gruesome job became an awful lot worse.

Along with data collection technology – the Home Office Large Major Enquiry System – HOLMES – that is used now by all UK forces had then only recently been developed and was still undergoing its first major review following the Yorkshire Ripper case at the time. Dumfries and Galloway Constabulary didn't possess it, but Strathclyde had acquired it and it was therefore despatched down to the investigation team; landing by helicopter with a senior officer to assist in operating it.

As well as law enforcement and security agencies, other resources soon started to arrive from across the world, given the scale and global impact of the disaster. Some were technical, others very basic, but they were all welcome just the same. Dunlop, for example, sent Wellington boots for those police officers involved in the search and others tramping over miles of moorland and muddy terrain. It was the middle of winter, after all, and many officers were not properly kitted out for the work nor the weather at that time of year. In recognition of the flight's commencement in Frankfurt, BMW offered a fleet of vehicles. Many other smaller and more local enterprises acted likewise, not simply large multinational companies. When the Salvation Army went to the cash and carry store in Dumfries to replenish supplies for the mobile kitchens they'd assembled at Lockerbie, as they do at other such tragic scenes, they were waved through without payment being sought and told to return if more supplies were required.

The tragedy devastated the lives of many but it also brought out great humanity. The local police and the community were the real heroes and heroines. Many showed kindness not simply in those few hours after the event, but in the days and weeks beyond. Homes were opened and hands of friendship and generosity extended. Clothes that had been scattered to the wind from luggage jettisoned from the plane were washed and ironed by some local ladies before being returned to the families along with other personal effects. One victim's family even recalls that a journal kept by their daughter was also meticulously ironed and returned to them, providing an invaluable memory of the child they'd lost. Similar acts of kindness were displayed in a multitude of ways and the links that were forged as a result remain.

Some of those attending the disaster faced subsequent challenges. Post-traumatic stress disorder was known about but not provided for as much then. Many officers suffered, some left the service and others endured in silence. The community itself saw an increase in

issues and incidents as people struggled to cope with the consequences. Some were health problems such as respiratory problems
caused no doubt by the fuel and other chemicals from the plane that
lingered and affected people for years to come; others were alcohol
abuse and other social problems as people self-medicated to cope
with the trauma they had endured and experienced.

Within a few days terrorism was identified as the cause. The black
box, which all planes carry to record data in the event of any problem, was quickly located by those scouring the hillsides. It was then
accessed by the Air Accident Investigation Branch, who pored over
it. Their investigation showed that there were no technical problems
for the plane or issues with the flight itself. It did, though, disclose
the explosion that was clearly audible and not able to be explained
by any technical data recorded. That, along with fragments of both
the plane and other items on the ground, confirmed it had been a
bomb. But who had done it?

TURBULENCE IN THE AIR

The Lockerbie bombing was the worst terrorist attack sustained
by the UK and the deadliest upon US civilians before 9/11, but it did
not occur in a vacuum. There was anger, vengeance and conspiracy
in the air as the plane took off that evening; and it had been about
for quite some time.

It's easy to view terrorism as a more recent phenomenon. Atrocities
in Madrid, London and Paris, in 2004, 2005 and 2015 respectively,

as well as numerous other examples elsewhere in the world, most recently in Brussels, have shocked the world. Innocent citizens simply going about their business in Europe, spectating in the US or lying on a beach in North Africa, have been targeted and slain. Terrorism over the last two decades has dominated media coverage and political and public debate. Our day-to-day lives have been affected, too, in small ways, such as the restrictions on luggage and taking liquids when boarding a plane, and in larger ones, the considerably increased security powers of the state being a major example. Age or the vagaries of memory may result in many viewing the 1980s almost as halcyon days. That, however, would be a mistake.

Terrorism has changed and adapted since then, but it still existed in the latter decades of the twentieth century. Faces and organisations may have altered; Iraq and Syria replacing Israel and Palestine as the backdrop, Al Qaeda and ISIS for other acronyms, but the risks and the bloodshed were just as real. The Lockerbie bombing was a seismic shock, but there had been tremors felt and turbulence in the air before the events of 21 December 1988.

Initial suspicions about who was responsible for the attack fell upon the Palestinians and, in particular, the Popular Front for the Liberation of Palestine – General Command (PFLP-GC), founded by Ahmed Jibril, not without good reason. They were not alone, however, in being identified as possible suspects by police and Western intelligence services. Other Palestinian groups, along with Libyan Intelligence and even Iran, who were under constant monitoring and had been involved in many prior incidents, were all considered potential suspects for the atrocity.

It wasn't simply the pre-existing tensions in the Middle East or terrorist actions in Europe or elsewhere that gave credence to this theory. The Palestinian Liberation Organization (PLO) warned security services in Europe of a likely terrorist attack upon an airline by extremist groups just days before the bombing. At that time, the PLO were in preliminary discussions with the US, seeking to break the logjam in the Middle East. Those talks would ultimately lead to the Oslo Accords signed in the early 1990s, but, at the time of the warning in 1988, the dialogue was at an early and delicate stage. Keeping the Americans and the West informed would not only avoid an atrocity that might harm them, but would doubtless show them in positive light. Perhaps, they may have reasoned, it might even earn them some favours that they could then call in at a future date.

Another advance alert, this one received sixteen days before the incident, which became known as the 'Helsinki warning', implicated yet another Palestinian group. On 5 December, over a fortnight before the attack, the Federal Aviation Authority (FAA) had issued a security bulletin warning of a terrorist threat. This followed a telephone call made to the US embassy in Helsinki, Finland by a man with a Middle Eastern accent. He stated that a Pan Am flight from Frankfurt to the US would be blown up by the Abu Nidal Organization within the next two weeks. The Abu Nidal Organization was another dissident Palestinian group. The warning was taken seriously by American authorities and despatches were sent urgently to American embassies. That concern was mirrored by the FAA, who contacted all US airlines, including Pan Am. The US embassy

in Moscow apparently posted warnings on bulletin boards and notified the city's entire American community.

A few days after the crash, a Swedish-language newspaper in Finland reported that a State Department official in Washington had
confirmed that a warning had been given to the Helsinki embassy by
an anonymous caller. The article suggested that the caller had said
that a bomb would be transported from Helsinki to Frankfurt and on
to New York on a Pan Am flight. It was apparently to be carried
on by a woman who would not even be aware she was transporting
it. The newspaper reported that a similar warning had been made to
the Moscow embassy. The Finnish Foreign Ministry, though, insisted
that they had no evidence of any link with Lockerbie.

The article also speculated about the involvement of a Finnish
woman who had been married to a member of Abu Nidal's organisation, Samir Muhamed Khadir, who had been reportedly killed
earlier in the year in an explosion that was caused by the premature detonation of a bomb they were carrying. This occurred earlier
on the same day and at the same quayside as a terrorist attack against
the *City of Poros*, a Greek cruise ship that sailed between Athens
and Hydra, in which three armed men boarded and opened fire
indiscriminately. Nine passengers were killed and ninety-eight were
injured in the bloodbath that followed. The assassins escaped on a
speedboat. The Abu Nidal Organization was believed to have been
involved, with support from Libya, given that one of the killers had
entered Greece on a Libyan passport and the weapons used were of
Libyan origin. The ferry attack was believed to be retaliation for the
incarceration of a known Abu Nidal member, Muhammed Rashid,

who was fighting extradition from Greece to the US on terrorist charges. He was subsequently released by the Greek authorities and went to Libya after the incident.

The wider backdrop for the attack on the ship, however, as with other attacks at that time, had been revenge for the US military's attack on Libya that had taken place in April 1986 and had involved US air strikes on various military sites in Libya, though, ostensibly, civilian areas were also struck. Colonel Gaddafi's compound in Tripoli was also targeted, but he had fled after prior warnings had been given to him by other states of the raid, moments before it was about to occur. It's thought that sixty Libyans died, including Gaddafi's newly adopted daughter, Hanna. Whatever the precise death toll, it had certainly provoked anger and cries for revenge from Gaddafi and his allies, both in Libya and elsewhere.

These air strikes had themselves been retaliation for the Libyan-sponsored bombing of the 'La Belle' nightclub in Berlin, where three people, including an American serviceman, were killed and 229 were injured. That took place on 5 April 1986, just ten days before the Tripoli raids. Libyan agents who were subsequently prosecuted were shown to have operated from their country's embassy in East Germany. That bombing was seemingly the final straw for President Ronald Reagan and his Secretary of State Alexander Haig. Concern had been mounting for some time over Colonel Gaddafi and Libya not only in the US, but this attack brought matters to a head and air strikes swiftly followed.

The hostility towards Gaddafi was longstanding. Disputes had arisen under previous US administrations and presidencies. As far back as 1973 Libya had claimed the Gulf of Sidra, off its coast, as a closed bay and an integral part of its territorial waters. That was disputed by the US. In 1981, President Reagan had despatched a US Naval Task Force and in August of that year the Gulf of Sidra incident occurred, when an aerial confrontation took place in which two Libyan planes were shot down. The relationship between the West and the North African country had been deteriorating; as the knowledge and fears of the West towards Libya and vice versa were compounded both by actions and misunderstandings on both sides. Moreover, there were fears of Libyan access to nuclear weapons as their involvement in neighbouring and uranium-rich Chad continued apace. All in all, the United States vented their anger and showed their intention and capability to act.

That was the open confrontation, but there was also a covert one going on at the same time. Gaddafi had long made it clear that he would continue to support terrorist organisations, whether the IRA, Red Army Faction, Red Brigades or whoever. Terrorist attacks had taken place at Rome and Vienna airports on 27 December 1985, almost three years before Lockerbie, in which the Israeli airline El Al's counters and check-in desks at both airports were targeted simultaneously. Seven terrorists were involved and four were ultimately killed in the attacks and their aftermath. Nineteen civilians were killed, including a child, and over 100 others were wounded before El Al security guards and police brought it to a conclusion. The attacks had been blamed on the PLO but Yasser Arafat vehemently denied responsibility and denounced the actions of the perpetrators. Responsibility was later claimed by the Abu Nidal Organization in retaliation for Israeli attacks on the PLO headquarters in Tunis in October of that year. Reports suggested that Libyan Intelligence had supplied the weapons and organised the attacks and Libya was accused of funding, supplying and supporting the terrorists. Whilst Libya denied the first two charges, they did express their public support for the operations.

In addition, on 1 November 1987, the ship MV *Eksund* had been intercepted by the French Navy in the Bay of Biscay carrying weapons and ammunition for the Provisional IRA. The consignment contained not just firearms and explosives but also rocket launchers. Gaddafi had stated he'd support the Provisional IRA along with other terrorist organisations, and it's suggested he'd been doing so since 1985, and though the MV *Eksund* was intercepted, many other shipments from Libya reached their destination and were used in Northern Ireland against police and security services. There may have been an additional edge to the supply of armaments and munitions to the Provisional IRA at that stage, however, as many of the planes used in the US bombing of Libya in 1986 had taken off from American bases in England.

Added to that, and further fuelling the detestation of Libya by the UK and the West, had been the shooting of PC Yvonne Fletcher outside the Libyan embassy in April 1984. An unarmed officer, she had been on duty during a demonstration by opponents of the Gaddafi regime. It had been a vocal but peaceful demonstration and she and her colleagues were simply on crowd-control duty. A counter-demonstration by pro-regime supporters had been orchestrated and police were separating the groups. Suddenly, without warning, shots from an automatic weapon were fired from the Libyan embassy. They struck PC Fletcher, who fell to the ground where she was comforted by colleagues, including her fiancé, who was also a serving officer. She died shortly afterwards in hospital.

A siege commenced. The Libyan embassy was diplomatic territory and both it and its staff had internationally agreed immunities. British forces could not go in and Libyan staff could not get out. After several days' discussion, the staff were allowed to leave under escort and were immediately expelled to Libya. The embassy was subsequently closed as the UK ended all diplomatic relations with the country, after which a tit-for-tat situation arose in Libya as retaliation, with UK nationals being held hostage for several months. There was, therefore, a legacy of dislike and mistrust between the UK and Libya. Relations between the two governments had reached a new nadir from which they were not going to recover for quite some time, and certainly not by 1988.

As ever, there had been some claims of responsibility for the Lockerbie atrocity communicated via telephone calls to newspapers and others in both Europe and the United States. These invariably happen after all such events, whether credible or crank. None in this case appeared definitive or particularly credible. They varied in origin and substance but none appeared to have been made with any clear authorisation or to have come through what may be described as 'formal channels'. There was a call from the Ulster Defence League claiming responsibility, an organisation that was treated with scepticism if not open disdain by the authorities; as well as a suggestion in a call to ABC News in New York that the Islamic

Jihad Movement had planted the bomb. In those years before the Iraq War and ISIS, such names were less prevalent and it too, whilst doubtless checked, was ruled out. There was also a claim that the bomb had been detonated by an organisation called the Guardians of the Islamic Revolution in revenge for the shooting down of the Iran Air flight 655 by the USS *Vincennes* that July. The CIA along with the investigation team seems to have quickly viewed the first two as entirely incredible and the latter, though less so, as being unlikely and somewhat premature.

Somewhat more credible, however, was the involvement of the PFLP-GC, who had recently been active in Germany. On 26 October 1988, just under two months before the Lockerbie tragedy, two members of a faction linked to PFLP-GC were detained in a small town near Frankfurt. Other raids on homes and houses in Germany had followed in the weeks thereafter and sixteen suspects were ultimately detained. Bomb materials were located, including radio cassette players, timers, and barometric pressure devices. As well as arms and ammunition, airline timetables (including one of Pan Am flights) and unused Lufthansa luggage tags were also recovered. The motive, it was suggested, apart from the ongoing issues in the Middle East and Palestine, was the downing of the Iranian airliner by the USS *Vincennes* in the July of that year. The same issue referred to by the caller on behalf of the so-called Guardians of the Revolution. The radio cassette player and the timers were different models from those used in the downing of Pan Am flight 103, but were similar in many other ways. To many it seemed more than just coincidence and these raids gave those investigating a perpetrator, a method and a motive; all good enough reasons to initially point the finger of suspicion at the PFLP-GC.

The downing of the Iranian Airbus A300 airliner had occurred on 3 July 1988. A civilian aircraft, it had been flying across the Persian Gulf from Tehran to Dubai, carrying 290 people, including sixty-six children and sixteen crew. The war between Iran and Iraq had been going on for many years though was drawing to a close after horrendous loss of life on both sides. The Strait of Hormuz was an essential waterway for oil supplies to the West and the US. Accordingly, American Navy ships had been in the area seeking to protect their interests and skirmishes had been regularly breaking out with the Iranian Navy and military forces. The warship, USS *Vincennes*, was reportedly in Iranian waters, entering them after a confrontation between one of its helicopters and Iranian speedboats in the Strait of Hormuz. Tension was high and fingers were on triggers. The warship apparently mistook the plane for a military craft and fired surface-to-air missiles with catastrophic effect. The plane was still in Iranian airspace. All aboard were killed. No adequate explanation has ever been given as to why the crew acted as they did. It seems clear that the plane was still gaining altitude after take-off and that its identification was civilian not military, though down it came. The US issued notes of regret but never apologised for it nor acknowledged any wrongdoing in its actions.

Iran was outraged and understandably so. Their representatives raised it at the UN Security Council later that month asking for condemnation of the US attack. Then US Vice-President George H. W. Bush defended the action in the debate, saying it was a wartime incident and that the crew had acted appropriately. It was only in 1996, following a case at the International Court of Justice, that a settlement of $131.8 million was made to Iran for the victims' families. The Western world was oblivious to it in many ways. A tragedy had occurred but little else it would seem. That's not, though, how it was viewed in Iran or doubtless across the Muslim world. Then, as now, sadly, there seemed to be a differential view in much of the developed world as to the loss of Muslims lives or those from developing countries, as opposed to those in the West. Bitterness was being sown and a harvest would be reaped amongst many around the globe. Western intelligence seemed to suggest there had been a meeting shortly thereafter, where not just the Iranian Foreign Minister and the head of the Iranian Intelligence Service, but also Ahmed Jibril, head of the PFLP-GC, had convened. Sources suggested that a contract had then been put out by Iran to avenge the loss of their plane by bringing down an American one.

The suspicions that the police and security services had, whether about Palestinians, Libyans or Iranians, were understandably and correctly passed on to government ministers. This was a huge investigation and those politically responsible and accountable would need to be in the loop and given interaction with other governments and international agencies. Not just those dealing with justice and security, but other portfolios with security implications would need to know too. Initial suspicions about the PFLP-GC, therefore, along with other such sources and snippets of information, were therefore transmitted to the UK government. Paul Channon was the UK Minister for Transport at the time, having been appointed in June 1987.

In March 1989, he met with senior political correspondents from major UK newspapers at the Garrick Club, favoured by many in the British establishment. The meeting was supposed to be off the record, or, as the Westminster political reporters say, on strict lobby terms, for background information only. However, for whatever reason, that was not to be and contents of the meeting were made public. It was reported that Dumfries and Galloway had carried out a brilliant criminal investigation; the government were evidently delighted at the police work and with the European intelligence agencies that had assisted. Additionally, it was inferred that not only did they know who the perpetrators were, but that arrests could swiftly follow. When a story broke along those lines, Channon initially denied that he was the source. He was denounced as a liar by a major London newspaper but declined to sue and in July 1989 he was quietly removed from office. The implication in the articles did seem to be that it was the Palestinians who had carried out the atrocity; and that was certainly the impression given in the press. Channon sought to roll back from that position, stating that the Lord Advocate was in charge and that his knowledge was limited to where and how the bomb had been placed on the plane. However, the damage had been done: the Palestinians were now in the frame.

It's been suggested in some articles that have appeared since that his misdemeanour was not the story given naively to the press, but another discussion that occurred that same day; albeit not involving him and occurring a few hours before. The US investigative columnist Jack Anderson had revealed in January 1990 that on the very day Channon was at the Garrick Club, Margaret Thatcher took a call from President George H. W. Bush, who asked her to 'cool it' on the subject. For whatever reason, and it was probably time constraints, that message was not relayed to Channon, and he went with the information that he'd already been given. Whether the request to 'cool it' related to the Palestinians or something else is not known, but the assumption seems to be that American intelligence was now moving from implicating the Palestinians to incriminating others.[5]

Channon, though, was not alone in his speculation. Early on, US government spokespeople had laid the blame on the Palestinians. Moreover, in early 1989, shortly before Channon's comments, CBS ran a news piece that 'conclusively' placed the blame on Ahmed Jibril, the leader of the PFLP-GC. CBS stated that their information had come from 'reliable sources within the international terrorist community'.[6] Exactly who or what the source was never stated, though it did not appear that the speculation was repudiated by the US government. The motive was said to be an attempt to discredit Yasser Arafat and collapse the talks that had been going on between the US and PLO. Though never properly formulated or publicly promulgated, the early speculation was that the bomb had been placed by the PFLP-GC. The sources seemed credible and the level at which it was being mentioned was significant.

Matters, however, were not clear cut. As preparations were made for the First Iraq War and the liberation of Kuwait, an alternative theory to the Channon gaffe arose from security agencies. As Western

---

5   Paul Foot, 'Taking the Blame', *London Review of Books*, 6 January 1991
6   *Michigan Daily*, 14 February 1989

relationships with Syria and some other Arab Nations hostile to Iraq improved, information became forthcoming from Syrian intelligence sources. They suggested responsibility lay elsewhere and began to point to Libya, not the Palestinians or Syrians.

Suspicions of Libyan involvement also increased when the bombing of a French airliner over the Sahara desert on 19 September 1989 was taken into the equation. The circumstances surrounding the atrocity committed on UTA flight 772 bore remarkably similar hallmarks to those of Pan Am flight 103. Both bombs appeared to have been placed on board in a Samsonite suitcase and used a sophisticated timing device as a trigger. Intelligence sources suggested that the atrocity was as a consequence of France's support for Libya's neighbour Chad in a border dispute. A French investigative journalist uncovered that a tiny fragment of the timer taken from the wreckage allowed the FBI to link it to Libya. Six Libyan nationals were subsequently convicted in absentia in 1999, including Abdullah Senussi, head of Libyan Intelligence and brother-in-law of Gaddafi.

A covert war was being waged but it was innocents who were suffering. For each and every action it seemed there was an equal and opposite one and the bitterness and hatred was growing on all sides with each new atrocity committed in the pursuit of 'an eye for an eye'. The world was being blinded to the consequences of this conflict, that was, until Lockerbie. The hunt for the perpetrators was on, and the finger from the highest sources seemed to be pointing at the Palestinians, the PFLP-GC in particular – but were they really responsible?

THE INVESTIGATION –
TO THE ENDS OF THE EARTH

After the black box had been discovered and the cause of the atrocity linked to an explosion, the crash site was redesignated as a crime scene, and there began an investigation that was to reach international proportions.

Led by Scottish Police under the direction of the Crown (as the Crown Office and Procurator Fiscal Service (COPFS) is known in Scotland), the investigation was assisted by an FBI Task Force that had been established and led by Chief Richard Marquise.

The intention of the terrorists was to have detonated the bomb over the Atlantic Ocean. That would have made recovery of much, if not most, evidence well-nigh impossible. However, a departure delayed by minutes meant the explosion occurred over Lockerbie and not the North Atlantic.

For the officers at Lockerbie and elsewhere, the work remained the same. It was about recovery, recording and analysis. Much of the focus was on body recovery and identification. They were starting from scratch, building up a picture and a profile of what had happened and anyone who had been involved, whether with the flight itself, any of the airports or any other possible way. Given the scale of the crash scene and the size of some fragments, it was a long and often lonely process.

Helicopter surveys and satellite imaging, as well as extensive and methodical searches, took place over much of the area by police and soldiers. Around 4 million pieces of wreckage were retrieved and painstakingly recorded and entered into computer systems. In addition, 10,000 pieces of debris were located and also meticulously entered into the system. As well as physical evidence, 15,000 witness statements were ultimately to be taken. It was to be a process that would take years to complete, not days or months. Entire careers were almost dedicated to it. Over the course of the investigation, the plane's fuselage was reconstructed piece by piece. Test explosions were even undertaken to try to find out the exact position of the explosion, as well as the precise amount of explosives that had been involved. Such tests concluded that a twenty-inch hole had been punched in the left side of the forward cargo hold. They also disclosed that remains of a Samsonite suitcase, which had been nearest the hole, showed signs of residue and other marks consistent with an explosion having taken place inside it. Pieces of a circuit board were also located and were recognised as being parts of a Toshiba radio cassette player.

That electronic device was similar to another that had been used by the PFLP-GC in West Germany in an attempted bombing only a few months before. In addition, items of baby apparel shown to have come from Malta were thought to have come from the same suitcase. Those were the initial conclusions and were to form the basis of the Crown case at future trials. The suitcase, the circuit board in the cassette player and the clothing from Malta were to be constants throughout the prosecution's case.

In conjunction with the ongoing criminal investigation, a Fatal Accident Inquiry (FAI) was held. A standard practice in Scotland, it is a legal procedure to deal with sudden deaths, and its use here was both perfectly normal and appropriate. Akin in some ways to the English equivalent of the Coroner's Court, it is more investigatory than adversarial; its purpose being to establish the facts of what happened and, if thought appropriate, recommend further actions be taken. Though normally a criminal prosecution would precede an FAI, that was obviously not possible here. In an FAI, the standard of proof is civil, taken on a balance of probabilities (i.e., it's more likely than not to have happened), whereas in a criminal trial the standard of proof must be beyond all reasonable doubt.

However, the nature of the tragedy at Lockerbie made it far larger and much more high profile than even the biggest of such inquiries in the past. The normal venue of the Sheriff Court House in Dumfries was too small not simply for the media and public interest but, also, for all the legal teams that would need to be accommodated. Though FAIs are led by the Procurator Fiscal (as the local prosecutor is known), others with an interest can seek to be represented. This was to be the case here, with several legal teams for victims groups, along with those from Pan Am, British Airports Authority and the Department of Transport in attendance. The venue was therefore moved to the Easterbrook Hall at Crichton Royal Hospital in Dumfries, which provided a space of suitable size that could be altered to suit the needs of the court and its entourage.

The proceedings were significant, running for over fifty-five days; from October 1990 until February 1991. One hundred and thirty-one witnesses gave evidence. In his judgment, Sheriff Principal John Mowat laid out what had been the case for the Crown: a brown Samsonite suitcase containing the Toshiba radio cassette, which in turn contained the timer and a Semtex-type explosive, had been loaded as unaccompanied luggage on flight KM180 from Malta to Frankfurt, where upon arrival it was interlined through to Heathrow; and there loaded onto Pan Am flight 103. Ground crew and baggage manifests at both Frankfurt and Heathrow airports showed the suitcase containing the bomb to have been located in container AVE 4041 on the plane, along with other luggage that had been loaded in Frankfurt. The FAI concluded that the plane had been airworthy, and the cause of death was murder.

The main points at issue were how the suitcase had got onto the plane and whether there was any negligence on the part of the airports or airlines. Even at that time unaccompanied baggage was supposed to be subject to special scrutiny and passengers and their luggage were in the main meant to travel together. The agents for the victims' families were keen to see the blame laid at the door of Pan Am. The company was painted almost as a failing company, riddled with defects and slackness in operation. Pan Am, in its defence, countered that it was being pilloried for one very small area of its operation, which was the security measures taken relating to interline baggage at Frankfurt and Heathrow. The company was equally eager to avoid potential civil liability that could and would eventually bankrupt it. Its defence in many ways was simply that its methods were no different from other airlines, and the Sheriff Principal seemed to accept that.

As it would be with the later trial, the problem of clear and overwhelming proof was an issue. Though an inquiry and not a criminal trial, however, assumptions could be made on the balance of probabilities and, as such, Sheriff Principal Mowat found that what had most likely happened was that the bag containing the bomb had come in on a feeder flight 103A from Frankfurt. It had then been taken directly to flight 103 without any counting or weighing to establish whether the baggage being transferred corresponded with what had been checked in at Frankfurt for passengers going on to New York. Nor was it reconciled or checked in any other way to ensure it belonged to ongoing travellers or could otherwise be accounted for. It was also not X-rayed there. He went on to decide that the luggage had been unaccompanied on both flight 103A from Frankfurt to Heathrow and flight 103 from Heathrow to New York, and that it had probably arrived in Frankfurt on a flight or airline other than Pan Am and so was interlined to Pan Am there. It had simply been loaded on in Germany without any attempt to identify it as an unaccompanied bag. He pointed out that, though interlined bags for Pan Am were X-rayed, there was no reconciliation procedure to ensure that passengers and baggage travelled on the same flight; and he added it was probably the same at Frankfurt.

He was unable to make any formal finding about whether the bomb had been placed on a plane initially in Malta. That would be an issue that would return later, at the criminal trial in the Netherlands. Instead, the evidence and interest at this point was focused on what was or was not done at Frankfurt, Heathrow and upon general airline security measures. Even then there was a clear acceptance in the aviation sector that attempts to place bombs via unaccompanied baggage posed a significant risk and one of the easiest ways for this to be accomplished would be by interlining luggage through another airline and airport. As a consequence, Sheriff Principal Mowat concluded that reconciliation between bag and passengers was a vital aspect of security to minimise the risk of unaccompanied baggage slipping through. X-ray screening alone had significant limitations. An electrical item with a plug, for example, would not arouse suspicions and Semtex could not be detected by the equipment used. In this case, the procedure of transferring bags between flights 103A and 103 was a particular risk and therefore precautions such as a reconciliation of the bags to ensure no unaccompanied luggage would have been appropriate both at Frankfurt and Heathrow. This, Mowat said, was a defect in the security system that contributed to the deaths of those aboard. Pan Am was subsequently convicted in a US Federal Court in 1992 of wilful misconduct due to lax security screening. Two subsidiary companies of the multinational were also convicted, including the firm that handled its security at Frankfurt.

The investigation, meanwhile, marched meticulously on. The dynamics of both tension and camaraderie between various agencies continued, though in the main all worked well with each other. The Metropolitan Police soon overcame their consternation that the lead agency was to be Dumfries and Galloway Constabulary and realised that they simply had to get on with it. The Scottish officers quickly earned their respect and, likewise, there was an understanding amongst the Scots, whether from Dumfries and Galloway or elsewhere, that they needed the skills and expertise that the Met and others offered. The exchange of officers to work in their counterparts' offices also helped to forge relationships between the two constabularies.

The span of the inter-police cooperation was not simply within the UK, but was international in scope; traversing ideologies as well as borders. Other than the obvious involvement of the FBI, other agencies from the home countries of victims, along with others with vested interests, also entered the fray. Of course, given their recent brushes with the PFLP-GC as well as the likelihood that the bomb had been routed through Frankfurt, the Germans had a significant interest in the investigation. Accordingly, Germany's Federal Criminal Police Office, the Bundeskriminalamt (BKA), became actively involved, sending officers to Scotland. The Israelis also saw a need to assist and to be kept appraised as a result both of their knowledge and expertise as well as the dangers they themselves faced from terrorism. Other international allies were likewise on the scene and provided support. The Arab nations that were aligned or at least friendly with the West were also involved, the Jordanians in particular having an interest given the number of Palestinians in their land.

One of the victims on board the plane was Hungarian and officers recall engagements with the Hungarian Police at a time when that country was still behind the Iron Curtain, conscious of the fact that there were probably officers from Hungary's security services and no doubt even the KGB amongst the officers they met. Exchanges, however, were cordial and assistance was given freely and frankly.

Though at that time officers were focused on the recovery of evidence, they were still conscious of the investigation gathering pace in other ways and through different agencies. The security services were present but, in most ways as is their norm, operated at a background level. This focus changed over time. A move was made from the recovery of bodies and evidence to the analysis of that evidence and the pursuit of leads and information. The Scottish Police presence also began to change in character. Hundreds of uniformed officers scouring fields for clues were replaced by teams of detectives in Lockerbie and later elsewhere working through and thoroughly analysing what had been discovered. Moreover, there was the arduous task of trawling through the manifest and passenger lists to interview the families of victims as well as others who might hold valuable information, whether in aviation, airport or air traffic control. This kind of methodical work can seem tedious, but was vital if they were to build a picture and a profile of the individual; as well as to exclude various individuals or factors from being the cause of the explosion. Much of it unglamorous and just dogged detective work; interviewing people which is, though, an art and craft in itself. What differed in this instance from the mundane gumshoe work of Hollywood movies was both the volume of it and the international dimension to it.

The structures were established to carry out all that work and ensure it was logged and collated. Detectives came from far and wide in Scotland as a crack team was set up, for Scotland's biggest case. John Boyd, the Chief Constable of Dumfries and Galloway, remained nominally in charge of the investigation, but day-to-day operational control was ceded to Detective Chief Superintendent John Orr, then serving with Strathclyde Police. He became what is known as the Senior Investigating Officer (SIO). It was a big task but he was an extremely able detective. His deputy was Superintendent Stuart Henderson, an experienced officer from Lothian and Borders Police.

Under them, teams of officers were established to take responsibility for the site, to cover the issues and aspects of the case in the town and well beyond.

The Lockerbie Incident Control Centre (LICC) moved into an old primary school in the town and from there officers began to span out across the globe. The relatives of the deceased passengers and crew had to be interviewed to rule out any involvement in the bombing or reasons to suspect that they were a target. Most of those interviewed understood that such lines of enquiry were routine, but for some it was distressing. People were still grieving and the hurt was raw. Given the wide range of nationalities of those involved, the distances clocked up by the officers in the investigation team were huge.

Some of these lines of enquiry brought spasms of tension between police forces used to working in specific ways. Scottish officers, for example, were accustomed to interviewing every witness fully and at length, even if it was thought at the outset to be of little likely consequence. These formalities had to be followed rigidly, they argued, or there was a risk of missing some gem or nugget of information. They also reasoned, by extension, that if standards dropped in one instance, how could they be maintained in others? There was logic within the longhand method of the Scottish constabularies to ensure the consistent high-quality standards of evidence-taking. That logic, however, was not shared by some other forces, and in particular by the FBI. They saw such lines of enquiry as a hindrance at best and a total waste of valuable police time at worst. Some of the paperwork returned to the LICC from the US was perfunctory to say the least, causing some angst amongst the Scottish officers who had laboriously carried out their own enquiries, even if they ultimately turned out to be fruitless.

Within the broad passenger and crew manifest list, there was also a higher-profile category that needed to be approached with even greater care and diligence. This included the US State Department officials and their military and security colleagues who had been on board the plane. Others in that category were the senior executives from Volkswagen and Bernt Carlsson, the UN High Commissioner for Namibia. It was thought, given their profile, that there was greater reason to suspect that they had been targeted specifically. The investigations were extensive and, despite conspiracy theories that circled the tragedy both then and afterwards, no particular link was found by the investigating officers at the time and nor has one been discovered since.

The allegation that it was the security services of the old South African apartheid regime assassinating Bernt Carlsson, aggrieved at his work in Namibia, seems entirely without foundation. The South African regime was ceding influence in that country, as it was to do spectacularly within a few more years in its own country. The risks involved for limited gain seem to argue against that. Also, whilst the apartheid regime was brutal both at home and abroad, there is no credible evidence of this being an assassination. Carlsson had faced a previous attempt on his life, but nothing came out then or has materialised since to indicate that there is any basis to it. The apartheid regime has long since passed into history and an ANC government has been in power for many years; truth and reconciliation hearings have also taken place since, allowing those involved in atrocities and the crimes of the regime to confess their guilt. Yet, no material or credible evidence has arisen to give any credence to a suggestion that is fanciful to say the least.

There have been other conspiracy theories suggesting that some Americans had knowledge in advance of a bomb on board and so had cancelled their flight. This would take involvement by their security services to a new and deadly height against their own citizens. There seems no credible evidence at all for that and there are many other factors that militate against it. The Americans on the flight had probably seen the warnings too but had no reason to remain grounded especially at that time of year when they would wish to be home with family. The fact that it would involve so many in such senior positions, never mind just ordinary citizens, would make this one of the greatest ever Machiavellian acts. Moreover, in today's age of WikiLeaks and other sources within the National Security Agency (NSA) and American intelligence, nothing to suggest such a conspiracy has ever come to light. It appears that the deductions of the Scottish officers following their methodical research at the time appear correct. These were all conspiracy theories and just that; no facts or evidence have been found to support them.

Another passenger given special attention in the initial investigation was Khaled Jaafar. He was a young Arab who had boarded the feeder flight at Frankfurt. That extended journey, together with his nationality and Islamic faith, immediately gave rise to suspicions about whether he was a suicide bomber or unwitting carrier. Whilst he had Lebanese friends and had visited the country many times in preceding years, however, there is no evidence of any terrorist or other criminal connection.

Another theory, that said Jaafar was drug running and that, unbeknown to him, his bag had been switched from contraband to an explosive device, was the subject of a television documentary (*The Maltese Double Cross*) and a book (*Trail of the Octopus: From Beirut to Lockerbie – inside the DIA*). It has continued to run on the internet, as is so often the case with such theories and suggested (even more implausibly) that Jaafar's activities were known to a few operating within the CIA, who condoned them or were even complicit. Such conspiracy theorists hold that it was linked to attempts to release Americans and Israelis held as hostages in the Lebanon, and that Major Charles McKee, who was killed aboard Pan Am flight 103, was going back to the US to expose the agency or the rogue elements within it. The theory goes that, to avoid that, those involved allowed the flight and, therefore, the tragedy, to proceed.

The US Drug Enforcement Agency, however, was clear that, though it had run controlled drug deliveries or 'stings', none had been carried out in Europe during or immediately before December 1988. Moreover, evidence clearly showed that Jaafar had checked in two bags at Frankfurt, both of which were accounted for and neither of which was the suitcase containing the bomb. Other suggestions of him being met by handlers at the airport were shown to be equally fanciful and false. The evidence for the theory simply doesn't exist, and nor has any new information come to light over the years that would seem to give it any credence whatsoever. Whatever personal failings he may have had or suspicious company that he kept, Jaafar was neither a mover nor a martyr. The investigators were right to conclude that he was just another tragic victim.

The instigators behind the programme included a notorious US hoaxer called Oswald LeWinter, who had been convicted of drug offences and sentenced to six years' imprisonment in his own country. He had also been responsible for a previous hoax known as the 'October Surprise', which had suggested that the Republican candidates for the presidency Ronald Reagan and George H. W. Bush had arranged to delay the release of US hostages from Tehran for their own political benefit. A Congressional Task Force established the claims to be entirely unfounded and, indeed, indicated that LeWinter had admitted that under oath. Another contributor was an Israeli, Juval Aviv, who claimed to be linked to the intelligence services but whose employment record seemed to show that he had simply been a security guard for El Al Airlines. His evidence was questioned not simply over Lockerbie but other issues he was involved in, which saw him arrested over allegations over fabrication of information. Others involved, including Lester Coleman and Steven Donohue, were also shown to have dubious backgrounds and doubtful testimony. The former pleaded guilty to perjury charges related to civil actions between Pan Am and flight 103 families and admitted the falsehood of the evidence. The latter had an equally murky past, with convictions for drug offences and involvement with the drug world.

Allegations of evidence-tampering, or even that evidence had been planted at the scene, have no basis in fact. The suggestion that CIA or other American agents planted the timer for the bomb at a very early juncture in the inquiry is entirely fanciful and would in effect be dependent on a degree of complicity in the bombing.

Rumours of Americans being onsite within a matter of hours appear entirely unfounded, too, the recollections of Scottish officers on the scene being of methodical bagging and tagging after meticulous searches had been conducted. The involvement of the Americans was peripheral and not at the grassroots level. Moreover, Scottish Police would not have countenanced the falsification or deliberate placement of evidence. The Americans simply didn't plant evidence nor did the Scots connive with them in it. The support provided by the FBI and America in specialist forensic analysis was of evidence both diligently and lawfully recovered.

The methodical detective work of the Scottish officers and their colleagues around the world began to focus. It was looking certain that there was no link between the cause of the bombing and any of the passengers or crew as individuals. So, as well as the background of the passengers and crew, the investigation now needed to consider the backdrop to the flight itself: where it had flown from, which flights it had linked with and what baggage might have been aboard. The security situation at each site and with each airline also needed to be considered, visited and reviewed, as did the international state of affairs. The links with the BKA, FBI and other services would be invaluable given their specialised knowledge of the events, interests and politics in their respective countries.

Forensic enquiries were also diligently being conducted and began to harmonise with the dogged detective work. One of the early lines of enquiry that was pursued by the investigating team related to the suitcase. The analysis by the Royal Armaments Research and Development Establishment (RARDE), a specialist section of the

Ministry of Defence based in Kent, examined parts of what appeared to be a suitcase shell. The damage indicated that it was probably the suitcase that had contained the bomb, and closer investigation revealed a piece of its patterned lining, which led the team to identify the brand as Samsonite. Further fragments were located and analysed, including a piece of its locking mechanism. A Scottish officer, accompanied by an FBI colleague, flew to the Samsonite headquarters in Denver, Colorado. There it was confirmed in May 1989 that not only was it a Samsonite product, but that the case in question was a 26-inch Silhouette 4000, a model which sold significantly in the Middle East market.

Further investigations at RARDE were carried out on other items, including fragments of circuit board. Links with the bomb-making equipment that had been planned for use by the PFLP-GC in Germany were investigated, but, although there were many similarities, eventually proved fruitless. However, what these investigations did disclose was a link to a Toshiba radio cassette player. There were some seven types of player manufactured by Toshiba that had similar circuiting, but again in May 1989, shards of damaged paper were examined that turned out to be from the manual for a Toshiba BomBeat RT-SF 16 model. That gave the police both the suitcase and the radio cassette that had carried the bomb. Similar in-depth analysis by specialist forensic scientists also led to the discovery of the timer. A piece of cloth that had been recovered from the crime scene was found to have blast damage and, more importantly, there were tiny pieces of electronic circuit board embedded in it. Searches were carried out amongst the other pieces of recovered evidence to try to locate other shrapnel and to build up a picture of what it was. Discussions took place with RARDE, who had their own experts not simply in explosives, but in such specialised areas as Improvised Explosive Devices. The assistance of the FBI was thereafter sought and officers passed the information they possessed onto specialist forensic investigators employed by them in the US. In June 1990, they confirmed that the circuit board was the same as another that had been recovered from an arms cache seized in Togo, Africa a few years before, following the attempted coup to overthrow the Togolese government by left-wing exiles. They confirmed that the timer was known as an MST-13. The CIA then provided information that indicated that a similar device had been found upon the persons of two Libyans in Senegal in February 1988. They had been charged with conspiring to bomb French military bases there; the motive apparently being revenge for French support for Chad in their war with Libya. Investigation of those timers led the investigators to a Swiss company called MEBO, which was owned by Edwin Bollier and Erwin Meister. A request was then made to the Swiss authorities to interview these men, who were based at their company's offices in Zurich. It was during the course of these interviews that investigators established a possible link to Libya, and to Abdelbaset al-Megrahi in particular.

As well as the suitcase, its contents would be integral in the investigation, and therefore every piece of evidence that showed definite or likely signs of explosive damage recovered from the crash scene had to be identified and thoroughly examined. A fragment of a Baby Gro suit that was found with traces of explosive on it clearly indicated that it had been inside the suspect suitcase, and its label (miraculously still intact) confirmed that it had been made by a company in Malta. In August 1989, officers went to the Mediterranean island and located the manufacturer on an industrial estate there. The link to Malta was further strengthened when another piece of recovered clothing, again tainted with explosive, was reviewed. A brown piece of cloth initially labelled as tartan was found to have a label that identified it as being of the 'Yorkie' brand. Initial enquiries in the English city of York from which it springs were fruitless. However, a search for the brand name in Malta resulted in the discovery of a 'Yorkie Clothing Company' on the island. The manufacturer there was not only able to identify the label and cloth as belonging to him, but could say definitively which batch of cloth it had come from. This fabric, he confirmed, had been used to make six pairs of gentlemen's trousers, and they had all been supplied to the same shop – Mary's House in Valletta, Malta's capital city. It had, in fact, closed, but on investigation they discovered that the business had relocated to Sliema, a town a few miles away. There they found the shop and inside met Tony Gauci, whose family owned it. He was to become a critical witness.

Gauci was happy to speak with Scottish officers, and said he remembered the sale of one of these pairs of trousers well. Being off the main road, the shop was not prominent in the town or well known on the island. Significant sales, therefore, were few, and customers would invariably be locals rather than foreign tourists. Gauci initially identified the purchaser as being of about fifty years of age and six feet tall. He also said he was Libyan.

Malta's proximity to Libya has been a significant draw for many visitors from that country. Only 200 miles from its shores, with easy and regular access, many came to the island to shop or relax. In many ways, for the isolated people and state of Libya, Malta was also a window that led into Europe. The sanctions against the state, as well as some of the restrictions imposed by its Muslim code, made it a venue where items could be bought that were otherwise unobtainable and pastimes (such as alcohol) could be indulged in that might otherwise be frowned upon. Business could be conducted there and its airport was often used as a transport hub for onward connections. Its language, being an amalgam of both Arabic and Latin, also meant that Libyans could get by in Malta with relative ease. They did so in such numbers that islanders were often able to recognise them, and therefore for Gauci to be able to state that a purchaser was Libyan was no great surprise, and can be compared to someone from the UK or the US knowing whether someone was French rather than Spanish or Italian.

In addition to the transaction with a man identified as Libyan, investigators noted that the clothing shop in Sliema was located a short distance away from the Libyan People's Bureau, which was the Libyan equivalent of an embassy. The timer, though manufactured by MEBO in Switzerland, was principally supplied to the Libyans. Similar types had been located in Togo and Senegal. That on its own may not have been surprising. After all, Libya was not only involved in funding terrorist groups but, as past atrocities had shown, had actively assisted in providing arms and materials. In addition the MST-13 model, known as an ice-cube timer, was different to the ones usually used by the PFLP-GC, which had a very limited time delay from when the charge was set and were known to be affected by temperature and other factors. In the main, they could be set for only around sixty minutes before detonation, whereas the MST-13 timers were much more sophisticated and could be set to detonate up to a maximum of 9,999 hours, approximately 416 days, in advance. A battery would probably have expired by then, but this did not negate from the accuracy of these Swiss-made timers.

As mentioned earlier, the Toshiba radio cassette player was of a different type to those that had been located in Germany and linked to the PLFP-GC. In October 1988, 20,000 of these cassette players had been supplied to Libya. Indeed, that country accounted for 76 per cent of worldwide sales for the six months up to the end of October 1989. The senior Libyan official involved in the purchase had also been involved in the purchase of the MST-13 timers. The difference between these and those cassette players found in Germany was that rather than having twin speakers, there was only a single one. A PFLP-GC bombmaker was later to suggest that he did not use radios with double speakers as there wasn't enough space for an improvised explosive device (IED).

The evidence of a link with Libya was mounting, but precisely what form it took was still to be established.

The clothes that had been traced as being sold by Tony Gauci would be vital in the prosecution's case against Megrahi, though at this early stage of the investigation, and despite some questions as to Gauci's identification of Megrahi, there seems to be no doubt about his evidence concerning the sale of clothes to a Libyan man.

Gauci was interviewed by a Scottish Police officer on 1 September 1989. Officers had first spoken to his brother, who had been serving in the front of the shop and who had initially stated that he had no idea what they were talking about. Tony Gauci, who had overheard the conversation from the back of the shop, shouted through that he could help and could recall the incident. He said he remembered the sale, which had occurred the preceding November or December, as it had been substantial. In addition, though it had been a sizeable transaction, the purchaser, according to Gauci, had appeared disinterested in what he was buying. He'd bought two pairs of trousers (one of which was of the 'Yorkie' brand), as well as a rather strange collection of other clothing, including an imitation Harris Tweed jacket, a woollen tartan cardigan and a blue Baby Gro. The bill came to 76.50 in Maltese pounds and the man paid in cash. He then left the shop but, as there was some slight rain, he had popped back in to buy a black umbrella. Gauci thought the man had then got into a white taxi parked up the street, but could not be certain of that. He was on his own in the shop at the time, his brother having left to watch AC Milan, his favourite Italian football team, play in a big European fixture that was being televised.

The information Gauci had provided about the sale of the umbrella prompted officers to check whether one had been recovered at the crash scene. Sure enough, further investigations uncovered that a small, black umbrella had been found amongst the other debris at the site. It had initially flummoxed colleagues responsible for the collation of evidence, and only then seemed to have any bearing or relevance.

Tony Gauci's statement regarding the transaction remained consistent throughout the investigation and subsequent trial. It is his identification of Megrahi and some of the timings, however, that some have since found troubling. During the first interview, Gauci had described the purchaser as about six feet tall and well built; not fat and with black hair. He gave other details about his appearance to an artist who composed a sketch that was later digitally enhanced.

On 14 September 1989, Gauci was interviewed at police headquarters in Malta at which point he was shown nineteen photographs of potential suspects. He identified a man named Mohammed Salem, but caveated his choice by saying the man was similar but too young. He was interviewed again on 26 September, when he was shown even more photographs. On this occasion he identified someone (not Megrahi) he said was similar to the man he saw. He was shown further photographs in interviews with the police the following year, on both 31 August and 10 September 1990. In both interviews, he could identify no one out of the fifty photographs produced over the two interviews. He did, however, tell officers that he had recognised a man whose picture he'd seen in a newspaper article about the tragedy, who had been captioned below the headline 'The Bomber' as the man who had been in his shop. The man in the photograph, though, was a Palestinian, Abo Talb, and he'd failed to identify him in the collection of images shown to him earlier. Gauci still held that the man was Libyan, and that he was around fifty years of age.

It wasn't until an interview on 15 February 1991, when he was this time shown a set of photographs that included Megrahi, that he finally identified him. Even then, however, there were issues. It had been a long time ago, Gauci said, adding with what seemed like some exasperation that, of all the photos shown, his seemed the most similar. There were differences, though, and he again referred to the likeness of the man he'd seen in the newspaper, Abo Talb.

Despite reservations on the part of some about Gauci's testimony, his identification was not the only link to Megrahi. After the first interview back in September 1989, a team of officers flew to Malta to pursue links. They would be there for quite some time, assisted not just by the local Maltese police but by the BKA and FBI. The Germans had provided them with the information that Air Malta flight KM180 had departed from Luqa Airport, as the main airport on Malta is known, for Frankfurt on the morning of 21 December. The Germans also had a computerised print-out from Frankfurt Airport of the passengers and cargo that showed that an item of luggage from that flight was unloaded from the flight from Malta and destined for Pan Am 103.

And so the focus moved from Tony Gauci to Luqa Airport. Given that the clothes in the suitcase had been traced to Malta, it was logical to think that it was there that the bomb had commenced its journey. However, both then and at the trial, evidence of the suitcase containing the bomb being placed on board flight KM180 was limited and difficult to find. Checks were made of all passengers on that flight from Malta and especially those who were continuing on to Heathrow and the US. The investigations were thorough and rigorous but it was clear, though, that the one family travelling on to the US through the German hub had no link whatsoever with events. Similar checks cleared all passengers on that plane regardless of their final destinations.

Checks moved on to those who worked at the airport, whether baggage-handlers or security staff. The Scottish officers, assisted by Maltese counterparts, methodically interviewed every available witness at the airport, which, given the linguistic challenges and the need to be incredibly thorough, was a time-consuming process. Frustratingly (and treated with some amount of suspicion by the Scottish officers), the log book kept by the army for the period 20–21 December 1988 was not available, and had apparently been accidentally destroyed. A local paper had run an article suggesting that two strangers had been seen by military personnel that evening, though subsequent investigations into both the missing log book and supposed incident proved fruitless.[7]

Alongside the interviews, they also made sure to meticulously scour the complexities of the baggage and security regimes.

These, however, only revealed to the investigators that the security and systems operated at Luqa were stringent and, indeed, included some additional checks that even Heathrow and Frankfurt did not include in their security systems, as a result of past issues with terrorism. In 1985, a hijacked Egyptian plane had landed on the island. The hijackers targeted the Israeli and American passengers and several were shot. An American and Israeli subsequently died from

---

7   John Crawford, *The Lockerbie Incident: A Detective's Tale* (Victoria, British Columbia: Trafford Press, 1992)

their wounds. The plane was stormed by Egyptian Special Forces, which only caused a fire to break out, killing sixty trapped on board. That and previous incidents were no doubt a salutary lesson for the Maltese. Tourism being vital to the economy, the military accordingly took over responsibility for internal security and perimeter patrols at the airport.

There were the usual check-in desks, after which luggage destined for the hold was tagged and placed on a conveyor-belt system that transported it to the airside of the airport, where it was checked for explosives. This involved pressing the case to expel air to allow the machine to register any particles displaced (unfortunately even there the security machinery was not able to identify Semtex, the technology for which simply did not exist at the time). Once checked, all luggage was loaded onto a trailer and delivered to the plane, at which point there would be another check to make sure nothing that hadn't been booked in was being boarded. If the records did not tally then the protocol dictated that the baggage was to be unloaded and, if need be, each item identified by passengers, who would have to disembark. That was standard procedure at most airports, and there was no suggestion that Luqa was anything other than thorough. It had the added protection of being guarded by the military and had greater perimeter site security.

The information from Germany was also clear on the fact that a piece of unaccompanied baggage had disembarked from an Air Malta flight KM180 that had departed from Luqa Airport; and later that day was transferred to Pan Am 103A, the feeder flight for the Heathrow to JFK route. It was not accompanied on the flight from

Malta as the luggage and passengers were all accounted for other than it. However, the computer logs clearly showed that this mysterious piece of luggage had arrived in Frankfurt from Malta; even though it could not be traced to any individual or records at Luqa.

As it was an interline bag, arriving at an airport with one airline, but departing thereafter with a different one, it was subject to an X-ray check only as it travelled through the international system at Frankfurt and Heathrow. The case was significantly different when it came to online baggage, which is carried by passengers and to which more stringent checks would apply.

There was the possibility, alluded to at the FAI but for which no evidence could be found to confirm, that it had been marked as a rush job, such is the case when luggage gets lost in transit and has to be fast-tracked to its owner. Such situations are obviously quite regular and the bags in question are doubtless treated as urgent, generally marked as such to notify baggage crew to move them expeditiously. The records and evidence from airport workers were unable confirm whether that had been the situation or not.

The analysis carried out on the luggage recovered at the Lockerbie crash scene provided evidence that the Frankfurt system was efficient in most other ways, however. Baggage belonging to American students who had boarded at Frankfurt for connection to the JFK flight was shown to have been properly tagged and recorded; moreover, to have been located in the same container as the Samsonite suitcase. The evidence seemed to further strengthen the link to the mysterious lone suitcase travelling from the island in the Mediterranean. Once landed at Frankfurt, it would have been treated as interline baggage and meander through the system. The incoming item from Malta, together with the baggage of the American students from Vienna, was logged into the system there. Evidence showed that the interlined baggage was the last loaded onto flight PA 103A from Frankfurt to Heathrow. There the interline bags were the first off, having been the last on at Frankfurt. Most of the baggage, including the items interlined, was placed on a container AVE 4041, which was shown to have been where the suitcase had been located, and the seat of the explosion on board.

The locus may have been Malta, but, with the suitcase's contents pointing in this direction, the focus of the investigation now moved to Libya. Interviews that took place both in Switzerland and in Scotland with Edwin Bollier and his partner, owners of MEBO, the manufacturers of the timer, revealed that a Libyan company called ABH had offices in the same building. Not only this, but a partner at that company was someone who often visited Malta. His name was Abdelbaset al-Megrahi, and searches disclosed that he had entered the country under a false name and passport at around the same time, and, on some of the critical dates, had stayed in a hotel close to Gauci's shop.

So who was Megrahi? Though much has been written about him, still more is unknown when it comes to this individual. There are some facts, however, that are clear and undisputed. What is accepted by all is that he had been head of security for Libyan Arab Airlines (LAA). In this role he had been responsible for training the Libyan Security Service staff (JSO), who were in charge of security on the planes. He had subsequently moved to become Director of the

Centre for Strategic Studies in Tripoli but retained links with LAA, and no doubt the JSO. Accordingly, he not only trained them but was, at least, a not insignificant figure within the organisation. The JSO had a fearsome reputation both within and without the country, known to carry out or support terrorist attacks.

Libya, as much if not more than other nations, had cause to fear hijacking and terrorist attacks. Libyan planes, therefore, travelled with what are now known as air marshals, armed and ready to protect the aircraft and its passengers.

Megrahi pursued other business interests in addition to this role, whether for himself or the state. The nature of the country at the time made it a place where personal external business interests could be cultivated and, indeed, would be supported by the state as a method of trying to circumvent international sanctions. How much was for personal gain and how much for national interest may never be known but the truth is probably a bit of both. As a result, he had several business ventures, including his involvement in ABH in Switzerland, and so travelled extensively. He did, though, maintain a senior role within LAA during this time. That role gave airline accreditation and access to many areas inaccessible to an ordinary businessman. It also appears that the Libyan government sought not just to acquire timers from MEBO, but considered buying into the company. Megrahi had been a conduit for the government, having met Bollier on several occasions and also having acquired mobile radio transceivers for the Libyan military.

Some of his links with both the Libyan administration and its security wing should be of no surprise. Libya was of course no ordinary state, being both totalitarian and tribal. As has been seen recently with the descent of the country into lawlessness and anarchy following the toppling of Gaddafi, it had major regional and tribal differences. Under Gaddafi, an elite was in charge and certain tribes predominated. It wasn't just political elite but a clan loyalty that ran and still runs deep. Megrahi was tied in with them perhaps through ideology but certainly through blood, which ran thick indeed. He was a friend of Abdullah Senussi, Gaddafi's head of intelligence and brother-in-law, and belonged to the same clan. His involvement with JSO is clear even if the extent of it is disputed. Megrahi by his own admission sought to do significant business transactions for the Libyan state and substantial amounts of money passed through his personal accounts.

It was Megrahi that then linked the inquiry to another Libyan, Lamin Fhimah. He had been the LAA manager for Malta and was based at Luqa Airport. He had been identified as someone with whom Megrahi had met and had a connection. In April 1991, attempts were made to interview him but by this time he had returned to Libya. A search of his flat was then carried out by the investigation team along with accompanying Maltese officers. This uncovered a diary from 1988 which, once translated, included a note that read: 'Take/collect tags from the airport (Abdulbaset/Abdussalam)'. Later on, under 15 December, was a note to 'Take tags from Air Malta'. There was even a further entry on that date noting that 'Abdel-baset arriving from Zurich'. Fhimah was also a JSO agent. Given the nature of the Libyan regime and Fhimah's critical job membership, nothing less could be expected.

The connection between Megrahi and the bomb had been made, and thereafter his movements were tracked. He had travelled under his own name into Malta often, but importantly for the investigation, he had been there from 7 December until 9 December, whereupon he left for Prague, returning again from Zurich on 16/17 December, when he headed back to Tripoli. As mentioned previously, whilst he'd been in Malta, he'd stayed at a hotel very close to Tony Gauci's shop. Further investigation also disclosed that he had a false passport under the name of Ahmed Khalifa Abdusamad, but this had only been used sparingly, and never again after this visit. He had gone to Malta under his assumed name on 20 December and had departed the following day, flying out on the LAA flight to Tripoli at the same time as the Air Malta flight to Frankfurt was departing. In addition, both he and Fhimah had security passes that would allow them airside access at the airport.

The net was closing in on Libya – two Libyans in particular – and so the investigation gathered pace in Malta through the year of 1991. Tony Gauci was re-interviewed. In February, after numerous interviews and many photographs being shown to him, he eventually identified Megrahi. An identification of sorts though hardly cast iron.

But, at least from a police point of view, it was something to go on. They now had Megrahi in Malta on those dates and records indicated that a telephone call was made by him to Fhimah from the Holiday Inn that he'd been staying at just after 7 a.m. on 21 December.

Given their nationality and status as Libyan agents, the police had a link between the two suspects and a motive – now they needed to pin down the dates; specifically, exactly when it was that the clothes had been bought. To link him to the identification that had been given by Gauci, Megrahi would have needed to have been in the country at the time. There was no suggestion that he had been in Malta on dates other than those they'd discovered, nor has it ever been suggested since. The purchase, therefore, had to have occurred in that window or else it couldn't have been him that bought them. Gauci was sure that the sale had taken place, and he was sure of the time of the purchase, but less certain of the exact date. There was doubt over whether the Christmas decorations were up or not, which would have cast some light on the timing, and the reference to his brother having gone to watch a match involving his favourite Italian team in a major football fixture restricted dates to being either 23 November or 7 December. The mention of rainfall seemed to preclude the 7th, but possibly allow for the 23rd. Once the purchase had been made by Megrahi, the investigators' assumption was that he then placed the clothing in a suitcase which he had brought with him on his later visit under a false name on 20 December. They and the bomb were then loaded into the case. The following day, he took the case to the airport where he and Fhimah, with security passes and knowledge of the airport, would load the bag. Thereafter, the suitcase made its way through the baggage system through Frankfurt to Heathrow, where it would be placed aboard flight 103. That was the basis of the outcome of investigations that the police handed to prosecutors.

The case had been pulled together, looked at and analysed not just by the Scottish Police and the FBI, but by the Crown Office and US Department of Justice. Circumstantial though some of the evidence may have been, they felt they had a case and indictments were issued accordingly against both Abdelbaset al-Megrahi and Lamin Khalif Fhimah on 13 November 1991, just under three years after the atrocity. The police and prosecution thought they'd got their men, but a trial there would still have to be; and that was not going to be any easier to arrange than the evidence had been to uncover. Libya was not accepting the blame and nor was it going to hand over its citizens.

CHAPTER ONE

DIPLOMATIC DIALOGUE AND INTERNATIONAL INTRIGUE

T he two Libyan suspects were formally indicted in November 1991 and, along with being a necessary legal procedure whereby the accused and the charges are publicly narrated, it also had the additional benefit of increasing international pressure on Libya.

Requests for extradition were made to Libya for the two suspects at the outset. Understandably, given the relationship between the countries, no formal treaty existed between Libya and either the UK or the US, and therefore no formal, internationally agreed routes could be invoked. Requests were made to the Libyan authorities to have the accused simply handed over for trial, despite the lack of formal legal mechanisms, but they were refused by the North Africans. An offer, though, was made in turn by the Libyans to detain them for trial in their home country if evidence was provided. That in turn was rejected by the UK and the US, neither of whom were prepared to hand over their hard-gathered and highly technical evidence, nor trust a trial on Libyan soil. An impasse remained and so it was to remain for several more years.

During this time, the pressure continued to mount. Sanctions had been taken against Libya by the United Nations and other states since the 1970s, and these were augmented by a further UN declaration in 1992 as a result of the Lockerbie allegations. These additional sanctions widened in terms of scope, bringing in many more countries, as well as heightening the level of compliance. This wasn't, after all, a case of allegations of subterfuge or links through weapons and bombs to others that they could just simply deny. Now there were two real individuals accused of a mass atrocity, with names and faces that had been shown around the world. Libya's friends and allies were reducing as the world opprobrium towards them increased, and more and more, neighbouring North African nations began to feel the heat. Even Colonel Gaddafi could see that some resolution was needed. But, given the make-up of the Libyan regime, he couldn't simply bow down and throw two of his citizens, wider clan and, indeed, security officials to the waiting western wolves. There were both tribal ties and political necessity to be overcome if he were to broker the deal his country needed, but he was willing to parley.

The will and resolve of Gaddafi and his Libyan colleagues were being sorely tested through the sanctions policy. It wasn't simply trade boycotts but the daily life of ordinary citizens that was being affected. Travel to Libya was difficult. Medical supplies in hospitals were restricted, causing problems for the sick and vulnerable. The maintenance of machinery and vehicles were all suffering as repairs could not be made due to the limited supply or unavailability of parts. The price of oil had been falling and the Libyan economy was reeling. Once inured to a great deal through oil wealth, the costs were now being felt in their society. The changing international world also impacted on them. The collapse of the Soviet Union played a part. Soviet support had made access to military hardware and other support accessible and often available at a discount price. The fall of the Berlin Wall and the breakup of the Soviet Union made much of that no longer available or affordable. In addition, the world, though still turbulent, now comprised of one, not two, superpowers; and the one left standing was the US. The noose was contracting and a deal was needed. But, it was not one that could be done at any price – but one Gaddafi could pay.

Despite the international situation, the standoff between Libya and the UK/US showed no sign of abating. The war of words continued, as did the battle between client organisations and security services in Africa and Europe. But diplomacy was being embarked on as it was clear that the pressure was biting on Libya and Gaddafi was prepared to talk, albeit privately. Attempts to broker a solution were being made publicly as well as through back channels. In November 1994, President Nelson Mandela of South Africa offered his country as a neutral venue for the trial. This was rejected by the then British Prime Minister John Major. Several more years elapsed until, in July 1997, at the Commonwealth Heads of Government Conference in Edinburgh, Mandela reiterated the offer, this time to Tony Blair, who had succeeded Major as Prime Minister.

Indeed, the South African President was clear in subsequent meetings that 'no one nation should be complainant, prosecutor and judge' as he strived to assist in breaking the deadlock. He was keen to effect a settlement but one that was acceptable to both sides.

The diplomatic dialogue gathered pace. It wasn't just President Mandela trying to break the logjam, but many others, including powerful representatives for both countries and international organisations. The United Nations became involved not simply in terms of its resolutions on sanctions, but in seeking to broker a compromise. It came from the very top, with Kofi Annan, the UN General Secretary, directly involved along with his legal team. Other nations too were trying to ensure a settlement. Saudi Arabian officials were going back and forward to North Africa as well as linking with other diplomats in New York and elsewhere. The UK and US wanted a trial, the Libyans wanted sanctions lifted.

In the UK, the Tory government was swept aside by New Labour under Tony Blair in 1997. The incoming administration had inherited a problem. Business interests were lobbying for a solution to allow access to trade and resources in Libya, whilst from a foreign policy perspective some new thinking had started. Moreover, Islamic fundamentalism began to rise as a problem in many areas in the Middle East and North Africa. Libya, though a pariah state, was also a state, which not only didn't support, but very often opposed, fundamentalists. As ever in international relations, the old adage that my enemy's enemy is my friend held some sway. Libya offered opportunities commercially but also politically and militarily as the spectre of Al Qaeda and others began to rise.

International opinion, however, was split on both sides. Some African states felt that the West had to lessen their demands and be more supportive of the efforts being made by President Mandela and others to secure an agreement. There were limits on the levels at which sanctions could be imposed as well as the timescale for which they could run without some breaking in ranks by African countries. If the West and UN wanted to retain some element of international solidarity, a solution would need to be reached soon or the current consensus would fragment.

In Libya, Gaddafi sought to address the challenges he would face if he were to turn Megrahi and Fhimah over. It's been suggested that he struck an agreement with at least one prominent dissident to use his good offices with the Megaraha tribe, to whom Megrahi belonged, to accept the deal.

The main stumbling block yet to be overcome concerned the location, and therefore the law, that would be used for the trial proceedings. The UK and the US were not prepared to accept a trial under a jurisdiction that wasn't their own. The International Criminal Court in The Hague would not be established for another five years and, in any event, the US has to date refused even to participate in this court. Libya had also, ironically, opposed it. Would an ad hoc court or tribunal, even if it was under another jurisdiction, suffice? The offer made by President Mandela had been rejected, and so it seemed clear that a neutral third country playing host to the trial was not going to be acceptable to the US and perhaps not even to the UK. The Libyans, despite their opposition to the International Criminal Court, were more sympathetic to the offer articulated by Mandela. However, that was not to be. Those seeking the prosecution wished for something more formal and established.

The two main, most likely jurisdictions were Scotland and the US. For obvious reasons, the Libyans would not consent to the latter. They would, though, consider a trial under Scottish law, but not within a court in the UK. Hence, the drive towards a Scottish court in a neutral country. Professor Robert Black, a Scottish lawyer and academic, had been involved from an early juncture. He had flown out to Libya to meet the accused and is viewed as the architect of this Scottish law/neutral country solution. Along with Lord Trefgarne, a former Tory government minister and then head of the Libyan British Business Council (LBBC), Black had initially been approached by British engineering firms eager for a solution so that they could access lucrative contracts. He was to provide advice to the Libyan government on Scots law as well as solutions to the impasse. It also resonated with a newly elected Labour government keen to both espouse an 'ethical foreign policy' trumpeted by the then Foreign Secretary Robin Cook and make the breakthrough on the Lockerbie situation, which remained an emotive and highly public issue. The American Secretary of State Madeleine Albright was prepared to accept a third country as the solution if it would bring about a trial. The Libyans, too, were prepared to compromise as the pressure mounted.

By the summer of 1998, Colonel Gaddafi had agreed in principle to the outlined deal. There were still other issues, though, and not all of them inconsequential. In early February 1999, a delegation that included Jake Gerwal, a Mandela aide, and Rihab Massoud, a Saudi Arabian diplomat, had sought to mediate further as the stumbling blocks both focussed and narrowed. These were issues that went right to the heart of the Libyan regime. They were looking to maximise the benefits for their two citizens and at the same time minimise the risks for themselves. The Libyan state and its leader-ship needed to be protected.

The intermediaries met separately with both Gaddafi and Cook. It was agreed that, if convicted, the suspects would serve their sen-tence in Scotland, but that there would be UN supervision as well as Libyan diplomats based there. They would agree to a trial in a neutral country as they had said for quite some time. It has been suggested by some diplomatic and intelligence sources, though, that other cri-teria were added as part of the final deal. Scots law would prevail, the accused would not be interviewed by the police and no other suspects in Libya would be sought. The suggestion has also been made that Gaddafi got a concession from Kofi Annan, 'who provided him with a letter allegedly assuring him the proceedings would not be used to justify regime change'. It's also been suggested by those sources that 'the suspects would not be exposed to those who might try to gain testimony from them that might implicate Gaddafi personally'.[8] In August 1998, both the UK and US governments wrote to Kofi Annan stating that they'd be willing to accept a trial before a Scottish court convened in the Netherlands. That country, they felt, since it was already hosting many international Justice Agencies, had the credibility and capacity, as a well as the willingness to oblige.

---

8   Ethan Chorin, *Exit the Colonel: The Hidden History of the Libyan Revolution* (New York: Public Affairs Books, 2012), p. 67

The UK and the US would get the trial they had been demand-ing and Libya would get off the hook on which it was squirming. The two accused were being offered up as the price of peace. Things were beginning to move at some pace after all the delay and impasse and a few days later the UN Security Council passed a resolution establishing the international basis of the trials. The resolution also required Libya to accept responsibility for and pay compensation to the victims' families of the crime. This was passed before any trial in any jurisdiction or under any format had occurred; but was the precursor for the events that followed. The dialogue and intrigue had delivered both a deal and the accused.

And so, on 5 April 1999, the UK Foreign Secretary Robin Cook made a statement in the House of Commons in which he outlined the terms of an agreement that had just been reached between the UK and Libya. Discussions, he said, had been ongoing for some time, but a trial would now take place under Scottish jurisdiction but in a neutral country. The venue would be Camp Zeist in the Netherlands, which he told the House he'd already visited and then outlined its facilities. He thanked the government of the Netherlands for their willingness to host the trial. The two accused, if convicted, would serve their sen-tences in Scotland, though there would be UN monitoring of their incarceration. That, he explained, had been the final stumbling block, and one on which the UK was not prepared to move. With the final obstacles resolved, the two suspects were now in transit to the Nether-lands where they would quickly be handed over to Scottish jurisdiction.

It was also made clear that the United Nations sanctions would now be suspended and, after ninety days with Kofi Annan's support, would be formally lifted. The UK and the US were to get the trial they so very much wanted, and the Libyans were to have the sanctions lifted that they very much needed. But, what of the two suspects within all this and now en route to the Netherlands to be handed over to Scottish authorities?

HOLDING OUT IN LIBYA

Amidst the high-level diplomacy and intrigue, the two accused had engaged their own lawyer in Libya early on in the investigation and when they had become formal suspects in 1991. There were to be many different lawyers from different jurisdictions over the coming years, but the announcement of the trial still came, though, as a surprise to the Scottish lawyers, who had been engaged to represent the accused.

As the net began to close in and a trial became more likely, legal agents had been hired in any jurisdiction where proceedings might occur. Scotland and the US were most likely, but other areas were theoretically possible. Hence, in the summer of 1993, Alistair Duff, a leading criminal defence lawyer in Scotland, received a phone call from Dr Ibrahim Legwell, a leading Libyan lawyer who represented Fhimah and Megrahi. It appeared that he had contacted agents in London who had meticulously trawled through the names and CVs of Scottish criminal defence lawyers before alighting on him as the best and most suited. After expressing an initial willingness to consider acting for the accused, Legwell and a London lawyer travelled to Edinburgh to meet him and explain matters in greater detail. Scotland, as in England, has a system of barristers (or advocates as they are known in Scotland) who appear in the higher courts. Legwell and the London lawyer made it clear that not only had they researched and chosen Duff, they'd already pre-selected their advocate of choice, who was to be Donald McAuley QC. In due course, Duff, McAuley and the London lawyer went to Tripoli to meet their new clients.

The initial discussions concerned not just the Scottish legal system but, of course, their prospects if a trial in or under Scots law were to be held. It was clear that the accused did not wish to go either to Scotland or the US. A neutral venue would be not just Gaddafi's choice but theirs as well. The two suspects were under some sort of house arrest in Tripoli; not under lock and key, but not free to do everything as they pleased. The Scottish legal team met them and their Libyan agents alone; there was no sight of any obvious involve-ment of the Libyan government or their security services. However, their liberty and options were still curtailed and the government had no doubt a major role in their lives and destiny.

The lawyers returned to Scotland having given advice not to offer themselves up for trial. If there was to be any trial, then it should be in a neutral country and with an international panel of judges. Perfectly understandable and advice that would have been given by any competent legal agent. A few months passed and, as 1993 turned into 1994, the Scottish legal team was contacted again and asked to return to Tripoli. They did so and on this occasion they were joined by other legal teams from different jurisdictions.

They included an American attorney from Miami, Frank Rubio, who had represented the Panamanian dictator General Noriega, amongst other previous clients.

The journeys there and back offer an insight into the ongoing international intrigue that was taking place. Libya, after all, was by now a pariah state. The Lockerbie bombing was simply another reason for international disdain; the cold-shoulder treatment and specific sanctions had been in place for quite some time. A few weeks prior to departure on the second occasion, Duff received a phone call from Lord Trefgarne, who said that he understood that Duff and others were due to be going out to Libya very shortly; and indicated that he and Professor Robert Black were due to be going as well. They were also going to meet with the accused and their lawyers. This was at the behest of British business interests keen to end the impasse and see sanctions lifted. Their costs were being met by those same business interests and, indeed, Duff and the others were offered seats on the Babcock & Wilcox private jet that was taking Trefgarne and Black to Libya. That flight was declined. Though representing commercial interests, they appear also to have been working for the Libyans as, in 2007, Trefgarne wrote to Saif Gaddafi seeking an additional $1.5 million that he said Black and he were owed for work done over a considerable number of years between 1993 and the conviction at Camp Zeist.[9]

When Duff and the others in the Scottish legal team had concluded their meetings, however, they encountered a delay before they could

---

9   *Daily Telegraph*, 11 September 2011

fly home. Sanctions were indeed biting in Libya and access in and out of the country could be complicated. But another major UK business figure was there as well – the enigmatic Tiny Rowland. Rowland, who died in 1998, was a significant business baron who had been Chief Executive of the Lonrho Group. It had a reputation for sharp practice with even the former UK Premier Ted Heath describing the company as the 'unacceptable face of capitalism'. He subsequently acquired the *Observer* newspaper as well as maintaining many other business interests worldwide. Despite his somewhat shady reputation in the UK, he made many powerful friends in Africa, where the Lonrho Group had considerable mining interests. He is said to have sold hotel interests to Libya several years after Lockerbie and was also awarded South Africa's highest honour by President Mandela in 1996.

Rowland was in Tripoli on business and, hearing of the frustration faced by the Scots in being able to depart, offered them his own private jet that was standing idle. The offer was accepted by the Scottish delegation and Rowland's plane subsequently conveyed them back to the UK. Libya may have been a pariah state in diplomatic circles, but it offered huge commercial opportunities for trade interests. Lord Trefgarne may have shunned them whilst a government minister, but was he was more than willing to fraternise with them whilst acting on behalf of big business. A lot has been said and written about subsequent deals in the desert for oil, however it wasn't just oil companies, and it wasn't just subsequently but throughout the entire period of sanctions being imposed that commercial interests were lobbying. Those concerned about commerce, therefore, not just politics, were pushing for a settlement.

After their sojourn across the Mediterranean, things went quiet for the Scottish legal team. Time passed as the political arguments and intrigue ebbed and flowed, but they had no standing instructions and could neither comment or act, only watch from afar and read what was happening in the papers or was reported on TV. Then, in September 1998, they heard of a change in the Libyan defence's legal team. Dr Legwell had been removed and was replaced by Kamal Maghour. The new agent was a former Foreign Affairs Minister in the Libyan government and also an experienced lawyer who had served as a judge on the country's Supreme Court.

Despite his qualifications, however, the change in representation led to a great deal of speculation that the pressure and intrigue that had been mounting on the international stage had been matched within Libya. Dr Legwell was clearly unhappy at being removed, stating that the Libyan government had decided to set up a consortium for the accused's defence. He had refused to join it and indicated that he had already been chosen by the suspects themselves. It seemed a strong signal that the defence case for the two suspects was moving away from legal considerations of the accused to political concerns of the state. The removal of Dr Legwell appears to have been carried out at the behest of the Libyan administration, rather than the accused themselves. It had always been made clear that the accused's defence was to be paid for by the Libyan legal aid system, and it seemed that those who paid the piper were now calling the tune. Legwell had opposed a return for trial, but all that was soon to change.

Weeks passed before the Scottish legal team were contacted by a new law firm in London, who had in turn been contacted by the new agents in Libya. The Libyans were seeking a meeting and one was duly arranged to be held in Paris, where the Scots were re-hired for the defence. However, the process of gaining access to their clients wasn't to be so quick and easy. Despite repeated requests to meet with the accused, the Libyan lawyer was evasive and thwarted all the Scots' attempts to do so until March 1999, when a meeting eventually took place in Tripoli. Discussions then took place between the Scottish lawyers and their Libyan clients, both within the presence of the Libyan legal agents and without them. Once again, advice was tendered about the difficulties they faced and the likelihood that at least one of them would be convicted. The legal advice from the Scots team was clear: don't leave Libya and consent to a trial unless it was international in format and neutral in venue.

In many ways, however, it seemed as if the accused knew more about what was being decided about their trial than their Scottish legal agents. Indeed, not only did they anticipate being sent to a trial, but it transpired that their departure to the Netherlands was already scheduled for the coming weeks. They were stoic about their fate but the lawyers thought they knew more than they could or would tell. The diplomacy and intrigue had set events in motion and it was outwith their personal control. They were aware of the consequences of going to the Netherlands but the die was cast. Politics and commerce were usurping their legal considerations and as pressure had mounted on the Libyan state, it seemed it similarly was exerting pressure on its two citizens; and those supporting them were implementing it. Libya would support them in their legal fight to avoid conviction, and they'd also provide for them and their families, irrespective of the outcome. Nevertheless, Megrahi and Fhimah would be offered up for the greater interests of the Libyan state.

And so it came to be that, more than a decade on from the disaster in Lockerbie, there was to be a trial of two of the alleged perpetrators of the atrocity. The international brokering had resulted in a trial under Scottish law but at Camp Zeist in the Netherlands. The efforts of many, from Secretary General of the UN Kofi Annan to South African President Nelson Mandela, had broken the international logjam that existed. The UK and US would get their trial. The Libyans would have the sanctions lifted. Trade and commerce could open up for engineering or oil. Everyone seemed to be getting a little of what they wanted; other, perhaps, than the accused.

The world may have brokered the trial, but now it prepared to wait and watch. The trial was unprecedented in Scots law and the international focus likewise for Scotland but a global show waited for millions around the globe. Robin Cook had stated in Parliament that if the men were innocent they would have nothing to fear from Scottish justice. However, for many, if not most, this must have appeared not as a trial of two suspects, but of 'the Lockerbie bombers'.

A little piece of Holland was to become for ever Scotland, but it wasn't simply the accused that would be on trial; so would Scots law.

CAMP ZEIST – THE TRIAL BEGINS

Camp Zeist, a somewhat dilapidated former US Air Force Base in a small town east of Utrecht, was a strange site for court proceedings.

Despite this, it would become synonymous with the Lockerbie bombing; however, second only to the Scottish town itself.

A bilateral treaty was agreed between the UK and the Dutch that ceded the site for the purpose and duration of the trial and any consequent appeal. Importantly, the base had buildings that could be converted or adapted for court use and possessed the space to accommodate not just the judges, lawyers and accused, but the expectant media, who were likely to arrive in their droves. It still ostensibly remained the territory of the Netherlands but, to all intents and purposes, Scotland effectively took over. Armed Scottish Police guarded the perimeter and Scots prison officers guarded the accused. Scots judges presided and even the entourage who support the judiciary were imported from across the North Sea.

The old schoolhouse that had served the camp families' children was converted into the court house. However, it was to be a Scottish court like no other. The security alone made it more akin to a Mafia court in Sicily than the High Court of Justiciary, as the highest criminal court in Scotland is known. Though security for terrorist trials has tightened in Scotland, there has been no Scottish court before or since akin to what was established at Camp Zeist.

As well as security, the technology employed was like no other. Judges sat high above the proceedings, as they do in most courts in Scotland, the witness box in front of them. Slightly to either side were the seats for the defence and prosecution; and behind the defence rows of counsel, then solicitors and finally there sat the accused. The most up to date technology was fitted and security installed. The court itself convened behind a bullet- and bomb-proof screen. There was, though, a main large screen and microphones fitted. Moreover, judges and lawyers had their own visual aids as well as laptops. Those allowed in, whether victims' families or media, could see but were physically excluded from the main participants. Sound was relayed and amplified out to the waiting press gallery on the other side of the screen and to those outside the building.

There was a somewhat surreal atmosphere, but the stage was set for the show. The eyes of the world were watching. An entourage of those who had helped broker the deal supervised the departure of the accused from Tripoli. At the airport in Tripoli, the ambassadors of all the UN Security Council states, other than the UK and US, who didn't have a diplomatic presence in the country, gathered to see them leave. Also present were President Mandela's Chief of Staff and Prince Bandar from Saudi Arabia, who had both been pivotal in the arrangements. An Italian Air Force plane, bearing the UN emblem, landed to collect them for the journey to the Netherlands. Meanwhile, press entourages from around the globe flocked to Camp Zeist to await their arrival.

On 5 April 1999, Fhimah and Megrahi landed at The Hague, where they were detained initially by Dutch Police officers before being transported by helicopter to Camp Zeist. There they were handed over to the Scottish Police to be processed at Camp Zeist, where they were formally charged and detained. They appeared before a Scottish Sheriff Principal, who had been flown in especially for those proceedings, and arrangements were made for a further procedural hearing the following day, when a more formal examination could take place. On the advice of their legal team, Fhimah and Megrahi declined to comment and the world's waiting press had little but the events themselves to comment on. Thereafter they were formally remanded into custody to adhere to Scottish legal process.

Megrahi and Fhimah were initially held in temporary accommodation in the former camp hospital before later being moved to the more secure former guardhouse of Camp Zeist. After a slight delay, it was converted into the detention area for the accused. By all accounts it was not the normal military guardhouse. In many ways, the prisoners had the run of their building, though they were clearly under lock and key within it. For the prisoner officers, they offered no real challenge other than the dietary requirements of Muslims, which were different from the usual prisoners that officers dealt with, but this simply involved providing the appropriate food and leaving them to cook and prepare it themselves. The prisoners were well behaved and those looking after them got on well with them.

It wasn't simply the location, but the manner of the proceedings that was to be unusual, which, though under Scottish laws and procedures, would be unlike any other. The law in Scotland, as in most jurisdictions, has evolved over many years, and can be deeply conservative and loath to change, understandable in an area of life where precedent is so important. This situation, however, was totally unprecedented, and aspects of Scots law that might normally be viewed as sacrosanct were jettisoned. Firstly, this trial would not be, as is the norm in Scotland, before a single judge and jury. It's normally fifteen citizens in Scotland, not the twelve as in England and the US. The judge normally advises on the law to be applied and the jury decide on the facts that occurred. Instead, this was to be by three judges sitting alone without a jury at all. The judges would be deciding not just on the law to be applied but facts as they decided them. However, given the location and other factors such as security and pre-trial publicity that was understandable; and accepted by all participants.

Secondly, in Scotland, as in other legal systems, the accused are innocent until proven guilty. Reporting and comment is to be restricted and if there is too much and it is felt prejudicial then often there can be no trial at all. The accused, having been essentially tried and convicted in the press, cannot get a fair trial before a jury, as their minds will most likely have already been, if not made up, then at least tainted. Sometimes, if publicity is localised, then it can be moved to a different city or community. News of the Lockerbie bombing, however, was global, and there was hardly a site on earth, let alone one in Scotland, that was not aware of the hearing. Despite this, however, any argument that would normally be made that a fair trial could not be guaranteed as a result of adverse publicity ('a plea in bar of trial') was never going to be entertained, let alone sustained. It wasn't Scots law that had decided upon that, but international diplomacy.

Reporting on Scottish trials was tightly regulated, but so too was the broadcasting of them. Television cameras in Scottish courts remain very rare even to this day, and in the closing decades of the twentieth century they were almost unprecedented. This, however, was a world event and the world media wanted access. The Scottish court rejected the live broadcasting of the initial trial and many in the UK and especially the foreign press were not happy. Despite this, the press and broadcasting coverage was still huge.

The former gym hall was converted into the media centre. In the court room, significant space, albeit behind the glass security screens, was made available for the world's media to watch. It wasn't just the broadcasting centre that was created, either. Stands for broadcasters outside were established to allow interviews to be carried out and covered by the army of waiting reporters. Over 600 from thirty or so countries had descended upon Camp Zeist and they posed a huge challenge to the Scottish media staff on hand to assist and accommodate. The majority were from the UK and US, but there were journalists from all corners of the world in attendance. Given the nature of the trial it was hardly surprising that two Libyan press officers were clearly viewed more as representatives of the security services than the third estate.

There were insufficient seats within the formal court building, so a simultaneous transmission of proceedings was relayed to the media centre. It had been hoped that doing so would reduce tape recordings and other gadgets, which were precluded from being taken in. Despite these restrictions, breaches still did occur, such was the clamour for news. Despite the availability of live transmission to the media centre, many clamoured for a ringside seat even if it was to be behind the glass security screen, and so a rota system to allow the press access to the formal court room was arranged. Commendably, efforts were made to ensure that the reporters from both the Syracuse University paper and the local journal for Lockerbie were not edged out in the unseemly scramble. Their readers had, after all, suffered more than most, but were in danger of being elbowed aside by a world press corps eager for the front-row seats.

Efforts were also made to try to teach the international media about some of the technicalities of Scots law and to make them aware of the rules and requirements they were expected to adhere to. The challenges went from the very complex technicalities to very basic misunderstandings about language. Foreign reporters asking to be allowed to take a picture of the Crown were expecting some kind of diamond-encrusted tiara, not realising that the formal title for the prosecution in Scotland is the Crown Office and Procurator Fiscals Office, shortened to 'the Crown' in common parlance. It was also necessary to explain to journalists from different jurisdictions that Scotland had three verdicts in use. They were (and still are) 'guilty', 'not guilty' and 'not proven'. Both 'not guilty' and 'not proven' are verdicts of acquittal from which there can be no retrial. The reason for the three verdicts is historic, though common perception is that a 'not proven' is more akin to a 'we think you're guilty but cannot prove it'. However, explaining this system to foreign correspondents was no easy task. Indeed, the nightmare scenario for the media handlers was the return of a 'not proven' verdict and trying to enlighten an incredulous world to it. It's hard enough to explain in Scotland, let alone doing so via interpreters or to those used to different legal systems.

Other challenges continued on a daily basis as the trial proceeded. The usual reluctance of those involved in Scottish court proceedings to engage with the media was an issue to many from other countries,

but especially the United States, where they are used to daily briefings and interaction often directly outside the courthouse. The clash
in legal culture wasn't simply with those from outside the UK. Many
English reporters could not comprehend that Scots law was not simply English Law in a Scottish court, and that the rules that applied to
them varied from what they were used to in London or elsewhere.
Undoubtedly, though, the biggest culture clash was with those from
the US, where the system and media world were and are remarkably
different. Prosecutors and even judges can court publicity as their
re-election can depend upon it, whereas neither post is elected in
Scotland and both are forsworn from political activity. Requests were
accordingly made for interviews not just with witnesses but with
prosecutors and judges; something that is unacceptable in Scotland
but the norm in the US. They were of course politely refused.

Other reporting, however, was harder to restrict, even when it
clearly challenged and often broke the rules that were in place. On
the first day of the trial, comments were aired publicly by some of the
victims' families that clearly indicated their belief in the accused's
guilt; something that should not be commented upon until after
proceedings have finally concluded. Some victims' relatives had
come over for the trial along with American officials; many if not
all were convinced of the accused's guilt, whilst others still regretted that the trial was not being held in the US, where they felt it
belonged by right. A few were strident in their denunciation of the
accused and made their views public throughout the trial. Additionally, a daily précis of the trial on numerous channels drove a coach
and horses through normally tough media laws meant to restrict

comment to a factual recounting of what had been said that day. Many reports took it much further and made judgments, assessments and statements that would normally be precluded. Perhaps wisely and understandably, the court ignored what might usually have resulted in a finding of contempt of court for many a journalist and for some victims' families.

Many of those present at the proceedings recollect both moments of great solemnity and times of intense boredom. Some of the evidence, especially relating to the falling to the ground of passengers, was, understandably, deeply harrowing. Witnesses had to relate what they'd seen and other evidence disclosed the full horror of the atrocity. Some aspects were very scientific and technical and were hard for lay people to follow and comprehend.

A formal identification parade was the next procedural event. It was arranged by the Scottish Police, who had sought out some local Arab community members to act as stand-ins along with the two accused. All were dressed in identical tracksuits. The crucial witness, Tony Gauci, was brought in. The defence lawyers objected when formally asked if they had any complaints regarding the conduct of the parade, but these were clearly based on the pre-trial publicity given to the two accused and the photographs of them shown to the key witness. Having had those comments formally noted, the parade then proceeded regardless. Gauci was brought in to look at the line-up and after what appeared to be an eternity to those waiting and watching, stated that 'number four' was closest. Number four was of course the accused Megrahi, though it was hardly a ringing endorsement for his important identification evidence.

Scots law had at that time a procedure called the '110-day rule', which was meant to ensure that the accused awaiting trial would not rest interminably in custody pending proceedings taking place. The prosecution was therefore required to bring them before the court and commence the proceedings within 110 days of their formal remand. As a consequence, the trial should have begun in October 1999. However, it was clear that the prosecution would not be ready to start at that stage. A dilemma was faced by the defence, who, equally, would not be ready since much of their preparation depended on the case that they would be answering to. They faced a dilemma: should they insist that matters proceed expeditiously and see if the prosecution case unravelled, or seek an adjournment to allow for preparation that both they and the prosecution would require? Understandably, given the obligations on the defence, they opted for the delay rather than gamble that the prosecution case would fail. It allowed for more time for all to prepare but delayed the proceedings until May 2000.

The accused faced charges of murder, conspiracy to murder and a breach of the Aviation Security Act 1982. The indictment was substantial in size as much as in substance. As is normal in Scotland, the indictment (as the formal charge is known) detailed not just the crimes they were alleged to have committed but the names of each of the people they were accused of murdering – in the air and on the ground. There were several pre-trial hearings that took place at Camp Zeist and others at the High Court in Edinburgh. The accused were not brought to the latter venue as their attendance wasn't necessary and the security implications made it both unwelcome and impractical. There were initial legal challenges by the defence to some of the charges that the accused faced and descriptions of them in the indictment. However, after legal debate it was decided that they would face charges of conspiracy and could be described as members of the Libyan Security Services.

And so, on 3 May 2000, over eleven years after flight 103 had been destroyed, proceedings commenced. Another adjournment soon took place, but thereafter the proceedings would not finally conclude until 31 January 2001.

The judges were three of Scotland's most senior: Lord Sutherland, supported by Lord Coulsfield and Lord McLean. A fourth judge, Lord Abernethy, also sat as an alternate, lest anything should happen to another of the judges. The prosecution was led by Alan Turnbull and Alastair Campbell. The defence counsel were Bill Taylor and Richard Keen. There was also a plethora of lawyers there for both prosecution and defence, both advocates and solicitors. Officials from the US Department of Justice were also present, given the close involvement of them and the FBI in the investigation.

The prosecution's case was that the plane had been blown from the skies by a bomb planted in a Toshiba radio cassette player contained in a Samsonite suitcase on board. The bomb timer was one of the batch sold by the Swiss company MEBO to Libya. The clothes in the suitcase that had carried the bomb had been bought by Megrahi in Malta, where it had been placed on board at Malta and conveyed through Frankfurt and on to Pan Am 103 at Heathrow. Fhimah was in charge of the Libyan Arab Airlines security at the airport in Malta. Not everything could be proven or linked, but the Crown hoped that there would be what is described as 'a sufficiency of evidence to prove beyond reasonable doubt' that they were the guilty men.

The defence case involved the incrimination of others; in this case, several groups. Firstly, the Palestinian Popular Struggle Front (PPSF) was suggested by the defence, of whom several possible suspects were named. Secondly, the PFLP-GC. Thirdly, Parviz Taheri, who was a prosecution witness due to be called at the trial. In the absence of clear evidence and the unwillingness, understandably, of those incriminated to cooperate, it was a scatter-gun approach. It wasn't, after all, for the defence to prove the guilt of those they suggested might have done it. However, it did offer an alternative scenario to that put forward by the prosecution. It seems, though, that the general perception amongst the defence team was that the PFLP-GC were always the stronger suspects.

The Crown case was laid out over quite some time by witnesses from many different walks of life, but of which many of whom were police and forensic specialists. The accused did not give evidence on their own behalf and only a few witnesses were led for the defence. After all, the burden of proof rests upon the prosecution – it's for them to prove the guilt of the accused, not for the accused to prove their innocence. The legal advice to the accused in this trial, therefore, was to refrain from giving evidence, and this cannot be construed by the court as a sign of guilt. The prosecution were preparing for and relishing the very thought of cross-examining Megrahi and Fhimah, but it was not to be. Their legal team advised against it and, though sound legal advice, it would be seen within the court of public opinion (if not the court room itself) as if they had something to hide.

THE JUDGMENT

When the court reconvened before the eyes of the world on 31 January 2001, Lord Sutherland read out the judgment detailing the evidence they'd heard, the facts they'd found proven and matters they'd excluded or rejected before announcing their verdict. The full judgment ran to over eighty pages. To a packed courtroom, the watching media and the bated breath of the accused, they started by setting the scene that had been laid out before them and the legal consequences of it: that a bomb had detonated on board and, as a result, the plane had fallen to earth, killing all on board and others on the ground; that whoever was responsible for placing the device on the plane would be guilty of murder; and that, therefore, the issue before the court was whether the prosecution had proved beyond reasonable doubt that one or other or both of the accused was responsible, either as a principal perpetrator or even in assisting in the crime.

The judgment referred to the initial evidence given by the Air Accident Investigation Bureau, who had detailed the fracture in the forward cargo bay on the port side of the fuselage. A small, 20-inch square had been completely shattered and thereafter tore the plane apart. That was accepted by the court as the primary cause of the consequent tragedy. Further evidence had been led detailing where luggage containers had been located within that forward cargo area and as a result which one had contained the device. Testimony was given by forensic scientists at the Royal Armaments Research and Development Establishment (RARDE) as well as by experts from the Defence Evaluation and Research Agency (DERA). They were specialists in aircraft structures, who also confirmed where the bomb was likely to have been and the consequences as a result. They were able to identify not simply which container, but whereabouts within the container the device had been located. That on its own was sufficient to satisfy the court about the cause of the crash.

The RARDE witnesses also talked about the fragments of the Samsonite case that had been recovered on which damage from an explosive device was indicated. It was in their opinion that the damage had come from an explosion within the suitcase, not without. Fragments of a radio cassette player had also been located. Those forensic experts also spoke about a small piece of circuit board that had also been charred and tinged by the explosive device. This had pointed them to the PFLP-GC arrests in Germany in October 1988. They had then travelled there and examined the device that had been located there. It wasn't the same model but it was similar. Moreover, a fragment of an owner's manual for a Toshiba RT-SF 16 BomBeat radio cassette player was also recovered. The court accepted that as having been the model involved and where the bomb had been placed.

Further specialist evidence from RARDE disclosed clothing that was similarly likely to have been within the suitcase where the device was located. The clothing, including some labelled 'Made in Malta', was detailed, some of which was of distinctive brands. As well as the clothing, there was also a black, nylon umbrella. All of this evidence was fairly uncontroversial and rather matter of fact. The suitcase, radio cassette player and timer, as well as the clothing, were not the real issues of concern for the defence, as on their own they did not link directly to the accused.

However, evidence was then led that police investigations had traced some of the branded clothing to a shop in Malta operated by the Gauci family. Tony Gauci's evidence was critical to the prosecution case and he narrated how he'd been visited by officers in September 1989 and was able to relate to them that he'd made a particular sale a fortnight before Christmas the year before. His recollection was that the Christmas lights were just being put up and that it was mid-week and possibly Wednesday. He was particular that the time was about 6.30 p.m. He stated that the purchaser was a Libyan. Many Libyans visited his shop as indeed they did the island of Malta and he believed he could differentiate between them and other Arabs or North Africans. He stated that the man bought an assortment of clothing, including some of those now lodged as productions from the downed flight. The court expressed some mild surprise that he could recall the incident so vividly, but accepted his evidence that he recalled the purchaser taking little interest in the items he was buying.

They next turned to the charred piece of material from the neckband of a shirt found near Newcastleton. Embedded within it were fragments of circuit board. Despite challenges by the defence on how it had been recorded and labelled, the court was satisfied that there was nothing untoward about how it related to the circuit board.

Investigations into it had been extensive but fruitless until information was provided by the FBI that the device was known as an MST-13. Further investigations led to the interviewing of Edwin Bollier and Erwin Meister, the partners in the firm MEBO, which manufactured and designed electronic items. Timers were obtained by them which were in turn examined by forensic scientists. The RARDE witnesses were in no doubt that the minuscule items recovered were part of an MST-13 timer. That allowed the court to move their conclusions that the bombing had been caused by a device within the Toshiba radio cassette, which in turn had been located in a brown Samsonite suitcase along with various clothing from Malta; which was then detonated by the MST-13 timer.

They then turned their consideration to how the suitcase could have gotten onto the container loaded onto the plane. It was accepted that it had been on a specific container, which explained the precise location for the bomb damage to the plane. The loading of baggage they accepted as being a sophisticated process with security checking and tagging for interlining flights, in which baggage that is unaccompanied is specifically targeted. The records and witness testimony were able to show precisely where and in which container it had been located, but how had it got through security?

The prosecution were clear that the suitcase went on at Luqa Airport, Malta on the Air Malta flight to Frankfurt; where it was then transferred to the Pan Am feeder flight and was thereafter loaded onto Pan Am 103. The evidence for this chain of events, though, was not so clear-cut. They narrated the normal method for tagging and carrying luggage, but it didn't seem to fit here. Even back in 1988, unaccompanied luggage had special handling procedures and steps existed to ensure that transit baggage did not travel without the passenger. Moreover, in many aspects, the evidence became confusing, and some evidence was conflicting. Both witnesses and evidence seemed to indicate that all passengers from the Malta to Frankfurt flight recovered their luggage and records suggested that there was no unaccompanied baggage. Similar doubts and concerns applied regarding how it might have been loaded undetected at Malta and thereafter for onward transmission. The court was prepared, though, to accept that as no baggage was left at the gate, it must have been loaded and transmitted to Frankfurt.

Assumptions were made regarding how it had got through screening at that airport and subsequent others. Reference was made to the Helsinki warning and that systems operated for the screening of bags at Frankfurt; presumably heightened by the terror threat. Security at Luqa Airport was arguably tighter even than at Heathrow. They too had systems for screening and checking for explosives as well as procedures to try to ensure that luggage that was not checked could not get through. All in all, it appeared to remain unclear as to how the bag could have been placed on board the plane and get through the elaborate checks. It was all inference and conjecture; and much of the evidence simply explained the checks carried out to try to ensure such eventualities did not occur. But occur it had and aboard it was; even if no one could explain how or with any absolute certainty where this had happened.

The judges spent a considerable amount of time running through the evidence that had been before them. They accepted that if the bag was loaded at Luqa, the way in which it had been done was not established; and the prosecution couldn't show how it was done. The judges even concluded that it was a major difficulty. Assumptions can be made about how security may have been circumvented at

Malta, along with slack checks thereafter in the system, but there remained no clear evidence of it being placed on board.

Having left in abeyance how it was put on board, they then moved on to deal with the evidence that may link the accused to the crime. As regards Megrahi, they said that there had been three important witnesses. Adbul Majid, Edwin Bollier and Tony Gauci.

Majid was on the Crown list of witnesses and initially put up as a supergrass; a spy deep within the JSO that would expose the inner workings of the regime. This plan, however, soon fell spectacularly apart. The defence sought access to CIA cables, which was initially refused by the prosecution, but overturned by the court. The cables disclosed that even the CIA thought him a bit of a fantasist. He'd been employed by the JSO but initially in the vehicle-maintenance department – not a frontline unit. He'd subsequently been transferred to work for LAA at Luqa Airport in Malta as assistant to the station manager. This was a post normally filled by a JSO member, showing how the regime and its security arm ran throughout Libyan society. He'd been meant to implicate both of the accused and give a link to both the explosives being brought in and the suitcase being placed on the carousel. However, it became quite clear that the real driver for his evidence had been financial gain and a desire to leave Libya. He'd even wanted an operation to have a pin inserted in his arm which would have rendered him unfit for military service. He was by that time on the American Witness Protection Program, taken into protective custody when he finally left Libya, and had been handsomely rewarded. It was clear, though, that even the CIA were unflattering in their assessment of their own star witness.

The judges were brutal in their assessment of him, stating that some of his suggestions and evidence were at best grossly exaggerated and at worst simply untrue. They believed that his continued association with the American authorities was largely motivated by financial considerations (he was receiving a monthly payment that had risen to $1,500 per month, had sought the surgery for his arm and even tried to persuade them to finance a car-rental business that he'd wanted to establish in Malta). They stated that 'information provided by a paid informer is always open to the criticism that it may be invented in order to justify payment, and in our view this is a case where such criticism is more than usually justified'.[10] So, because of this, his evidence added nothing to the prosecution case. It may have been as embarrassing for the prosecution as it was expensive for the CIA, but it didn't destroy the Crown's case.

Next the judiciary turned their attention to the evidence given regarding the timers. They were also scathing about Edwin Bollier's evidence, though it was still of benefit to the Crown. They found him an unreliable witness and at times untruthful, but there were still aspects that they thought credible. They were satisfied that he'd supplied MST-13 timers to the Libyans. He was one of the founders of the firm MEBO AG in Zurich, Switzerland, which supplied electronic equipment, and one of whose principal customers was the Libyan military. MST-13 timers had been designed at the request of Said Rashid, who in 1985 had been head of special operations for the JSO and Ezzadin Hinshiri, who was Director of the Central Security

---

10   Opinion of the High Court of Justiciary at Camp Zeist. Case 1475/99

Section of the same organisation. Both those officials were linked to Megrahi. As a consequence of these links, Bollier went to Libya on many occasions. He also met Megrahi on several occasions, the first meeting of which was in spring 1987, and they met on some three or four occasions thereafter. It was also suggested that he supplied the Stasi in East Germany, though those particular timers appeared to be accounted for. He gave evidence that he attended tests carried out by the Libyan military in the desert which involved the use of the timers in connection with explosives and in particular air bombs. Indeed, he'd been in Tripoli on 18 December 1988 when he'd been in Megrahi's office, though he himself was not there for the purpose of supplying further timers.

There was a dispute over the circuit boards that made up the timers, with some being single- and others double-sided; and a dispute over whether the fragment of circuit board found at the crash site was from an MST-13 timer. However, much of that seems capable of being explained by the damage caused to the timers by the explosion. Forensic evidence showed that the effect of the explosion on the timers could be such that it would be difficult to differentiate as to whether they had single- or double-sided solder masking. The reason that this was of interest was suggestions that the timers located in Togo had double-sided masking specifically. It was suggested that the Lockerbie one was single-sided only. Solder masking provides a permanent protective coating for a circuit board and prevents short-circuiting. The Togo ones also had the letters MEBO printed on the surface of them. Significant and extensive tests were carried out, including controlled explosions. They concluded that it was the explosion itself that caused the apparent differences rather than them being specifically different timers.

There have been conspiracy theories running ever since regarding the timers. The evidence of James Thurman, one of the American experts working for the FBI, was challenged and accusations of perjury were made against him. However, significant investigations were carried out and though there may have been some lapses in procedure by him, there is certainly no evidence of any other wrongdoing or, specifically, seeking to pervert evidence in this case. The individual who was the source for the allegations was himself dismissed from his post. Likewise, allegations have been made about the timer evidence being planted. There is simply no substance to that allegation, however, and the fact that American experts knew about MEBO prior to the Lockerbie investigation is perfectly understandable given the seizures of timers in Togo and Senegal that occurred long before the tragedy. The CIA and FBI knew before Lockerbie happened, never mind the investigation, that Libyan intelligence had been acquiring timers from that company and that they appeared specifically made to order. Linking the two up at a later stage accordingly seems logical rather than suspicious. All the evidence shows that the American, along with UK forensic experts, acted appropriately and properly.

Bollier's partner Erwin Meister also gave evidence of having conducted business with both Megrahi specifically and Libya in general. Much of this evidence was very complicated and, indeed, seemed to take the story in different directions, never mind countries. Evidence was heard of timers being recovered in Togo as well as others in Senegal. As stated earlier, there were suggestions that the timer could also have come from East Germany, not simply Libya; though it did appear that checks disclosed that the Stasi-supplied ones in the former East Germany were all accounted for.

The court was scathing of most of the witnesses involved in the evidence relating to the supply of the timers. That's perhaps understandable given the nature of the business they operated in and the people with whom they traded. The supply of timers, whether to Libya, East Germany and possibly even other regimes, is not standard commercial fare and far more akin to underworld dealings. In these circumstances, it's understandable that the evidence is as murky as the world in which it operated. The issue of single- or double-sided timers, therefore, was oftentimes obscured by witnesses who probably had a lot to hide. Subsequent research by a filmmaker disclosed that Bollier's email address, featured on his website, was Mr.Lockerbie@gmail.com.[11] Insensitive and highly suspicious, confirming no doubt the basis for the court's scorn and circumspection regarding his and colleagues' evidence. Whatever the shortcomings of the evidence from Bollier and others, however, they were satisfied that it provided a link between the Libyans and the timers. It also linked them to Megrahi, who had travelled to Switzerland and whose name had been specifically mentioned by those who had visited Libya seeking to supply them.

This, then, brought them on to the witness Tony Gauci. He was the link needed to implicate Megrahi with the suitcase and, thus, the bomb. In the statement that they read out, the judges referred

---

11   Patrick Radden Keefe, 'The Avenger', *New Yorker*, 28 September 2015

to Gauci's comments at an identification parade for Megrahi on 13 August 1999. That set the scene for the problems with the reliability of his evidence. He stated that it was 'not exactly the man I saw in the shop. Ten years ago I saw him, but the man who look a little bit like exactly is the number five'. Asked to identify him in the court dock at the trial, he stated, 'He is the man on this side. He resembles him a lot.'[12] That might have given the impression that the court were sceptical of his evidence but this was not the case. The court qualified their statement by saying that it was important to look at the history, which they then proceeded to do; though it's hard to see how that gave any more clarity to already sceptical evidence. What followed in the narration of the responses by Gauci when asked to comment and identify the purchaser of the clothes was often contradictory.

To put it simply, the identifications made by Gauci could almost have been of different people. Indeed, he stated that he didn't have a great deal of experience on height and age. But the first interview with the police on 1 September 1989 had seen him detail a purchaser who had been over six foot in stature. A week or so later, in a further interview with the police, he placed the age of the individual at about fifty years of age. Initially, Megrahi was not identified by Gauci. Shown photos in September 1989, he initially identified someone else, though did caveat it by stating it was only similar to the man who was older. A subsequent attempt to have him identify the person a few weeks later also did not identify Megrahi but another person again, though

---

12 Opinion of High Court of Justiciary at Camp Zeist. Case 1475/99

that was caveated as only being similar in some ways. Further photos were shown the following year on more than one occasion and yet there was still no positive identification. At the trial it came out that, at around the end of 1989 or the early part of 1990, his brother had shown him a newspaper about the Lockerbie disaster. The article was headlined 'Bomber' and had photographs of two people. Gauci thought one of the men whose photograph was shown was the man who had purchased the clothes from him. However, that person was identified as Abo Talb, one of the Palestinians incriminated by the defence. The court itself acknowledged that by the time Gauci gave his statement on 10 September 1990, he had been shown many photographs indeed, but had not seen the man who had bought the clothes from him.

On 15 February 1991, Gauci was again interviewed by Scottish Police and shown a card of twelve photographs. He initially thought they were all younger than the man who had purchased the goods. He was asked to try to allow for age differences. Eventually, he stated that 'number eight' resembled the man who had bought the clothes. He qualified it by stating that he would need to be ten years or more older. Indeed, he added, 'I can only say that of all the photographs I have been shown, this photograph number eight is the only one really similar to the man who bought the clothing, if he was a bit older, other than the one my brother showed me.'[13] That was his first identification of Megrahi, photograph number eight being a passport photo of him from 1986. The court also heard that, at the end of 1998 or the beginning of 1999, Gauci had gone

---

13 Opinion of High Court of Justiciary at Camp Zeist. Case 1475/99

to the Maltese Police having been shown a magazine by a friend containing an article about the air disaster. At the bottom of the page there was a photograph of Megrahi, who Gauci stated looked like the man who had bought the articles from him, though he did again add a qualification that he was without glasses and that the man's hair looked shorter.

It wasn't simply the description of who he had seen purchasing the goods in the shop that differed, but the date on which the transaction was made. There again, the evidence was often contradictory and frequently difficult to follow. For sure, nobody doubted that the goods had been purchased by someone and that they linked to the suitcase and hence the bomb. But exactly by whom and on what date was the issue. The Crown was adamant that it was Megrahi and the date was important not simply for the veracity of Gauci's evidence but in order to make a further link with him and his presence in Malta.

Pressed about using the Christmas decorations in the town as a guide for giving a date, he initially stated, 'I wouldn't know exactly, but I have never really noticed these things, but I remember, yes, there were Christmas lights. They were on already. I'm sure. I can't say exactly.' When pressed later in his evidence, he stated, 'I don't know. I'm not sure what I told them exactly about this. I believe they were putting up the lights, though, in those times.'[14] In its judgment the court accepted that his position about the decorations was unclear but thought that it was consistent with his rather confused

---

14   Ibid.

recollection that the purchase was about the time when the decorations were being put up; which in turn they took as consistent with his evidence that it was about two weeks before Christmas.

Gauci had, though, been clear that on the day of the purchase he'd been alone in the shop. His brother, with whom he normally worked, being absent, watching a football match on television. It was a major European fixture involving his favourite Italian team AC Milan. So the dates were set. The prosecution and defence were both clear that if that was the case, then the matches broadcast on Italian TV that he'd watched would either have been 23 November or 7 December. Gauci was also clear that the purchaser had also bought an umbrella from his shop as well as the clothes for the suitcase. There were conflicting statements by him as to whether it had been raining or drizzling at the time and, indeed, whether the shower had stopped or not when the purchaser left. They, though, appear relatively minor details, confusion about which can be viewed as understandable given the passage of time. But it did appear clear that there had been rain and at least some drizzle. Whether it had stopped or continued was debatable. The importance related to the date of purchase.

Metrological evidence was led for the periods 7/8 December and 23/24 November. The latter period had light, intermittent rain at Luqa Airport, and the weather in Sliema, where Gauci's shop was located, was very likely to have been the same. On 7 December, there had been a trace of rain at Luqa Airport at 9 a.m., but no rain was recorded later that day. The meteorologist indicated that Sliema was about five kilometres from Luqa. He was asked if there was any likelihood of rain there between six and seven in the evening. His response was that it was 90 per cent that there wouldn't have been, though it was possible there could have been some slight drops of rain – far from an endorsement of rain having occurred.

All in all, it seemed a muddle as to who had bought the clothes and when they had been purchased. It hardly seemed a clear identification or a certain date. The court then turned its mind and its judgment to their opinion on Gauci and what they took from his evidence. They stated that

> the clear impression that we formed was that he was in the first place entirely credible, that is to say doing his best to tell the truth to the best of his recollection, and indeed no suggestion was made to the contrary. That of course is not an end of the matter, as even the most credible of witnesses may be unreliable or plainly wrong.[15]

They went on to add that they were 'satisfied that on two matters he was entirely reliable, namely the list of clothing that he sold and the fact that the purchaser was a Libyan'.[16]

That then took them on to the heart of the case about whether the purchaser was Megrahi. On that the judges themselves conceded that there were problems. They accepted Gauci's evidence that his brother was watching football, which focussed the date of purchase down to one of two days – 23 November or 7 December. They then formed the view that a brief, light shower was not impossible

---

15 Opinion of High Court of Justiciary at Camp Zeist. Case 1475/99
16 Ibid.

despite the evidence from the meteorologist. Despite having stated the 90 per cent likelihood of no rain, they decided that it must have occurred. To assist their conclusion, they regretted that Gauci had not been asked about the weather at any other time of the day on 7 December. That would have assisted, they thought, as it did appear to suggest that there had been a slight trace of rain at 9 a.m., but none apart from that. How, though, that would have assisted, given that Gauci appeared to link the rain with the umbrella made at the purchase (which was in the evening), is surprising to say the least. They appeared to focus on issues that he had not been asked about to give them the right to make a deduction that it was the day in question. The solution, in their view, was to simply assert that there must have been a light drizzle at the time. On the issue of the Christmas lights, they simply suggested that Gauci's rather confused recollection was consistent with his other evidence. As a result, the court was satisfied that the date of purchase was 7 December.

They then moved on to other contradictions in the identification. The first descriptions given by Gauci were of a man six feet tall and aged around fifty. The court accepted that at the first identification parade in December 1998, Megrahi was 5 ft 8 in. and thirty-six years old. They noted, though, that Gauci had indicated that he did not have experience of height or age but accepted that 'there was a substantial discrepancy'.[17] However, they believed that his doubts added to, rather than detracted from his evidence. They believed that he had picked out Megrahi at the identification parade and in

---

17   Opinion of High Court of Justiciary at Camp Zeist. Case 1475/99

court not because it was 'comparatively easy to do so but because he genuinely felt that he was correct in picking him out as having a close resemblance to the purchaser'.[18] They went on with a further caveat that they accepted 'of course that he never made what could be described as an absolutely positive identification'. That said they concluded that

> having regard to the lapse of time it would have been surpris-
> ing if he had been able to do so. We have also not overlooked
> the difficulty is in relation to his description of height and age.
> We are nevertheless satisfied that his identification so far as
> it went of the first accused as the purchaser was reliable and
> should be treated as a highly important element in this case.[19]

That not just closed the basis of the Crown case, but some might say sealed it.

The judgment then moved on to the defence case. They had lodged their notice of incrimination but still the court correctly pointed out that it was not for the defence to prove anything – the burden of proof still remained with the Crown. Some evidence was led about Parviz Taheri, the third person incriminated, but it was of little relevance and quickly dispensed with. They quickly moved on to the PFLP-GC. Understandably, they conceded that no member of the organisation was there to give evidence, but they did hear testimony from others and, in particular, from German Police

---

18 Ibid.
19 Ibid.

officers, that a cell of the PFLP-GC was operating in the former West Germany at least up until October 1988. They also accepted that it showed 'that at least at that time the cell had both the means and the intention to manufacture bombs which could be used to destroy civil aircraft'.[20] They further accepted that the raids on 26 October had 'found radio cassette players, explosives, detonators, timers, barometric pressure devices, arms, ammunition and other items, including a number of airline timetables and seven unused Lufthansa luggage tags. From other evidence it appeared that one of the airline timetables was a Pan Am timetable'. They recognised that there was considerable evidence of the 'bombs being manufactured to be concealed in Toshiba radio cassette players'.[21] However, they did point out that they were a different model from that used in Pan Am 103 and that the timers were also different. The ones recovered in Germany being considerably less sophisticated than the MST-13s used in the Lockerbie bombing and hence no doubt the need to use them along with the barometric pressure devices.

The court went on to explain that many members of, but not the entire cell had been detained. At least one of the principal agents was not captured and was at liberty at the time; before being detained and ultimately convicted in relation to bomb attacks in Germany, at which point he was sentenced to fifteen years in prison. They concluded, therefore, that it may have been possible for the cell to have regrouped and restocked. They conceded that in April 1989 three further explosive devices were found at a cell member's home

---

20 Opinion of High Court of Justiciary at Camp Zeist. Case 1475/99
21 Ibid.

in Germany, but they concluded that these were part of the stock from October but which had not been discovered. They believed that there was no evidence that the cell had the materials to carry out the Pan Am bombing and in particular did not have MST-13 timers. That, they thought, was important. It had been an MST-13 timer that had been used and, indeed, without barometric devices or other required aids. The timers were primarily supplied to the Libyans, though a few did go to the East German Stasi security service – their clear assumption being that the timers did not, therefore, get to the PFLP-GC and so they could not have been responsible. This seemed to ignore, though, the evidence of previous atrocities where Libya was providing arms and ammunition, such as the *City of Poros* cruise liner attack or even the La Belle night club bombing in Berlin, where the Libyan embassy in East Germany appears to have been the base. However, the court took the view that there was other evidence to assist in that assumption. The cell's principal bomb maker, Marwan Khreesat, was in fact an agent of Jordanian Intelligence and had been instructed that any bomb made must not be primed. Moreover, it was suggested by FBI agents that he'd said he never used twin speaker radio cassette players as explosive devices, which the Toshiba on Pan Am 103 was.

Finally, with regard to the PFLP-GC, they considered the situation relating to Khaled Jaafar, the young US/Lebanese national who was killed aboard the flight. There had been suggestions that he may intentionally or unintentionally have taken the bombs aboard in his luggage when he embarked at Frankfurt. There had even been evidence from another passenger of his being nervous when queuing to board. However, the court rejected this theory due to lack of evidence.

That then left only the first incriminees: the Palestinian Popular Struggle Front (PPSF). One of their members, Mohamed Abo Talb, did give evidence and admitted having been a member but claimed that he'd left it many years ago and was now residing in Sweden. However, in 1989, he was convicted of bombings in Copenhagen and Amsterdam and was sentenced to life imprisonment, which he was still serving when he gave evidence. The court accepted and narrated that PPSF and PFLP-GC not only shared many of the same objectives but often cooperated and worked together. There were also links with individuals who had been in Germany with PFLP-GC comrades and had been detained at the time of the police raids in October 1988 when in fact buying electronic components. Abo Talb, it was also accepted by the court, had been in Malta from 19–26 October 1988. However, there did appear to be other evidence that he thereafter returned to Sweden and was there during November and December 1988, though he remained in contact with other colleagues in Malta. The court therefore concluded that 'whilst there is a great deal of suspicion as to the acting of Abo Talb and his circle, there is no evidence to indicate that they either had the means or the intention to destroy a civil aircraft in December 1988'.[22]

Having dispensed with the special defences of the accused, the court then moved to their assessment of their guilt or innocence. They dealt firstly with the second accused Fhimah. They stated

---

22 Opinion of High Court of Justiciary at Camp Zeist. Case 1475/99

that the principal evidence against him was from two entries that he'd made in his diary in 1988 that had been recovered. One entry was 'take/collect tags from the airport (Abdulbaset/Abdussalam)'. This was written in Arabic, though the word 'tags' was in English. In addition, on 15 December, there was an entry, preceded by an asterisk which said 'Take tags from Air Malta', and at the end of that entry, in a different-coloured ink, 'ok'. The clear inference that the prosecution were making was that Fhimah's job was getting the tags for Megrahi to place on the bag. Further entries confirmed that Fhimah was expecting Megrahi to arrive from Zurich on 15 December, though it transpired it was in fact 17 December that he passed through. Fhimah did, though, go to Libya on 18 December and returned aboard the same flight with Megrahi on 20 December. The suggestion obviously being that, given his job at the airport, it would be easier for Megrahi to get through airport security carrying the explosive devices. This tied in with the evidence of the supergrass Abdul Majid and a telephone call from Megrahi to Fhimah supposedly regarding a lift to the airport in the morning.

The court indicated that they were satisfied that he'd made the entries in his diary and that they could be inferred as having a sinister connotation. They accepted, though, that it might be a step too far to infer that the tags were going to be used to destroy an aircraft. However, they gave themselves an opt-out from having to make that leap by excluding the evidence of the supergrass Abdul Majid that he'd seen both Fhimah and Megrahi arrive at Malta with a brown suitcase. They decided they couldn't make any inference at all as to why Fhimah had gone to Libya on 18 December, returning on

20 December in the company of Megrahi. Similarly they couldn't make any inference regarding his job and attempts to circumvent security at Luqa Airport. Nor could they even conclude that he'd even been at the airport on 21 December. Despite his work and the telephone call from Megrahi supposedly seeking a lift, they formed the view that no legal deduction could be made. Many other harder inferences had been made, in particular as to how the suitcase had been loaded at Malta, but none were to be made here. That conclusion, however, led them to believe that there was insufficient evidence. Fhimah was then formally acquitted.

That then led them on to deal with Megrahi. He had been charged with a conspiracy, but, in an incongruity that was later to exercise one of the UN observers, Hans Kochler, the release of Fhimah meant that he was left conspiring alone. It is, though, common for people to be charged with conspiring along with others as yet unknown and the court accordingly allowed amendments to be made. That was surprising in some ways, though, given the acceptance that the suitcase was placed on board at Malta.

Despite this initial hiccup, they started by indicating that the notes in Fhimah's diary could not be used as evidence against Megrahi. Having acquitted him, it would have been inappropriate to use them against what to all intents and purposes would have been a co-accused. But what other evidence did they conclude existed? Firstly, they referred to the false passport that he travelled on. It bore a false name: Ahmed Khalifa Abdusamad. It had been issued to him at the request of the Libyan Security Services in June 1987 and had been used by him to visit Nigeria that year, returning to Libya via Zurich and Malta. On the journey, at least between Zurich and Tripoli, he had been on the same flight as Nassr Ashur, who was also using a coded passport and who Bollier had said had been the person that had bought the timers. Further journeys had been made that year to Saudi Arabia and Cyprus. The only use made of it in 1988 was to travel in and out of Malta on 20 and 21 December. It was noted that it was never used again. He had also used his own genuine passport on other occasions, including visiting Malta between 7 and 9 December, when he travelled on to Prague, before returning to Libya via Zurich and Malta on 16 and 17 December.

That may have been suspicious, but what the court felt was a major factor was the identification of him by Gauci. They stated that 'we accept the reliability of Mr Gauci on this matter, whilst recognising that this is not an unequivocal identification'.[23] From that they assumed that Megrahi was the purchaser of the clothes which were in the suitcase and surrounding the bomb. They accepted the date as 7 December when he'd first arrived in Malta and had stayed in a hotel near Gauci's shop. From that they inferred he must have known what the purpose of the purchase was for. They accepted the evidence that he was a high-ranking official in the Libyan Intelligence Agency, the JSO; also, that as head of airline security it could be inferred that he was aware in general terms at least of security precautions at airports where Libyan Arab Airlines operated from. They also believed that he was involved in military procurement and had a relationship with MEBO, who manufactured the timers.

---

23   Opinion of High Court of Justiciary at Camp Zeist. Case 1475/99

They then went on to conclude that he entered Malta on his false passport on 20 December; a visit for which there was no reason. They stated that it could be inferred 'that this visit under a false name the night before the explosive device was planted at Luqa, followed by his departure for Tripoli the following morning at or about the time the device must have been planted, was a visit connected with the planting of the device'.[24] As far as the court could see, there was no innocent explanation for the visit; and the only evidence had been a denial that he had visited Malta or had a passport in a false name. The false passport had been used before in 1987 for a trip to Nigeria. Part of that trip had seen him travel along with Nassr Ashur, another high ranking JSO official who according to evidence from Bollier had been present at tests in Libya where MST-13 timers were used to detonate bombs in mid-air. Moreover, the time of his presence at the airport and an acceptance that it was an unaccompanied bag that had been placed on board the feeder flight at Malta put him firmly in the frame. The judges were of the view that had there been an innocent explanation for his visit to Malta on 20 December then they could not have made that inference. However, in the absence of one, they felt entitled to draw it.

The court then summed up its verdict:

> We are aware that in relation to certain aspects of the case there are a number of uncertainties and qualifications. We are also aware that there is a danger that by selecting parts of the

---

24 Ibid.

evidence which seem to fit together and ignoring parts which might not fit, it is possible to read into a mass of conflicting evidence a pattern or conclusion which is not really justified. However, having considered the whole evidence in the case, including the uncertainties and qualifications, and the submissions of counsel, we are satisfied that the evidence as to the purchase of clothing in Malta, the presence of that clothing in the primary suitcase, the transmission of an item of baggage from Malta to London, the identification of the first accused (albeit not absolute), his movements under a false name at or around the material time, and the other background circumstances such as his association with Mr Bollier and with members of the JSO or Libyan military who purchased MST-13 timers, does fit together to form a real and convincing pattern. There is nothing in the evidence which leaves us with any reasonable doubt as to the guilt of the first accused, and accordingly we find him guilty.[25]

It was a unanimous verdict and Megrahi was convicted.

Given the gravity of the offence and the number of deaths involved, a significant sentence could always have been anticipated. A conviction in Scotland for the crime of murder carries a mandatory life sentence. That is the only judgment that the bench can lay down. They can, though, give directions as to the minimum period that needs to be served behind bars before an application for release on

---

25   Opinion of High Court of Justiciary at Camp Zeist. Case 1475/99

parole can be made. In Megrahi's case, they specified that it needed to be at least twenty years.

That minimum sentence to be served was later increased in 2003. This was a consequence of European Human Rights legislation requiring prisoners serving life sentences to be told the minimum period they required to spend behind bars in what is termed the 'punishment' part of the sentence. He was not alone in this requirement and as a result his sentence was increased to twenty-seven years, with judges stating that they took into account his age and the fact he was detained in a foreign country. However, the nature of the crime and the deaths involved required a significant sentence to be imposed and increased the period of years to be served.

As Fhimah departed, Megrahi remained at Camp Zeist. He was to stay there behind bars, pending an appeal that was immediately lodged by his agents.

THE APPEAL

The Crown had been as hopeful of a conviction as the defence had been as pessimistic of acquittal. They believed that at least one of their clients was going to be convicted; and so it came to pass. However, if there was scepticism about the outcome of the trial, there was perhaps more cynicism about the prospects for an appeal that had been speedily marked by the defence. Indeed, a sweepstake was being run on how short the decision of the Appeal Court would be. That feeling of pointlessness came from all sides: defence, prosecution and bystanders. The prospects on appeal looked slight, if not non-existent.

However, regardless of what was thought by those involved, due process had to be followed. The legal procedure provided that an appeal needed to be marked within fourteen days, which was duly done. The grounds of appeal expanded on over a further six weeks to provide further clarity regarding the basis of it; which was that there had been a miscarriage of justice. The composition of the Appeal Court had caused some administrative difficulties for the Judiciary and the Scottish Court Service. That wasn't simply in the logistics of getting further judges over to the Netherlands but in the practical operation of it. As it had been a court of three judges that had imposed the conviction, it could only be considered and overturned by an even larger court. Hence a court of five judges had to be assembled. Given the limited number of judges in Scotland and the need to excuse those who had sat previously in the decision, it was complex and demanding in the very composition of it. However, under the auspices of the Lord Justice General Cullen, Scotland's most senior judge. He was joined by Lords Kirkwood, Osborne, McFadyen and Nimmo Smith.

Though the trial had been a media frenzy, live transmission of the proceedings had not been allowed. That, though, was to change for the appeal. The Lord Justice General indicated that live reporting of the appeal as it happened would take place. The BBC would transmit it and it would also be broadcast over the internet, in English with Arabic translation. The expectant eyes of the world continued to be trained on Camp Zeist and this time they would be viewing Scots justice live as it happened.

This case was different from the norm as it was judges themselves who had been deciding not simply on law, but fact and evidence. Given that it was a panel of judges, the circumstances were changed from the normal course, where a jury's verdict on fact is virtually impossible to challenge. The defence for Megrahi in the original trial also represented him in the appeal. He made it clear that he felt the presiding judges had reached a verdict that no reasonable jury, in an ordinary trial, would have made. He specifically felt that the relevance of significant evidence had been ignored and that facts that were unreliable had been accepted. The view usually being that their decision is final and absolute. However, this case was different with the hybrid role of the judges and a challenge was therefore made to their interpretation of the evidence. In particular, the defence focussed on the evidence of the witness, Tony Gauci where, despite doubts that the court itself had expressed and clear contradictions contained within it, they had accepted his identification of Megrahi as the purchaser.

In addition, they referred to the bomb's journey to Pan Am 103, where they sought to lead fresh evidence that it had commenced at London Heathrow, not Malta. That particular evidence had not been led at the trial but purported to show that sometime between 2200 hours on 20 December and 0030 hours on 21 December 1988 a padlock had been forced on a secure door at Terminal 3 in Heathrow which potentially allowed for access air-side. No explanation could be given for that but there was equally no suggestion of necessarily any access having been gained or by whom. Moreover, notwithstanding the breakage, security staff were on site and, indeed, it was them who had logged and recorded it.

That evidence had not been available at the trial, as it had only latterly come to light. The clear suggestion being made by the defence was that it was where the bomb could have or was planted and as such it did not lead back to Malta and Megrahi. Presumably, even if not able to show precisely that it had been placed at Heathrow, it was an attempt to sow seeds of doubt that it might have been; as, after all, the onus of proof is one beyond reasonable doubt.

However, the court rejected this as a possible ground of appeal. No suggestion of subterfuge other than the damaged padlock could be made. It was also accessed from an area within the airport that was already semi-secure in many ways. With the clothes being accepted as having been bought in Malta it appeared absurd that they'd have been brought to London then secreted at Heathrow rather than transported on the Air Malta flight. Moreover, it does not explain the unaccompanied piece of luggage at Frankfurt that had come from the inbound plane from Malta.

Whatever difficulties there were in arranging the composition of the bench that presided, there was no impediment to their speedy decision-making. When the appeal finally concluded and the judges returned to give their verdict, it took all of three minutes for the Lord Justice General to deliver the formal decision. They rejected the appeal, finding none of the grounds established or having any real basis. The following day a helicopter took Megrahi from Camp Zeist to Barlinnie Prison in Glasgow to serve his sentence.

That helicopter journey itself required intense security. Contact was made with constabularies and airports in England over which it would fly to ensure the presence of armed officers in the event of requiring to make an emergency landing or any attempt to free the prisoner. The high security that had been created at Camp Zeist was continuing. Megrahi had been the world's number one suspect and he was to become the world's number one prisoner.

SCOTTISH JUSTICE ON TRIAL

A great deal of criticism has been levelled at both the decision and Scottish justice itself. But is that either fair or justified? This was a trial that had only come to fruition after over a decade of both investigation and then international negotiations. It was a hugely difficult investigation given where and how it happened and considering the international dimensions to it. Moreover, there was significant evidence implicating Libyan involvement, as well as a great deal more circumstantial evidence to damn Megrahi. Many cases are dependent on circumstantial evidence and that does not invalidate them. But, did the evidence link together and was there proof beyond reasonable doubt?

The initial reporting was mostly, if not entirely favourable. Justice had been done and some closure afforded to families and the community affected. Praise was heaped on police and prosecutors in many countries who had collaborated to bring the perpetrator to justice. Victims' families expressed their relief that at long last justice had prevailed. Libya had a different perspective but had a lifting of sanctions and the opportunity for trade to console it. One of their citizens had been acquitted and the other convicted. They would seek to support him and would certainly ensure the welfare and wellbeing of his family. All seemed satisfied; justice had been delivered even if no one thought the crime had been perpetrated by just one man.

Later, though, criticism of the trial and the verdict began to emanate, slowly at first and initially from the margins. That castigation has grown, as has its intensity. For some it was a miscarriage of justice that needed review, for others the conviction of an innocent man. This contributed to the public debate that ran on Megrahi and Lockerbie and has continued ever since. Newspaper articles, books and even television programmes have all been written and made on the subject.

Dr Jim Swire, who had lost his daughter Flora in the tragedy, began vocally to raise concerns about the trial and subsequent conviction. His efforts and campaigning have kept both the Lockerbie bombing and the conviction of Megrahi in the public eye. His genuine decency and sincerity have impressed many. Opinion on his views vary from those convinced that given Dr Swire's views Megrahi must be innocent, to others who saw his aligning with the perpetrators of the crime as the result of some Stockholm-type syndrome.

Dr Hans Kochler, one of the UN-appointed observers at the trial at Camp Zeist, became a persistent critic of both it and the outcome. There had been five UN observers at the trial from a variety of organisations. They included the EU, the League of Arab States and the International Progress Organisation based in Vienna. Kochler was the president of the latter organisation as well as being a professor at the University of Innsbruck. His criticisms were trenchant, though some seemed to be of the very set-up that his sponsoring agency, the UN, had supported. They had been accepted by all at the outset and not challenged thereafter. He made it clear that he felt that the rule of law had been jeopardised, if not jettisoned. He was strident in his denunciations of the use by the UK government of Public Interest Immunity certificates, which were used to restrict and, indeed, stop access to information being placed before the court. Rumours abounded as to what they related to, but there could be no publication or comment in the press or courts on them. Others joined in the chorus, including Professor Robert Black. He and others have united in a campaign against the conviction and in pursuit of the innocence of Megrahi.

Edwin Bollier also sought to interject, and he and others raised issues over the timer. His evidence and that of others was rejected, perhaps understandably by the judiciary. Some of the challenges to the evidence relating to the timers were based on an assertion that evidence had been planted or concocted. Those allegations were rejected emphatically by all whether at the Appeal Court or Scottish Criminal Cases Review Commission (SCCRC). However, the latter did see some issues pertaining to the timer. Was it the MST-13 or another? If it wasn't that one then another link to Megrahi and maybe even Libya was lost. It still remained a very tenuous challenge to the conviction, however, given the strength of the forensic evidence that had been assembled by the prosecution for the trial.

A further criticism came from an unusual source, namely, the former Lord Advocate Peter Fraser. He had been in office when the tragedy had occurred and was in situ during the initial investigations, including when the decision was made to pursue the Libyans. He was reported in the *Sunday Times* as decrying the evidence of Gauci and being scathing of his testimony.[26] He was quickly slapped down by his successor. Though his comments may have been an unguarded aside, it further fuelled those campaigning for a further investigation or appeal.

It was not simply in the court of appeal, but in the court of public opinion that the debate would ebb and flow. Many were convinced of Megrahi's guilt and refuted any suggestion otherwise. They included individuals who had been involved in the investigations. The agencies worldwide were loud in their condemnation of allegations of misdeeds in the investigation and defended their own and colleagues' work. Officers who had worked on the case were understandably concerned at an impugning of their professionalism, never mind integrity.

Nelson Mandela, who had been vital in brokering the deal for the trial in a neutral venue, took time out from a visit to Scotland in 2002 to go to see Megrahi in his Barlinnie Prison cell. Whilst having no sway with courts or commissions it certainly had a significant ripple effect on the news agenda and for those convinced of Megrahi's innocence; for not only did he visit, but he convened a press conference in the prison itself. There he indicated that doubts had been cast

---

26 *Sunday Times*, 23 October 2005

on the conviction by the Organisation of African Unity; though he was diplomatic enough not to say so himself. He did, though, indicate a clear view that a further appeal or review seemed right. Given his involvement in brokering the arrangements for the trial added to his global status as a statesman and man of great integrity, it did have a significant impact. He also went on to express concern for Megrahi's welfare and sought to have him moved to serve his sentence in a Muslim country closer to Libya. It was early days then but symptomatic of the pressures building – pressures that would neither diminish nor dissipate.

However, the court had been agreed on an international basis. Monitors from international agencies were there and represented. A great deal of thought had gone into its structure and composition. Three judges were there to compensate of the lack of a jury; which clearly could not be established given the pre-trial publicity, never mind the location in a different country, making the practicalities impossible. The judges who presided were experienced and of a high calibre.

There was suspicious and even damning evidence of Megrahi's involvement in highly dubious affairs that were linked to the disaster, but was it sufficient in law for a conviction?

Many have questioned that. They have formed the view that, whilst suspicious, the evidence does not link together to lead to proof beyond reasonable doubt. Scots law, as with most legal systems, can be complex and perplexing to those that do not know it. It has its own quirks and idiosyncrasies aside even from the paraphernalia that accompany the judges in their ermine robes and horse-hair wigs. Its three verdicts, never mind the evidentiary requirement for corroboration, can be baffling to the uninitiated.

The problem, however, was not with the system of law, but the case itself. It was circumstantial evidence and weak in many ways. However, there was evidence for the court to consider all the same. There are issues, though, that have raised concern. The court itself commented on the lack of evidence of the Samsonite case with the bomb being placed on board the Air Malta flight. It certainly seems that is where it started and that Megrahi was at the airport at the time with a pass that allowed him access. But, beyond that, there really is no evidence other than that he was there. It's understandable how once loaded at Malta it would work its way through the system unchecked and with only cursory checks at Frankfurt and Heathrow. But, there is no direct evidence that Megrahi placed the bag on board.

Even greater doubts are expressed regarding the identification of Megrahi by Tony Gauci. Again, the court itself expressed its own concerns but was prepared to put them aside, having been persuaded of what they saw as his general honesty and good intentions. However, beyond that, his identification is far from clear. The court was required to deduce that 7 December was the day of the purchase even in the face of evidence that cast huge doubts against it due to the lack of apparent rain in Sliema. That does appear much more problematic.

It's very easy to look at pieces of evidence in isolation and be critical, but those deciding must look at the case in its entirety. There may be aspects that cause concern but they need not be fatal.

There may also be parts that can never be explained but, again, it need not always result in an acquittal.

Would a jury have convicted the accused? Most certainly they would have. Though research on Scottish juries is non-existent, juries are similar in many ways whichever legal system they are sitting in. They are not asked to consider the legal technicalities but make what they sense is the right moral judgment. They would have almost certainly been swayed by views that had already been formed in the court of public opinion long before the trial in Camp Zeist convened. It was for that reason that a court of three judges, after all, had been established – a jury was seen as already compromised and could not be trusted to be impartial.

But, the question was, could a panel of judges be any less so? Of course, they are trained well and assiduously to put extraneous matters aside and to concentrate on the evidence and not be swayed by other factors. In the main they do it well. The legal training does focus the mind and create a special way of thought, as well as action. It can allow for greater clarity and the desired judicial independence. However, judges are human beings too. They live and breathe the same air and atmosphere that the rest of society does. They can seek to inculcate themselves and rigidly focus their thoughts, but there are limits to what that can achieve or realistically be expected to deliver.

Despite initial refusals to do so, the accused's own government had even been complicit in handing them over, assisted by international organisations as prestigious as the UN. Those who criticise the verdict often take a sideswipe at Scottish justice, but that ignores the fact that Scotland and its system never sought to have the tragedy that befell it let alone the investigation and prosecution that followed. Both the event and the subsequent trial were unprecedented in Scotland. The terms of the trial were negotiated at an international level, well above the ranks of those who ultimately presided or acted. Would another court in another land have been different? Most certainly not.

This was more than the trial of the two accused; so much more. Prospects for peace and trade depended on it; as much as the closure for some victims' families and vengeance for others. Further pressure would have mounted on Libya and perhaps even Gaddafi himself if not nominals in his stead. The thaw in international tensions would have receded and fast, and the hoped-for lifting of sanctions and resumption of trade would have faltered and evaporated. Both Libya and the West both wanted and needed it. The world would have become a less certain and less secure place. The die was cast when the trial was established.

Those who took part did so to the best of their abilities and to try to uphold justice. This was no ordinary trial and in no ordinary court. It's hard to imagine how there could have been any other verdict in the circumstances. In many ways, as with Megrahi and Fhimah, Scots law and its judges were simply actors in the theatre that had been created to circumvent and solve both a diplomatic impasse and political problem. Scots law convened the trial, and yet found itself on trial.

CHAPTER TWO

THE CASE REFUSES
TO GO AWAY

And so justice had been done. A man had been convicted. The victims' families had some closure. The international world had some peace and accord. But, still, the case would not go away and many of the Lockerbie questions remained unanswered. Those believing in Megrahi's innocence maintained their campaign and those sceptical of the Lockerbie case retained their cynicism.

Libya settled with the victims' families, paying compensation in 2003 amounting to $2.7 billion; doing so on the basis not just of the trial verdict but the UN Security Council resolution. Libya, though, made it clear that the settlement was not an acceptance of guilt but a compliance with UN diktat. They needed to do so to end the sanctions that were crippling them and that was conditional on settlement of the outstanding compensation due to the victims' families.

The police and prosecutors indicated that they accepted that Megrahi could not and did not act alone and so the case files remained open and the investigation would continue. But against who? If this was state-sponsored terrorism, then surely it would be Gaddafi who had authorised it and senior ministers or figures in the regime like Abdullah Senussi or Moussa Koussa who would have directed it. Nothing would have been carried out or sanctioned by a Libyan agent without their approval. But that would be an investigation too far. The era of deals in the desert was arriving and so the Libyan leader was to be courted for a while. Both Gordon Brown and Tony Blair would embrace Gaddafi, whether in tents in the desert or at the UN; Clinton would meet with the Gaddafi family and Obama himself would shake Gaddafi's hand just weeks before Megrahi's release. Commerce and security would take priority. The Lockerbie case file would remain open, therefore, but gather dust.

Fhimah had returned to Libya after his acquittal at the trial, whilst Megrahi, after the failed appeal, was taken to serve his sentence in a prison in Scotland. However, the Libyan authorities, though having been complicit in arranging for him to stand trial, did not forget about him after his conviction. The Libyan state made arrangements for his welfare whilst in prison in Scotland pending continued efforts to have him if not exonerated then at least returned to their own land in the future. Libyan officials decanted to Glasgow as, initially, did Megrahi's family.

Prison authorities in Scotland needed to consider Megrahi's welfare and personal safety as well as ensuring that he remained securely detained. He was initially to be detained at HMP Barlinnie in Glasgow. Similarly to many Scottish prisons at that time, it was an antiquated and austere building. It was the major prison for the City of Glasgow and had previously held many high-profile prisoners, though none with a global profile as great as Megrahi's. Concern understandably was initially for his own personal safety. A convicted mass killer of a foreign nationality and religion could have been a target for revenge and or simply someone seeking to make a name for themselves within the prison environment. The judgemental nature of many prisoners allied to a strange hierarchy of perceived culpability can result in targeting and bullying. Scottish prisons, like all such institutions, can have issues with violence and bullying.

Significant resources, therefore, had gone into preparing Barlinnie for his arrival. A special suite had been established and arrangements even made to allow for Arabic TV to be accessed. Larger than the usual prisoner accommodation, it was made even more secure by the installation of camera surveillance. Labelled 'Gaddafi's Café' by some in the press, its costs raised both queries and ire. However, what may have seemed like more favourable treatment in reality meant that Megrahi received even less privacy than the other prisoners. It was still a prison, after all, and the security regime to both protect and contain was significant. However, he caused no significant issues to those supervising him other than the special nature of his status and his particular religious requirements. Other prisoners, too, seemed to quickly become accustomed to his being there and all was well in the prison regime.

The Libyan government made arrangements for staff to be present in Glasgow to monitor his needs and liaise with authorities. A consular corps was established. There were very few Libyans in Scotland. There were some students at university and college and others working in the oil industry but, to all intents and purposes, the legation was established for Megrahi. The consular staff would be regular visitors of Megrahi, as were his family who had travelled from Libya and moved to Newton Mearns, a popular and wealthy area to the south of Glasgow. The house was retained there through to his ultimate release, though the family's use of it was to vary. Initially, the move was thought to be on a permanent basis, and some of his children had even been enrolled in local schools. However, his wife and family's twelve-month visa for residency was not renewed by the UK authorities and they left at the end of the year. The UK was not comfortable with the family residency and difficulties were experienced in the children's schooling. The family settled for regular visits and the house was maintained as a place to stay during these trips.

Meanwhile, Libya and Megrahi settled down for the long haul. Though the unsuccessful appeal itself could not be further reviewed, a Scottish Criminal Case Review Commission (SCCRC) had been established in 1999. Its purpose was to consider miscarriages of justice and, where appropriate, seek to direct cases back for further appeals on the basis of new evidence or other specified grounds. The Commission included both legal and lay members; an august body with individuals of many skills and talents. Megrahi changed his Scottish legal team and a new stage in the proceedings commenced. The application for a review was lodged in autumn 2003 but took until June 2007 to consider.

The SCCRC justified the time they had taken to reach their conclusion as being necessary given the complexity of the case. After all, they had to consider not just the evidence that had been before the court but also fresh information that had not. In their decision, announced on 28 June 2007, they explained the basis of what the Commission had been established for and what it was expected to do, in this and other cases. The statutory test came in two parts for them. Firstly, whether a miscarriage of justice may have occurred; and, secondly, whether it was in the interests of justice that a reference should be made. Importantly, the Commission does not sit as a further court of appeal; it just considers applications made and decides whether, following those two tests, a referral should be made to the Court of Appeal. It is ultimately then for the courts to decide whether to accept the referral and, thereafter, if they wish to hear a further appeal.

The Commission rejected the more fanciful and Machiavellian grounds of appeal that had been made. In particular, to those allegations of tampering with evidence and the wilder theories relating to the timer, Jaafar or Major McKee. They saw no evidence to conclude there was any basis in the assertions of security service implication in the placing of evidence or, indeed, removal of it. The investigation in its conduct was vindicated by the Commission. It remains a slur cast against the police and investigators but is entirely without foundation.

Moreover, in recent years, there has developed a ground of application for referral that basically accuses the initial defence team of errors to justify an appeal. That was submitted here but was also rejected. Whatever may have been wrong with the trial, those charged with the defence of the accused at Camp Zeist acted properly.

The Commission, though, rejecting most of the submissions, did uphold the challenge to the reasonableness of the verdict on some grounds. They decided that there were six grounds for referral or areas that they thought should be considered. These were primarily related to the evidence of Gauci and the clothes having been bought on 7 December. Though not the only points, they did seem critical. The evidence of Gauci had been commented on by the court at the time; not just whether he'd identified Megrahi, but the difficulties over the weather and alleged rain that related to the specific date. This also concerned the Commission. They were clear that the purchaser could only have been Megrahi if the date of purchase had been 7 December. That was the only date where his presence in Malta coincided with the possibility of it being the date of sale. But, referring to the issue over when and whether the Christmas lights had been illuminated, that would appear to have suggested the date was 6 December. There was doubt over the date, given the meteorological evidence. They also commented on the initial identification parade, where evidence had subsequently come to light that Gauci had seen a photo of Megrahi in a magazine in which he was linked to the bombing.

They also referred to other issues that challenged the credibility of the evidence of Gauci. They had not been before either of the courts that had previously convened. Further information had come to light indicating that he had subsequently been paid by the US authorities for his evidence. That was significant and new. In Scotland, witnesses get limited out-of-pocket expenses for their evidence. Payment, however, is unacceptable. Instead, it is viewed as the duty of the citizen to partake, whether as a witness or a juror, not a paid emolument. Of course, there have been rewards given in the past and they can be referred to or challenged, but there have not been many in Scotland and the sums not usually significant.

It appears, however, that Gauci received $2 million and his brother $1 million.[27] These were sums that were unprecedented in Scottish criminal court proceedings. The Commission could find no evidence that the payments were a factor or that Gauci was aware at an early juncture of possible financial reward. Moreover, that of its own does not mean that it was false, but it certainly puts his evidence in a different light. At a minimum, it's something that should be able to be suggested to the witness as a reason for his evidence, if only for him to refute it. That had not happened here, as the existence of the payments had been unknown. However, given the points made by the judges themselves regarding the evidence of the supergrass Gaika being tainted by cash payments, that would seem to oblige them to reconsider Gauci. Allied with the issue over dates, it's clear to see why the SCCRC considered that there were grounds to consider the court's judgment as potentially unreasonable.

Many police officers and prosecutors have been at pains to state that much of Tony Gauci's evidence was provided prior to his even having been aware of a reward being offered. The usual descriptions from both those who support his identification or question it is of a simple man. Perhaps he was genuinely driven by a desire to help but also susceptible to influence or a perception of it. It would be natural to wish to assist the authorities in obtaining justice.

---

27 *The Scotsman,* 25 November 2013

Officers would have been at pains to explain how critical and crucial his testimony was. Human nature would lead to trying to do what was right or appeared to be. Given that payment was now known to be involved, however, his evidence needed to be reviewed, even if few were suggesting he was a barefaced liar.

The Commission had therefore found the basis upon which they could find that a miscarriage of justice may have occurred. But they still needed to meet the test of reasonableness, meant to be a failsafe so that even if there are grounds that could justify a referral, if it still appears that guilt would be shown or other actions make it inappropriate, they can decide not to. Here they alluded to Megrahi's defence, which they accepted had inconsistencies and contradictions, but for which there was insufficient reason to justify a refusal to refer. They also looked at the Libyan letter to the UN Security Council, in which they accepted responsibility for the actions of their officials relating to the Lockerbie incident. The Commission formed the view that this of its own was not an acceptance of Megrahi's guilt and did not justify a refusal to refer.

It was far from an acquittal, but it was a chink of light for the defence – and seen by many as a remarkably large one at that. The Commission therefore referred the case back to the Court of Appeal to consider whether to hear a fresh appeal. As mentioned, there were six grounds upon which the Commission had decided there was a case for a further appeal to be heard, but the key issue was related to Gauci's evidence.

So, it was back to the Scottish courts to see whether there would be a second appeal, and, if so, on what grounds it would take.

Procedural hearings commenced in the autumn of 2007 in which these grounds of the appeal were argued, as well as the scope of the evidence that could be included. The court decided that an appeal could go ahead, though it would not begin until the spring of 2009. In addition, the court allowed the defence to extend the grounds beyond those referred to by the Commission. However, some evidence viewed as secret and relating to US intelligence was addressed by a security-vetted defence counsel authorised to view the documents for the court. That was instigated by the Foreign Office and not the Crown in Scotland, as it related to national security, not the conduct of the case. This caused some concern amongst those campaigning for his release and many others who were following proceedings for whatever reason, but national security would always overrule court procedures and so it was to be. Whether it would have been crucial will never be known, though the Commission seemed in any event to have focused on Gauci, not secret intelligence, as the basis for the possibility of a miscarriage of justice.

So the case was going back before the courts and no sooner was the appeal under way when the Lockerbie story was to take yet another twist. Both the issues of prisoner transfer and compassionate release were looming on the horizon.

LOCKERBIE RETURNS

Little did I know then that two decades on I would have my own part in the tale of the Lockerbie bombing. As for other Scots, the memory of it was seared in my soul. As a lawyer I had discussed the case with colleagues and knew people who had been actively involved in a legal capacity, as well as prosecutors and police; natural in the small legal and political world that exists in Scotland. Moreover, the case was the biggest in Scottish history and was still subject to not just ongoing proceedings but heated debate in both public and professional circles. I had never even been to the town before the tragedy. Subsequently, my visits had been restricted to several brief stops en route to family holidays in France. All that, though, was about to change.

In May 2007, I was appointed Justice Secretary in the Scottish government and the first ever Scottish National Party (SNP) administration. As a consequence, I became accountable for the oversight of the Scottish Prison Service (SPS). I was also responsible for decisions both on prisoner transfer and on compassionate release.

Very early on in my tenure, the Lockerbie issue came to light as the UK government sought to enter into a Prisoner Transfer Agreement with Libya. Given that there was only one Libyan prisoner in Scotland and few elsewhere in the UK, the implications were clear. The issue quickly moved on from one of prisoner transfer to that of compassionate release. Abdelbaset al-Megrahi, the only man convicted of the bombing, had prostate cancer, and it was declared to be terminal. When he applied for compassionate release, it fell to me to decide.

In an early discussion with a Scottish government special adviser, I made it clear that it would be my decision and that the First Minister would be kept separate from it. It would be the only discussion that I would have with special advisers on it until my statement on his application for compassionate release on 20 August 2009. Scottish government officials representing the interest of the minister and the country correctly took the lead. That position was taken not only because it was the responsibility of the Justice Secretary, but at that early stage in the SNP administration, a Cabinet Secretary could be lost, but there was too much at stake for the government to allow the First Minister or administration as a whole to be damaged. For good or ill, therefore, it would be dealt with by me alone.

I decided that there were some guiding principles that would be followed. Firstly, Megrahi was a Scottish prisoner and would be dealt with by the Scottish government and its agencies; and no other. Though a very new administration and in a devolved, not sovereign Parliament, it would be dealt with ourselves. Scotland had not chosen for the tragedy to befall it, but it was our responsibility to address its consequences. It may have been the political equivalent of the black spot being passed, but at least this way we could ensure we would be in charge of our own destiny.

Secondly, due process would apply and Scots law would prevail. Megrahi had been convicted by a Scottish court. There was a second appeal ongoing against his conviction and that had to be respected until varied or revoked. There were specific laws and clear guidance on both prisoner transfer and compassionate release. The laws of Scotland would, therefore, be followed, not those of any other jurisdiction; and the values of the people of Scotland upheld, not the views of any other nation.

Thirdly, everything would be as open and transparent as possible. The eyes of the world were watching and therefore doing anything else would be foolish, never mind wrong. Throughout the proceedings, the Scottish government and its agencies have sought to be as free and frank as possible. A significant website with information posted thereon still remains for public viewing today.

Fourthly, there would be no cover-up for any errors or wrongdoing by anyone or any organisation. There was some concern and alarm in both police and prosecution circles that they may be pilloried; any decision made by me could, after all, have significant implications for them. Therefore, whilst I would not hide any wrongdoing, I would also not allow good people or their organisations serving Scotland to be needlessly maligned, trashed or traduced.

There was one minor caveat, which, without affecting my final decision, I had decided upon, which was that Megrahi would not be allowed to actually die in a Scottish prison cell. Having him as a prisoner here was one thing. After all, the SPS and other agencies had coped remarkably well to date. Continuing to keep him here, whether in prison or hospital, also could be managed. However, having him die in Scotland would be quite another. This would not, though, prejudice my decision. He could remain and be treated until his final moments – the rules would not be abrogated – and if need be we'd have him medevac'd out whether in a helicopter or a plane, but die in a Scottish prison cell or even on Scottish soil he would not.

It was to become rather an ironic situation in some ways. The Scottish government, who have no powers or competencies over foreign affairs, were left to deal with what was an international situation. To be fair, the SNP administration would not have wanted it any other way. It has always sought for Scotland to have the normal powers that apply to any nation. So, when a domestic Scottish issue became an international one, the Scottish government was not going to cede responsibility for it to the UK.

Equally, it suited the UK government for any such decisions to be the responsibility, and, if need be, the culpability of the Scottish administration. However, it was a strange position whereby the UK government's Foreign and Commonwealth Office were supposed to represent the interests of the whole of the UK, including the devolved administration. Yet the interests of the UK administration were not those of the Scottish government. They had a separate agenda and their departments would follow that, not the interests of Scotland or its government. Nothing, though, could have prepared us for the firestorm that descended.

In many countries and in the UK, through the Privy Council, there are mechanisms to deal with issues for which there is a need for some unity in the national interest, where non-partisan discussions can take place and governments can seek to involve and work collectively with the opposition. Political differences can be buried in the effort to come to some consensus for the common good. They occur not just in war, but other times of threat or difficulty. The possibility of release of Megrahi was clearly such an event for Scotland and for its people. There were significant risks to the country. Unfortunately, no such apparatus is available in Scotland. More importantly, however, the political climate meant that the opposition would not cooperate with their rivals, the chance to bring down the Scottish government being the imperative for opposition politicians, rather than the national interest. The Labour Party in Scotland in particular was shameless in its actions.

Though it was my decision alone, this story is not just about me. I was ably supported by official not political staff from the Scottish government officials and Scottish Prison Service, who dealt professionally and adroitly with issues that were unexpected and in areas where there was little collective experience. It was challenging for them as well as me, but I am, though, particularly indebted to the team that worked with me and were there throughout the events. My Private Secretary, Linda Hamilton, was a star. She was assisted by the talented Linda Pollock, the policy adviser on the case. They were diligent in their preparation for events I had to attend and policy decisions I had to make and dogged in their defence of me at every turn. Government ministers spend so much time on the road that your driver becomes an extension of the private office. My own, Ian Inglis, a kindly and deeply Christian man, began to take an almost fatherly interest in my welfare and journeys with him were convivial and fun despite the pressures. Indeed, those pressures created a comradely bond between us. My constituency office manager, Karen Newton, had worked with me since she had left school, initially when I was a lawyer and then later in my political office when elected to Parliament. My reputation as an assiduous constituency representative is mainly due to her, as she has dealt with the bulk of work that floods through the door. She was not privy to the inner deliberations, but was my local representative, especially when personal security tightened. There were risks to her, but she endured them with stoicism and good humour. They all faced the risks and potential dangers as I did. They supported me and sustained me in many ways. Whilst the times were challenging they were made enjoyable through their companionship. I was truly fortunate to have them.

A lot has been said or written about my decision. Some agree with it, whilst others do not. I have had to answer in Parliament and in parliamentary committees both in Edinburgh and in London. Some US senators even sought to have me brought before them in Washington, DC. There have been many who have been highly critical and that is their right, whether they were directly affected by the atrocity or simply commentating from an armchair or electronic device.

Others, though, have been supportive, both publicly and privately, and for that I am truly grateful. Emails, letters and just kind words and a handshake have been much appreciated. The support of many around the world was deeply important and remains so now. Some prominent public figures gave open support, which was very helpful in the media firestorm that engulfed me; others sent private words of backing or encouragement, all of which were much appreciated. But, in many ways, it was the simple and kind expressions of support or concern for my welfare from ordinary people that were most heartening. The overwhelming majority of correspondence, whether post or emails, received by my office were supportive and Linda would show me some of the cards or letters occasionally to try to sustain my spirits. Remembering the cards and home-baked goods still brings a smile to this day, but greatly heartened me back then. Those gestures were and still are deeply treasured.

In December 1988, I neither thought I would be Justice Secretary for Scotland nor have a significant role to play in the events that had tragically unfolded. However, it was a privilege to hold that office and it was my responsibility as the office holder to make that fateful decision. With the honour of holding high office comes the requirement to live up to its responsibilities, and I have always believed that, given that opportunity, it's incumbent on the individual to adhere to principle and to seek to do what's right. Nothing less should be expected; and those given such an opportunity have an obligation to seek to use it justly.

It was, as I said in my statement, my decision and my decision alone to release Abdelbaset al-Megrahi on compassionate grounds. I followed the rules and guidance of the laws of Scotland and upheld the values I believe are adhered to by the Scottish people. It is a decision I didn't choose to make, but was required to take. It's a decision I stand by now as then.

This, then, is my story of the Lockerbie bombing.

CHAPTER **THREE**

FROM LINLITHGOW
TO LOCKERBIE

was born in Edinburgh in 1958. My parents Donald and Betty
moved about quite extensively before finally settling in Linlithgow, the county town of West Lothian, in 1965. My father was a
management consultant and my mother had been a secretary before
giving up work on getting married. It was there that I grew up with
my brother Allan, who was three years older than me. I attended
the local primary and secondary schools. It was a happy childhood
and that is something I have never forgotten in my life when dealing
with others less fortunate. Sadly, neither of my parents lived to see
me elected as an MSP, let alone appointed Justice Secretary. However, I am indebted to them for the start in life they gave me and
the encouragement they provided throughout. I miss them more
than words can say. Alex Salmond, who was to become First Minister and appoint me as Justice Secretary, also lived in Linlithgow,
though he was a few years older.

In 1976, I returned to the city of my birth to study law at Edinburgh University. University afforded me not just friends and a great education but an opportunity to travel. The wages earned during summer work allowed me to travel with friends through Europe on railways as so many young people did, as well as cross the US and Canada on the buses. Those trips were not only great fun but highly enlightening and formative for some political thoughts. I became convinced that philosophically and culturally I was northern European rather than transatlantic and that was where Scotland's future lay; though I admired the beauty of North America and the energy of its societies. It also gave me the travel bug which I have encouraged in my own children, feeling it offers so much, in so many ways.

Graduating in 1980 I was one of very few students to make the move from Edinburgh to Glasgow. I was fortunate to obtain an apprenticeship at Levy & McRae in Glasgow. They provided a great breadth of work to learn in and from. They have remained a major firm in Scotland and, indeed, represented many of the Lockerbie victims' families in both the Fatal Accident Inquiry and compensation claims. They were part of the Air Disaster Group that had agents from many jurisdictions. That, though, was considerably after I had left the firm. Indeed, many of the leading partners had by the time of Lockerbie moved on. Neither, then nor now, do I have any contact or interest with them.

I had a good training at Levy & McRae and was sorry in many ways to leave. However, I had a desire to move back to the east coast. I was to become more involved in politics and my interests and most of my friends were there. Somewhat with a heavy heart I obtained employment back in the city I had studied in. I worked for several firms in the city before deciding to establish my own firm along with a partner. I enjoyed both my time there and the work undertaken. It was both challenging and rewarding. It was mostly court work and legal aid work at that. Not the best remunerated, but stimulating and rewarding all the same. The firm had a reputation for being radical and work from a variety of sources came in. My partner and other colleagues had a specialism and expertise in representing victims of domestic violence. Other staff did work in the higher courts located in Edinburgh for law centres elsewhere in Scotland, who needed agents in the capital.

A referendum had taken place in 1979 for a Scottish Assembly, albeit with very limited powers. The people had voted by a very narrow margin in favour of it but a duplicitous rule had been imposed, requiring 40 per cent of the electorate to have supported it. As a consequence it fell. During the referendum, the Labour Party was deeply split between an official line that was for the Assembly, and many leading activists who were bitterly opposed. Scotland was left powerless in the face of a Conservative government that it had not elected as a result. It would take another twenty years to get a Parliament to protect us and allow us to chart, at least in some ways, our own course in the world.

So, though the Labour Party was the dominant political force in Scotland, it was not for me. It had lost its way, I believed, not simply in its commitment to a Scottish Parliament, which had been a bedrock for the original founders, but on a variety of other social and economic issues. I was then, as now, committed to Scottish independence. For me, this was not about Scots being better than anyone else, but simply being ourselves. The tragedy of Scotland is not how bad things are; for me and many others life is remarkably good. The real tragedy is that, with all the advantages Scotland has, things should be so much *better* for our people. The levels of poverty, in particular, are appalling for a modern, Western European nation.

The opportunity to participate in mainstream party politics soon came along. The SNP, following its heavy defeat in the 1979 election, had, as many political parties do in such circumstances, turned inwards. A great deal of introspection as to what had gone wrong and what direction to take was under way, and a political grouping from the left had been established within the party. The local contact and the man who persuaded me to join was Alex Salmond.

The woes of the failure of the referendum and the defeat in the subsequent election continued and the SNP split in a myriad of ways, with disputes on left versus right, hard-line independence against gradualism and more powers for the country. It was not a happy time for the party and it was a baptism of fire for a relatively new member. As in every dispute, there was fault on all sides. Common sense and the onset of another UK election saw peace prevail. The SNP has since become a social democratic party in the Northern European tradition.

I contested elections at local level in 1982 and then at local, UK national and European level in the years thereafter. Most of those elections were in West Lothian where I had grown up, even if by the mid-1980s I had moved to Edinburgh. In those days, standing as an SNP candidate, and certainly in central Scotland, was simply a method by which the party flag was flown and the cause aired. The times were not favourable to the party, even if the period of internecine warfare had passed. The animus towards the Tories and their policies wreaking havoc on both Scottish industry and Scottish society saw the people of Scotland put their trust and faith in Labour as the only viable alternative.

My profile and position within the party grew. Elected office within the party followed. In the late 1980s, the Conservatives were facing issues with local taxation. The property-based tax needed to be reviewed and there was considerable disquiet amongst their members at increasing costs that would be borne by homeowners. Their solution was the appalling poll tax or, as they liked to refer to it, 'the community charge'. It moved the burden from the well-off to the poor; imposed a per capita charge unheard of almost since the Middle Ages; and from a Scottish perspective compounded by imposing it north of the border a year before it was due in the rest of the UK. It was a rallying call for not just left-wing groups and the SNP to mobilise politically, it also lit a fire in the slumbering Scottish population appalled at the excesses of Thatcherism.

I was asked by the SNP National Executive Committee to consider the proposed legislation and let them have thoughts and tactics. This formed the basis of the SNP's 'Can Pay, Won't Pay' campaign. It was a mass campaign of civil disobedience, encouraging people who could pay to withhold their payment; to ensure that the tax would be defeated and that those who couldn't afford to pay would not have to. There was genuine anger in not just the communities that would suffer but also amongst all right-minded people; the tax was not just wrong but hated. The campaign against it was spectacularly successful. Public meetings that hadn't been seen for a generation returned. The tax was crippled both in terms of legitimacy and in terms of collection; and it ultimately brought down Margaret Thatcher. It also gave a huge political boost to the SNP. That and other campaigning raised my profile within the party. I had been elected as a member of the National Executive Committee and was subsequently to hold positions as both Policy Convener and National Treasurer.

The Tories were eventually removed both north and south of the border in the New Labour landslide of 1997. It had been eighteen years of Thatcher and the Tories, and the hatred and contempt towards the Conservatives ran deep. In Scotland, they were left without a seat. Labour had been spectacularly successful, but the SNP had also made some more limited progress. Scotland had rightly celebrated the crushing defeat for the Tories, whilst Labour, however, were conscious of the desire for political autonomy in Scotland, whether via all-out independence or Home Rule. That had been expressed in election victories for the SNP, if not translated into major elections over many years. The SNP were accordingly a spectre that haunted Labour even if still not an electoral challenge. Labour realised that they'd benefited from that pent-up desire for a Scottish Parliament; and that it could all too easily be lost to the SNP if some form of self-government was not offered.

Accordingly, they held a referendum in 1997 where there was overwhelming support both for a Scottish Parliament and one with tax-raising powers. The powers, though, were limited and often not in any logical way; responsibility for justice but not drugs or firearms; powers over education but not over the economy that are fundamental to any society. The constitutional structure wasn't based on any logic that would have come from a federal structure, instead assembled so that Westminster retained the important levers of power whilst the Parliament in Scotland was restricted in what it could do. It could not deliver the change the Scottish people had either voted for or expected to happen. Initially, though, there was delight if not euphoria about a Parliament returning after 300 years.

The restoration of the Parliament meant some soul-searching and decision-making for me. I had to choose whether to stand for it or concentrate on business and personal affairs. The timing, with a young family and a relatively successful business, was not good; however I'd fought for Scottish independence for so long that I couldn't give up then. Whatever the costs, financial or personal, I felt I had to be prepared to pay them and play my part in building Scotland's new future.

So, at a late stage and with most of the seats already selected, I threw my hat in the ring for Edinburgh East and Musselburgh. It was the constituency in which I had been born and was near where I lived. It wasn't, though, at that stage, viewed as a potential Nationalist gain. In that election in 1999, I did not win the seat but was elected on the list system which the Scottish Parliament operates to try to provide proportionality. The SNP had done well, but not well enough. A Labour/Liberal administration was formed. The SNP, though, did for the first time in its history have a significant cadre of elected representatives and the staffing and resources that they bring.

I sadly said farewell to my legal practice. It was a job I had enjoyed and it was a difficult time to leave the business I had started with my partner. However, I have never understood the concept of politicians carrying out other jobs in addition to their elected office. I think it's an insult to their voters and cannot allow them to focus clearly on their priorities. So, Parliament and the ability to work for the cause I believed in beckoned. Ministerial office, though, was still not even on the horizon.

Though I was saddened in many ways to have left the legal profession, it was liberating to be able to become a full-time politician. No more was it trying to cram in what meetings you could between clients and cases; spending only evenings and weekends completely dedicated to politics. The volume of work did not diminish, instead, it was simply that politics took over from dawn to dusk. It was an enjoyable and stimulating environment, however, and I had a capacity for work, an eagerness to learn and a hunger to campaign for our cause.

The SNP had done reasonably well in the election, but it wasn't to be the easiest of times for the party even if I was thriving in the new environment. Initially, the SNP paid the price for the Scottish people's frustration at the failure of the Parliament to deliver all their pent-up hopes. They were associated with the concept even if not culpable for the reality. The party went through change and some internal turmoil. Alex Salmond stepped down at that stage as party leader and returned to Westminster. In the Holyrood elections of 2003, the SNP went backwards electorally, though I was again returned on the SNP list. The party needed to reassess and renew and it did both.

Time is a great healer and that is also true for political parties. Scotland came to terms with the new political landscape as well as the new Parliamentary Building at Holyrood, which had initially caused a furore. By 2007, Labour was in trouble. It was tarnished by the war in Iraq and devoid of vision in Holyrood. There was a desire for change in the land and it was a chance the SNP took. Alex Salmond returned once again as leader. He had energy and enthusiasm and, with the growing confidence of the Scottish people, it was time for a change.

Wednesday 16 May 2007 saw the swearing-in of the first ever SNP government. The party had won forty-seven of the 129 seats. Far from a majority, and only one more seat than the Labour Party, but it was a huge and symbolic result, breaking their seemingly perpetual dominance. I was also elected for the constituency of Edinburgh East and Musselburgh, parts of which had been Labour for three generations.

Efforts were made to try to block the SNP from forming an administration. Gordon Brown, then the Chancellor of the Exchequer, and soon to become the Labour UK Prime Minister, even suggested that Labour enter into a coalition with the Tories to keep the SNP out of power. The Liberal Democrats had refused to enter into a coalition with the SNP before the election and the SNP refused to countenance a coalition with the Tories. However, momentum and perception are vital in politics. It wasn't just in seats but in votes that the SNP had outpolled Labour. The latter was seen to have suffered a significant electoral defeat and the SNP to have scored a remarkable victory against the odds. In the absence of any viable coalition, the only option was a minority administration. The two Green MSPs and the Independent were happy to give their tacit support and the Tories were reluctant to bring it down. There was scepticism as to whether it would last even until Christmas. However, to hold another election would be complicated and would probably only increase SNP support. So, it was to be an SNP administration, but how long it would last was the question on everyone's lips. It was not only a minority government, after all, but an inexperienced one.

Relations between the British Labour government and the newly formed SNP Scottish Executive were always going to be difficult. The fear and animus between the two parties were historic. One of the first acts of the SNP administration was to change its name from the Scottish Executive to that of the Scottish government; moving subliminally from a subservient relationship to one of greater equality and independence. Tension hung in the air and it was assumed by political commentators that there would be a confrontation between the two administrations. It was to come very early on but was not, as had been assumed, instigated by the Scottish government.

In early June 2007, weeks into office, it came to light that the British government had signed a Memorandum of Understanding with the Libyan regime of Colonel Gaddafi. The deal was to establish judicial cooperation and create other formal legal links between the two countries. Whilst that on its own was innocuous, the links would also extend to extradition and prisoner transfer agreement which, especially given the very high-profile Libyan prisoner currently in custody, would be controversial.

Prisoner Transfer Agreements (PTA) are commonplace. The UK has entered into over 100 of such agreements with various nations around the world, which are used to arrange the repatriation of prisoners to their own land so that they can serve out their sentences there, rather than in the country they were convicted in. This has benefits for both the prisoner and politics. As a result of the PTA the cost of incarceration is borne by the prisoner's home state, which can alleviate public criticism about the funding being allocated to foreign prisoners. Also, it is believed that if the prisoner is incarcerated nearer to his or her home and family, this can help with their rehabilitation.

The number of Libyan nationals residing in British prisons, both then and now, is not significant, and they were virtually unheard of in Scotland until the arrival of Abdelbaset al-Megrahi. Entering into a PTA with Libya opened up the possibility of returning him. The atrocity for which he had been convicted had not simply disappeared from the public eye. Indeed, there was an outstanding appeal by the Crown against the leniency of the sentence as well as the ongoing consideration of Megrahi's application to the Scottish Criminal Case Review Commission, which was due to be decided imminently.

It was not only the timing but the sensitivity of the issue, as Lockerbie still resonated in Scotland as elsewhere. They had ignored the interests of the Scottish government in their deliberations and discussions. Whilst that may have been possible under a Labour administration it could not apply in the new world of an SNP government. Scotland's rights, and not just the UK government's interests, had to be considered. Though courts and prisoners were devolved, control over foreign affairs was reserved for Westminster. Concordats, though, had been entered into at the time of the establishment of the Parliament to try to ensure that the rights of devolved Parliaments not just in Scotland but also in Wales and Northern Ireland would be respected where international negotiations would impinge on devolved matters.

These concordats, however, had rarely been tested. Whilst previously it may have been acceptable to just act and thereafter inform the Scottish government, that no longer applied with the new administration. Moreover, with an issue as sensitive and significant as that of Megrahi, it could not simply be treated as before or nodded through once deals had been concluded. Scotland's rights would need to be respected.

When it came to the attention of Scottish First Minister Alex Salmond, he reacted angrily, writing to Prime Minister Tony Blair and raising it in the Scottish Parliament. The UK government, he alleged, was ignoring the concordats, being disrespectful to Scotland and interfering in the ongoing administration of justice. Moreover, specific assurances had been given at the time of the establishment of the Camp Zeist trial that, if convicted, both of the accused would serve out their sentences in Scotland. In many ways it was a political gift for Salmond, and he was not going to waste an opportunity to lay down markers when it came to the new political landscape. There was a justifiable constitutional issue here on which he could seek to flex Scotland's newfound political muscle, and so he initially led the charge on the issue of inter-governmental relationships as

First Minister, rather than myself as Justice Secretary on the PTA. Over time that would change as the issue moved on to the specific issue of Megrahi but, at that initial juncture, the debate was on the wider constitutional relationship.

There was a general consensus in Scotland, even amongst opposition members, that the British government had acted inappropriately and that Scotland's interests in the issue needed to be respected. The British government initially tried to fob off criticism of their actions, telling the Scottish Parliament that they were aware of the sensitivities over Megrahi and that ultimately rights would remain with Scottish ministers to decide on any specific applications. The First Minister was not prepared to let the issue go, however, or allow the furore to die down. He replied seeking clarification as to whether Megrahi had been specifically discussed with the Libyans or whether he was being excluded from the terms of the PTA. The UK was continuing to meet with the Libyans on the Memorandum of Understanding and further letters were exchanged. The UK seemed to imply rather disingenuously that, as there were outstanding appeals, prisoner transfer would not apply to Megrahi. The terms of PTAs are invariably that there must be no outstanding or ongoing cases and that would apply in this situation. They were well aware, though, that they could be dropped, at which point this criteria would be met. The Scottish government suggested that if a PTA was to be signed then Megrahi could be specifically excluded from its terms.

On 27 June 2007, Tony Blair was succeeded as Prime Minister by Gordon Brown. The policy position of the UK in seeking an arrangement with the Libyans remained the same but the tack seemed to

veer towards a charm offensive by the new regime. The new UK
Lord Chancellor and Justice Secretary Jack Straw came up to Scotland for separate meetings with both Alex Salmond and myself on
21 July. At my meeting he was cordial and obviously seeking to defuse
what was a contentious political issue. He enquired about Scotland's
position on the terms of the PTA and the specific concerns relating to Lockerbie and Megrahi were explained to him. In separate
meetings with both myself and the First Minister, he was advised of
the need for the Scottish government to be both kept informed and
involved where there was a clear impact on Scottish interests. That,
after all, was supposed to be the situation under the concordats. Jack
Straw indicated a willingness to take on board the interests of the
Scottish government and appreciated that Megrahi was the stumbling block. He recognised that if he were removed, then the issue
would be resolved.

Correspondence between Jack Straw and me as well as discussions between officials continued through August and September.
In my letter of 7 September to Jack Straw, I wrote:

> I welcome the confirmation that the UK has on a number of
> occasions made clear to the Libyan authorities that the PTA
> between the UK and Libya would not cover al-Megrahi. I also
> welcome the approach that your department, under your lead-
> ership, is now taking to this issue.
>
> Having considered the issue, including the risk of legal chal-
> lenge, we have concluded that the exclusion should be as specific
> as possible. Our view is that this will minimise the risk of legal

challenge by ensuring the terms of the PTA clearly reflect the position set out in the letter of 24 August 1998 from the UK and US governments to the United Nations Secretary General, which made clear that anyone convicted of the Lockerbie bombing would serve their sentence in the UK. It will also preclude the risk of legal challenge from any other parties inadvertently included within the scope of a more general exclusion.

While the PTA could specifically name al-Megrahi we would prefer that the exclusion be worded to refer to anyone convicted of the Lockerbie bombing as that would also cover any future prosecutions, should new evidence come to light. I would be grateful for confirmation that you are content with that approach.

It seemed Jack Straw and Justice Department officials were keen for a settlement that would allow the PTA to go through as smoothly and with as little adverse publicity or opposition as possible. They appeared willing to accept that specifically excluding Megrahi or preferably anyone convicted of the Lockerbie bombing from the PTA would achieve this aim. This formal exclusion was not suggested by them as being an obstacle, let alone a complete non-starter. They appeared quite relaxed about considering it and went away to speak to other colleagues in government as well as the Libyans.

That was how matters stood until, on 2 November 2007, I took an urgent call from Jack Straw whilst in a government car heading to Tulliallan Police College in central Scotland. He indicated that the call was highly confidential and asked me to speak to no one other than Alex Salmond about this. He told me that the Libyans would not accept a PTA that specifically excluded Megrahi, and that on this they were adamant. It was non-negotiable. He then went on to explain the crux of the matter as he saw it, which was British interests. A commercial deal for development of Libyan oil and other resources in the south of that country was of potentially huge financial benefit. The UK was very eager to secure the deal for BP, but it was dependent on the PTA. Jack Straw then said that the Foreign Office advice was that the Libyans were not bluffing and that if Megrahi were to be excluded from the arrangements, the commercial contracts would not be signed. Moreover, the contract would go to an American competitor firm, which, as I recall, was Halliburton. He emphasised how important BP was to the British economy. He also suggested that other deals may also become available that would be of commercial benefit to Scotland. At the time I was travelling along the M9 motorway, passing my home town of Linlithgow and approaching the refinery at Grangemouth, formerly operated by BP. I remember telling him that I appreciated the significance of BP to the economy as I was just passing their former refinery in the car. I listened politely and indicated that I understood the British position and would relay it to the First Minister, to whom I would speak urgently. I also arranged to meet him in London the following week for further discussions about it.

There had been rumours of ulterior motives. This, though, was the first time the UK government had specifically indicated that the memorandum with the Libyans was predicated on vested interests for BP and presumably other commercial interests. Justice officials seeking to get a memorandum and a PTA signed were now being overruled by Foreign Office and other commercial interests. Jack Straw was not phoning as Lord Chancellor or Justice Secretary but as a representative of a government seeking to ensure significant commercial gain for a major UK PLC. It was clear from not just the call but the intonation in his voice that this was wanted and they did not want it jeopardised. They wanted the British company to get it, not the American competitor.

When the call ended I asked my Private Secretary Linda Hamilton to make arrangements for a call to the First Minister, which I did later that day. Alex and I discussed the situation. It was clear that the UK were intent on signing the memorandum with Libya come what may. Our powers over that were non-existent. They could sign what they liked and whilst the Scottish government could object, it had no veto or right to vary. The memorandum would be signed and the deal for the commercial interests obtained by the British. We decided that we'd therefore try to seek concessions from the UK government on other issues, both political and financial, that would benefit Scotland. The least we could do was try, even if it was unlikely they'd accept.

Financially, the Scottish government was facing significant costs from a court decision in the House of Lords. Due to a legal quirk in the establishment of the Scottish Parliament, the Scottish government, uniquely amongst public authorities, found itself without the benefit of a time bar on court actions raised under the European Convention on Human Rights. Most personal injury cases in Scotland cannot be pursued if not raised within three years but that did not apply in these types of cases. Whilst not entirely open-ended, the period of time and the accordant costs would be significant. The Somerville case was a human rights case brought about by the failure of a previous administration to address the issue of 'slopping out' in prisons (when chamber pots are used in prisons where there are no sanitary facilities in cells). Though the circumstances had now been addressed, actions were being brought by prisoners who had endured such a situation. The number of cases was rising and the bill was mounting. It was therefore decided to ask the UK government to change the legislation under which the Scottish government was being pursued to limit the time bar and make it retrospective; and if not then to get them to underwrite the cost that would occur.

Politically, the SNP was committed to taking action on air guns. There had been several tragedies involving the use of air weapons including a high-profile case in which a young boy was tragically killed by the reckless discharge of one. Moreover, their unrestricted use was blighting communities across the land, affecting not just humans but animals both wild and domestic. Though Justice was devolved to the Scottish Parliament, Firearms, along with Drugs, remained reserved for Westminster. Air weapons were classified as firearms and, accordingly, only they had the power to legislate. Hence it was agreed to ask that power over air weapons be devolved to the Scottish Parliament.

It was agreed that I'd ask Jack Straw about support for those issues at the meeting arranged to discuss the PTA. I was to fly to London for the meeting on 8 November, but on that day high winds were causing disruption and there was the possibility that flights between

Edinburgh and London might be cancelled. As a member of a minority government, I couldn't risk being stuck in London and missing a vote. Accordingly, a conference call was arranged. It began with the usual pleasantries and platitudes before moving on to the substantial issue of the PTA. I indicated that I had spoken to the First Minister and that we were aware of the significance of the memorandum for UK interests. I pointed out, though, that, because of Megrahi, the issue remained sensitive and difficult in Scotland. Moreover, I explained that, given the vehemence with which the First Minister had opposed the PTA when news of it had first broken, there would be political difficulties in concurring now. However, I explained that this would be made easier if they were able to offer some concessions to assist us. I then broached the issues of both the Somerville judgment and the devolution of air weapons. Jack Straw was somewhat taken aback as I recall. He'd perhaps been anticipating the Somerville request as discussions were ongoing between the respective administrations regarding it, but the air weapons request seemed to come as a bolt out of the blue. A sharp intake of breath could be heard. He said he'd need to speak to ministerial colleagues and get back to me.

The Scottish government official who was in the room with me for the conference call and who is now a very senior civil servant was biting his wrist to stop himself laughing. He stated, deadpan, that it would never have happened under the past administration. Maybe not, but if they were going to impose a PTA upon us with all the consequent difficulties that would arise, we'd do our best to get something tangible for Scotland out of it.

The telephone discussion in November was followed up on

6 December with a letter to Jack Straw reminding him of our desire
to have anyone convicted of the destruction of Pan Am flight 103
excluded from the PTA's terms as negotiations between the UK and
Libya continued. Discussions between officials for the respective governments were ongoing. As the turn of the year approached it was
clear that our requests were not going to be met. Numerous calls were
going back and forward with a variety of ministers, but all to no avail.
It was always a forlorn hope as we had little bargaining power, and
though the First Minister was still hopeful and seeking calls to be made
to Jack Straw, frankly I viewed them as pointless. They were going
nowhere and it was clear that there was no give whatsoever in the UK's
position. The British government was intent on delivering the PTA
and on the terms that were acceptable to the Libyans. The Libyans
had always made it clear that Megrahi was part of their discussions
with the UK. They wanted their man back before he died. When
Gaddafi heard of the suggestion of excluding Megrahi from the deal
he was apparently furious and held up the signing of the oil contracts.[28] It was the reason for the PTA in the first place. As far as
Gaddafi was concerned, 'Megrahi's return to Libya was the price of
fully opening up Libya to the bankers and the oilmen.'[29]

Correspondence between the First Minister and Jack Straw continued in January, February and March of 2008. The line from the
UK was that Megrahi could be excluded simply by Scottish ministers
refusing to agree to a request from him for a transfer to Libya. The
Scottish government's response was to point out that such a decision

---

28 Chorin, *Exit the Colonel*, p. 155
29 Ibid., p. 157

could be challenged in court. A specific exclusion would have precluded that. Moreover, the opportunity was taken to remind Jack Straw that he had agreed to a general exclusion of anyone convicted of involvement in Lockerbie back in September.

The British government also made reference in its responses to the UK national interests, both economic and strategic. Jack Straw had made reference to Libya moving to dismantle its military nuclear capacity. The First Minister had in his response on 18 March taken the opportunity to welcome that and urged the UK to follow Libya's lead. It was clear that discussions with the British government were getting tetchy and going nowhere. Alex Salmond wrote: 'It is clear that a continuation of this correspondence would not be fruitful. The UK government has clearly decided to press ahead with a Prisoner Transfer Agreement without an exclusion, despite the concerns that we have expressed. We will simply have to deal with the consequences.'

Jack Straw had either been overruled or persuaded by Foreign Office and Trade Department colleagues that UK interests were such that he had to go back on his promises to the Scottish government. However, the discussion with the Libyans appeared to move slowly and in September 2008 the First Minister again wrote referring to previous discussions and asking for a specific exclusion of those involved in the Lockerbie bombing. He stated in his letter of 29 September:

> I understand that the proposed agreement has not yet been
> concluded. I hope that with the additional time you have had
> to reflect on the matter you may have come round to our way

of thinking and agree that a specific exclusion of the sort set
out in our earlier correspondence should be made. Even at this
late stage, I would urge you to reconsider.

Discussions continued but the Scottish government was clearly
on the margins of what were ongoing negotiations between the UK
and Libya. A telephone call took place between the First Minister and
Jack Straw on 13 October when the latter was seeking agreement
for the wording of a letter on jurisdiction that was to be sent to the
Libyans. The First Minister said he'd need to speak to both me and
the Lord Advocate and that he'd wish to see the formal wording.
A further call took place on 24 October in which the First Minister was advised that, though the signing was not imminent, it was
anticipated before the end of the year. The die was cast and there
was clearly going to be no exclusion.

The negotiations with the Libyans on the PTA may have been progressing slowly, but a charm offensive with them was well underway.
An energy summit was scheduled in London for 19 December that
year and the Libyans had been invited. The First Minister wrote to
Prime Minister Gordon Brown regarding the sensitivity of it given
its proximity to the anniversary of the tragedy on 21 December and,
indeed, had raised it in the call to Jack Straw the month before. Gordon Brown responded and, whilst acknowledging the sensitivity of
the time, clearly narrated the UK's interests in engaging with Libya.
His letter of 11 December stated:

As part of those diplomatic relations, we not only work closely with Libya in tackling today's terrorist networks in North Africa and more widely, but we are also able to include them in our dialogue with the world's oil-producing nations.

That dialogue is vital for Britain's economic interest, as we seek to keep the price of oil at a low and stable level, and as we seek to increase investment in alternative, more sustainable energy sources both in Britain and around the world. That will have a direct impact on the costs of energy and motoring for people here in Britain.

The PTA between the two countries was signed in November 2008 and ratified in April of 2009. No exclusion was inserted regarding Lockerbie or Megrahi.

The rights of the Scottish government, never mind the interests of victims, were ignored. They delivered what the Libyans requested and were going to leave it to the Scottish government to face the issue of accepting or rejecting a future application for prisoner transfer for Megrahi that would no doubt come in. Doubtless, if rejected, they would simply say it was the Scots that had decided that. It was the equivalent of delivering the black spot to the Scottish government and, indeed, its people. Some have questioned with hindsight whether it was wise for the Scottish government to have been so vociferous in opposing the PTA. Certainly, in the light of future events, it did limit options. The request for action on the Somerville judgment and devolution of powers on air weapons was simply an opportunity to try to gain some benefits for Scotland from decisions that were clearly going to be taken anyway.

As it was, the requests were not granted by the UK government. Somerville was eventually resolved through emergency legislation in the Scottish Parliament and air weapons were devolved after the SNP landslide victory in 2011. The Scottish government got absolutely nothing, financially or commercially, from discussions with Libya over Megrahi.

THE PROCEDURES BEGIN

In early September 2008, Megrahi was diagnosed with terminal prostate cancer. I was told by the Chief Executive of the Scottish Prison Service in one of the regular discussions that I had with him, and it was formally confirmed the following month. He had been unwell and had been undergoing medical tests. The disease had spread to other parts of his body and treatment was palliative only. The prognosis for his life expectancy was unclear though it was not anticipated that death was imminent. He was, though, required to attend hospitals on a regular basis for treatment and monitoring. I passed the news on to Alex Salmond's senior special adviser in an aside at a Cabinet meeting. It was not public knowledge and the situation was not critical, but it was appropriate that the First Minister should be kept informed. The appeal by Megrahi was due to commence in the coming months and it simply would not be kept secret. The news story finally broke on 21 October across the media, with both TV and newspapers carrying comments from his legal team as well as statements from the Crown and the Scottish government. The frenzy was about to begin. It was obvious that now, not only would there be an application for prisoner transfer, but in due course also one for compassionate release.

The Libyan government reacted quickly, with their chargé d'affaires in London writing to the First Minister on 23 October seeking a meeting to discuss Megrahi's ill health. The British government had also been aware at a very early stage. His illness was discussed in the telephone call between the First Minister and Jack Straw on 24 October. It subsequently became evident that the British were advising the Libyans on the criteria under Scots law for compassionate release. However, in that call, Straw made it clear that he was aware that it was a matter for Scottish ministers. He was happy to offer advice but would also appreciate being kept informed. The First Minister responded to the Libyans detailing the process for compassionate release as well as the relevant guidelines, including that the life expectancy criteria was three months or less. A meeting either with Alex Salmond or me was not offered but an early meeting took place with Libyan officials on 27 October.

Amongst the Libyan delegation that attended were Abdulati Alobidi, Minister for Europe, Omar Jelban, First Counsellor in London, and Moussa Koussa, then head of the Libyan Intelligence Services and subsequently Minister of Foreign Affairs. The involvement of the intelligence services and the high-level status of those in attendance confirming, if it wasn't already clear enough, how important Megrahi was to Libya. Gaddafi after all had made it clear that he wanted Megrahi back before he died in prison. The opening of the Libyan People's Bureau in Glasgow in 2002 had not only been to support him whilst in prison but to press for his release. 'There was never any doubt that Megrahi's release was one of Gadhafi's key foreign-policy objectives.'[30] The Libyans met with senior Scottish government officials and also two senior representatives of the UK Foreign and Commonwealth Office, including the UK ambassador in Tripoli. The FCO had insisted on being present at the meeting with Moussa Koussa, showing both the significance of the issue as well as the importance of those in the Libyan delegation to them.

Prior to the meeting, the FCO officer in Tripoli insisted on speaking to Scottish government officials on the phone over a secure line. The FCO official also flew over for the meeting along with the UK ambassador to Libya His name is redacted from the official minute of the meeting; no doubt confirming him as an MI6 officer. The notes of that meeting stated that the Libyans were aware of the legal processes and intimated that they were not seeking any special treatment for Megrahi. However, they emphasised that he'd spent nearly ten years in custody and that both his health and his morale were at a low ebb. They were waiting to see if he would be released on bail pending his appeal, for which a hearing was to take place on 6 November. They'd return to discuss matters with Megrahi after that. They had concerns about his care in custody and thought that a death in custody would be akin to a death sentence. They wanted 'a way out'.[31]

The application for Megrahi's compassionate release was refused

---

30   David Rose, 'The Lockerbie Deal', *Vanity Fair*, 27 January 2011
31   Scottish government note from meeting with Libyan delegation, 27 October 2008.
      Published on SG website

on 14 November by officials as the relevant criteria had not been met. A further meeting took place between a Libyan delegation and senior Scottish government officials, who were this time accompanied by Scottish Prison Service (SPS) officials on 18 November. Alobidi, the Minister for Europe, was the lead official for the Libyan delegation supported by Jelban, the chargé d'affaires in London and the Consul General in Scotland. The latter again expressed concerns regarding Megrahi's health and welfare. They regretted that it seemed that his release depended on deterioration in his wellbeing and emphasised how damaging this would be for UK and Libyan relations; again stating that, should he die in prison, it would be viewed as a death sentence. Scottish government officials detailed the criteria for compassionate release and for prisoner transfer. SPS emphasised the importance of Megrahi cooperating with medical staff. Earlier that day he'd refused to see his doctor as he was unhappy that medical reports for the court hearing on his application for bail had not been supportive enough. Alobidi asked if discussions with Scottish government ministers would be appropriate, but he was advised that whilst meetings and communications should continue, they would remain at this stage with officials.[32]

A further meeting took place in Glasgow on 22 January 2009. This time, Moussa Koussa, the Minister for Security, returned and was accompanied by Alobidi, Jelban and the Consul General for Scotland, as well as an interpreter and a legal adviser. Senior officials from the Scottish government were again joined by the Scottish Prison

---

32 Scottish government note from Meeting with Libyan Delegation, 18 November 2008. Published on SG website

Service. The Libyans indicated that they'd met with Megrahi that morning. His physical and mental health were poor, they said, and they thought him close to death. The Scottish Prison Service agreed that his health was not good and that test results carried out on him had been disappointing. They were clear, however, that he was not yet near death. The Libyans were assured, though, that the SPS and Scottish doctors were doing everything they could for him. The Libyans and, in particular, Moussa Koussa once again stated that his death in prison would be bad for 'Islamic, Arab and Libyan opinion' as well as the relationship between the UK and Libya. They indicated that they did not think that Megrahi would live long enough to attend the appeal in person and they asked who they should speak to if he wanted to abandon it. Scottish government officials told them that it was a matter for the courts. It was noted that the PTA had been ratified by Libya and now only awaited ratification by the UK. It was explained that once that had happened, an application could be submitted and it would be considered by Scottish ministers. It would have to be a provisional application as no final decision could be made whilst legal proceedings were still ongoing, and in this situation not only was there the appeal by him against conviction but also two appeals against sentence; by him and the Crown.[33]

A Libyan delegation again returned to Glasgow on 12 March to meet Scottish government and SPS officials. This time it comprised Alobidi, Jelban, and the Consul General in Scotland, who were also accompanied by the chairman of the Supreme Court, a judge and

33 Scottish government note from meeting with Libyan delegation, 22 January 2009. Published on SG website

another Foreign Ministry official. Concern over Megrahi's health was again expressed and reassurances given. The real issue for the Libyans was progress on the PTA. They were advised that as the UK had not yet ratified it, no action could yet be taken. The Libyans indicated that they would be speaking to the UK government about it the following day. Doubtless they were going to press more forcefully for progress to be made. The legal representatives explained how the sentence would operate for Megrahi if he was transferred back to Libya. It was also intimated by the Libyans that Bill Rammell, UK Minister of State in the FCO, had visited Tripoli in February. Alobidi indicated that the visiting minister been told how catastrophic the death of Megrahi in custody would be for UK and Libyan relations. The notes of the meeting recorded that Alobidi advised that 'Rammell had stated that neither the Prime Minister nor the Foreign Secretary would want Mr Megrahi to pass away in prison but the decision on transfer lies in the hands of the Scottish ministers'.[34] No formal applications, either for prisoner transfer or compassionate release, had as yet been lodged. My involvement had been peripheral up until this point, limited to simply being kept appraised of meetings and events. That, though, was about to change.

The US was not unsighted in all of this. They had asked to be kept informed and both myself and the First Minister felt it was right and appropriate to do so. The Libyans had advised them of their intentions and no doubt their own diplomatic and intelligence channels would have picked information up. Scottish and

---

34 Scottish government note from meeting with Libyan delegation, 12 March 2009. Published on SG website

US officials met at the US embassy in London on 27 October 2008 and the US chargé d'affaires met the First Minister at Bute House on 2 December that year. A further meeting between officials to discuss prisoner transfer took place on 27 April 2009, just before the PTA was ratified by the UK.

Though the news of Megrahi's ill health had broken with an initial flurry, he was soon once again off the front pages, if not out of the news. The meetings between officials were not made public at that stage and the second appeal had not yet started, other than for procedural hearings. It was, though, to be the lull before the storm. The pace was quickening. There was still very little public awareness of just how big this issue was going to be or who ultimately would be responsible for it. The complexity of it and its international dimensions were hardly considered, let alone understood. That even applied to those close to me. When out for a drink with my wife at New Year Megrahi had come up in conversation and she had flippantly said that it would be a decision for Westminster anyway. I said, no, it wasn't, it would be me; but even I had no idea just how significant 2009 would become.

GRIEVING RELATIVES AND GOVERNMENT INTERESTS

At the end of April 2009, the UK ratified the already signed PTA with Libya. The legal route to seek to have Megrahi repatriated now existed and the Libyans were quick to act on behalf of their citizen.

One unusual aspect of the agreement, for which no explanation has ever been given, was that the application could be made by a state on behalf of their citizen, but not by the prisoner, which was the normal procedure. Accordingly, at a meeting in Glasgow on 5 May 2009, a formal application was submitted by Libya for the transfer of Megrahi. The Libyan delegation was again led by Alobidi, the Minister for Europe, and Jelban, chargé d'affairs in London. The Scottish government was again represented by senior officials and the SPS.

The principal application in both English and Arabic was submitted by the Libyans together with supporting documentation and was accepted by officials on behalf of the Scottish government. It was explained to the Libyan delegations that it would be me, as Justice Secretary, who would be dealing with it. Discussions took place regarding process and procedures. The Libyans were aware that there would be opposition and indicated that the US government had already been in contact with them. Alobidi stated that the Americans wanted Megrahi to serve his sentence but that they would not put any pressure on the Scottish government. He also indicated that the UK government had said it was a matter for Scottish ministers. A discussion took place about Megrahi's health. The Libyans were anxious to know whether the public were aware of the gravity of the situation but were advised that medical information was private and confidential. They did, though, acknowledge that the condition had been diagnosed almost as quickly as it would have been in Libya and stated that they were grateful for the medical care. Though no significant deterioration had occurred, they emphasised that Megrahi wished to die surrounded by his family. In response, they were advised that if a significant decline in his health occurred, then compassionate release remained an option.[35]

And so the official process for considering the prisoner transfer request began. I would now be formally involved, as it would be my decision whether to grant it or not. Though I was considering it as part of my ministerial duties, it could not simply be a political decision, but would be one that was legal in nature, the role being more akin to sitting as a judge in a court or tribunal than a politician simply deciding on policy. As such, I would have to ensure that due process was followed and natural justice applied. Rights of all involved would have to be respected and laws and guidelines adhered to. Any decision such as this can be challenged in the courts and, given the stakes involved, this one certainly had the possibility of being so. It was going to be a lonely position to hold. Though supported by staff and encouraged by colleagues, the buck would fully rest with me. Some senior colleagues told me that they did not envy my task. That was indicative of the growing appreciation of the seriousness of the situation even if I was so caught up with the practicalities that I was oblivious to it at the time. There were two additional aspects as well as the legalities. One, related to the PTA, was whether any authorities had given assurances at the outset of the trial that Megrahi, if convicted, would serve his sentence in Scotland. That would need to be investigated to consider how relevant and binding they might be. UK and US governments had written a joint letter to the UN

---

35 Scottish government note from meeting with Libyan delegation, 5 May 2009. Published on SG website

Secretary General on 24 August 1998 stating that, if convicted, the accused would serve their sentences in the UK. That could have a material bearing on any decision that I would make. The second point was the backdrop of Megrahi's ill health and the likelihood that an application for compassionate release would be made. There was none before me at the outset of the investigation and accordingly I could not specifically seek evidence on it. However, it was self-evidently a factor and was lurking there in the background with one likely to come in sooner rather than later. Therefore, I decided that I would listen to any representations that might be made on compassionate release even if a formal application had not yet been submitted. That would avoid requiring a further round of evidence-gathering with the same people and which could be distressing for them. I would be supported at meetings by Linda Hamilton, my Private Secretary, Linda Pollock and George Burgess from the Justice Department and also at some meetings by Robert Gordon, the Director General of that department, all of whom were outstanding in their service and unstinting in their efforts.

The terms of the agreement were standard for all such documents other than the highly unusual ability for a state to apply on a prisoner's behalf. The conditions to be met were again standard and contained in Article 3 of the PTA:

- The prisoner is a national of the receiving state;
- The judgment is final and no other criminal proceedings relating to the offence or any other offence committed by the prisoner are pending in the transferring State;

- At the time of the receipt of the request for the transfer, the prisoner still has at least six months of the sentence to serve;
- The acts or omissions on account of which the sentence has been imposed constitute a criminal offence according to the law of the receiving State or would constitute a criminal offence if committed on its territory; and
- The transferring and receiving States agree to the transfer.

Other than the second condition (b), the criteria appeared to be met. With an outstanding appeal and an appeal against the leniency of the sentence by the Crown, there were still ongoing proceedings. The application could, though, be treated as provisional with that part able to be met at a later stage.

Prisoner transfers were not infrequent in Scotland. Scottish nationals who had offended abroad were often brought home, just as foreign nationals who had committed offences here were sent back. The procedures were more often routine than controversial, processed by the SPS and requiring only the final sign-off from the Justice Secretary, which was almost invariably given.

This transfer, though, was like no other, given the nature of the crime and the involvement of so many individuals and states. It simply couldn't, therefore, be processed in the usual way. Those governments and private citizens had a right to be heard or make written submissions. They were going to have to be met or engaged with and it was going to be very much in the public eye. That was going to involve meetings and calls with them. The normal timeframe for consideration was ninety days. The clock had started to tick and so the meetings commenced.

Scottish government officials therefore made contact with both victims' relatives and national governments, asking if they wished to make formal representations. Arrangements were made for calls and meetings that would take place over the coming weeks.

In order to try to get some early clarification on whether there had been specific undertakings given regarding Megrahi's prison sentence requiring to be served in Scotland, contact was made with the British government. On 22 June, the Foreign and Commonwealth Office were written to asking if they could advise on any undertakings that may have been given at the outset of the trial regarding where any sentence would be served and if so what the nature of them was. It was explained that if such undertakings existed, they may be reason to prevent a prisoner transfer taking place. It was pointed out that, as the Scottish government was not a party to those agreements, we had no information on them. After all, neither the Scottish government nor the Scottish Parliament had been established when the negotiations had taken place and, in any event, control over foreign affairs was specifically reserved for Westminster. Reference was made to the joint letter sent by the UK and US governments to the UN Secretary General on 24 August 1998 and which formed annex 1 of UN Resolution 1192 (1998), in which it's stated that if the two accused were found guilty they would serve their sentence in the UK. It was also stated that it was understood that the UN Secretary General had written to the Libyan government on 17 February 1999, stating that the accused, if convicted, would serve their prison sentence in Scotland. Finally, that there was reference in that letter from the UN to the Libyans regarding the monitoring of the prison sentence in Scotland. The FCO were asked for their advice on what had been intended by them, as it too could affect the decision on a transfer.[36]

A reply was received from the FCO on 3 July that was very cursory. It simply stated that:

> The FCO does not consider that either the joint UK–US letter, UN Security Council Resolution 1192 (1998) or the accompanying discussion between the UK government and the United States government regarding implementation of the trial initiative as set out in the joint letter, present an international law bar to such a transfer under the PTA where it is consistent with Scots law.

No expansion beyond that was given nor was any supporting documentation provided.

In a conference call on 26 June, I spoke with Eric Holder, US Attorney General, in the first of the evidence sessions. It was quite illuminating, and he was personable and polite, though the discussion was brief and to the point. He was aware that the decision rested with me, having been advised by both my officials and no doubt the British government. The USA, he said, was concerned about the prisoner transfer and opposed to any release or removal from Scotland. There was a slight genuflection towards compassionate release. That correlated with previous discussions had with the

---

36 Letter from Scottish government to Foreign and Commonwealth Office, 22 June 2009. Published on SG website

Americans, whether by officials or the First Minister, that appeared to show that, whilst opposed to both, that was less unpalatable than prisoner transfer. What I found particularly compelling was that he'd been Deputy US Attorney General to Janet Reno at the time when the arrangements for the trial in the Netherlands had been taking place. He was therefore not just speaking from formal records, but from personal knowledge. He advised that, given the significance of the atrocity, they had only agreed to the proposed trial arrangements on the clear understanding that it would be subject to Scottish jurisdiction and that any sentence imposed would be served in Scotland. He was clear that the British would have been aware of that.

After the meeting, Robert Gordon, the senior official in the Scottish Justice Department who had sat in on the call, surmised that it was the Libyans who had wanted Scotland as the place for imprisonment in the event of a conviction. I agreed. Even in more run-of-the-mill prisoner transfers, few, if any, ever go from Scotland back to the US. Returning means you become a prisoner of that country and become subject to their conditions for parole or release. These conditions are invariably more severe in America, and hence US citizens more often than not choose to remain prisoners here. Had Megrahi gone to the US, then the Libyans would have been aware that he would be unlikely to have seen the light of day ever again.

The next group to make representations were British relatives of victims of the tragedy, who came to see me at my ministerial office at St Andrew's House, Edinburgh. They were all remarkably nice people and included Dr Jim Swire, who had become a high-profile campaigner on Lockerbie. They stated at the outset that they were divided on their view on Megrahi's guilt or innocence. They were happy to meet collectively to make their points, though they had separate views and would detail them individually. There was clearly some tension between them, but the meeting was harmonious enough. Though I disagree with a lot of what Jim Swire argues, I have always found him a decent and sincere man; a kindly soul who has suffered an appalling loss but bears it with great dignity. Others who did not share his views were equally pleasant and dignified.

At the outset, as I was to do in every meeting with relatives, I thanked them for their representations and expressed my condolences for their loss. The process and procedures I was following were also explained. They were advised that the meeting was specifically to deal with prisoner transfer, not compassionate release, where as yet no application had been made. They were then allowed to make their representations. One lady made the very valid point of the need to take into account the rights of the victims, both those who died and those who had to live with the loss. They felt that they had been ignored throughout most of the other proceedings over the very many years since the tragedy. Though there was no single viewpoint amongst them, they were anxious, as they put it, 'that the truth be known'. They were keen for the appeal to continue irrespective of their view on Megrahi's guilt or innocence. Even those convinced of his guilt wished to know who had organised it. One of them said if the conviction was upheld they would have no issue with a transfer. Another indicated that it was always their understanding that the sentence, if imposed, would be served in Scotland.

The cost of all the legal proceedings was raised and whether that might be a factor. They were advised that the Scottish government did not cash-limit justice and it was not a consideration. Listening to the personal testimony of their loss was heart-rending. Both those convinced of his guilt and those persuaded of his innocence wanted further information and answers. They wanted to ensure that any actions would not interfere with the appeal and if it were to be abandoned for any reason that there would be some inquiry into the events of Lockerbie to try to provide the answers they were still seeking. Linda and I chatted after the meeting was over. Both of us were physically drained by the emotion of it but recalled our huge regard for the dignity of the families we'd met.[37]

The British government had not sought to make any formal representations and was clearly going to ground. It suited the UK for this to be Scotland's responsibility and my decision in particular. The British were happy to advise the Libyans on *procedures* but not to assist the Scottish government. However, there was information about what had transpired in the discussions at the outset of establishing Camp Zeist that only the UK could tell us. Accordingly, on 6 July I wrote formally to David Miliband, the UK Foreign Secretary. I explained that a prisoner transfer application had been received and that I was therefore seeking information and clarification as to what had or had not been agreed, as well as the release of any relevant papers and documentation relating to where Megrahi would serve his sentence. I specifically asked if an agreement was entered into

---

37 Note of meeting of Justice Secretary with Lockerbie victims' relatives, 1 July 2009. Published on SG website

whereby the sentence would be served in Scotland. If not, I asked what his understanding of the situation was. I offered to meet to discuss this and take any representations that he may have.[38] A letter was eventually received from Ivan Lewis, a Foreign Office Minister, on 3 August, which stated that neither international law nor previous agreements with the US or UN would prevent Megrahi's release. It was short and succinct but totally lacking in detail or information. He added: 'I hope on this basis that you will now feel able to consider the Libyan application in accordance with the provisions of the Prisoner Transfer Agreement.'[39] Of course a release could legally be made, but the question I'd asked was about whether any assurances had been given. That was never answered. The response from the Foreign Office did not clarify the points I had raised, though it did make clear the UK government's desire for Megrahi's release.

On 6 July I had my first meeting with the Libyans. The Libyans' arrival caused quite a stir in St Andrew's House as a fleet of large, expensive black cars swept in carrying all their entourage. Alobidi, the Minister for Europe, again led the delegation, supported by Jelban, the chargé d'affaires in London, and the Consul General in Scotland, as well as a judge, interpreter and a representative from the Gaddafi Foundation. That and other meetings with either me or officials were always carried out in English and their understanding of the language was flawless. The interpreter was clearly there in a different capacity as he was never used. They were quite charming

---

38 Letter from Justice Secretary to Foreign Secretary, 6 July 2009.
    Published on SG website
39 Letter from Foreign Office to Justice Secretary, 3 August 2009.
    Published on FCO website

and during the initial pleasantries I explained how I'd visited Algeria but never Libya, and they were eager to extol the greater virtues of their own land as opposed to that of their North African neighbour.

After the initial preliminary discussions regarding procedure and the current situation, the Libyans told us that it was on the grounds of Megrahi's ill health that they had submitted the application and that, moreover, if he were transferred, they had a signed undertaking from him that he would abandon his appeal. The Libyans were in turn told of the representations from victims' relatives, who wished the appeal to continue. The terms of the PTA were also stated, specifically that if there were an outstanding appeal at the time of final decision then the criteria set in the PTA could not be met.

I asked for their understanding of what had been agreed at the time of the establishment of Camp Zeist as to the location for imprisonment in the event of conviction. The judge who was part of the delegation then said that he'd been part of the Libyan negotiation team at the time of those discussions between the UK and Libya. He told us that they'd originally asked for the accused to serve their sentence in Libya and if that was not possible, then another Muslim country or even the Netherlands. The UK refused that request. The Libyans thereafter agreed that, if convicted, the sentence would be served in Scotland. That had been included in the letter written by them to the UN, but there was no other agreement. In any event, their view was that circumstances had changed and we should deal with the current situation. Interestingly, they indicated that all these negotiations had been with the UK and that the US had not been party to them. Finally, the issue raised by some relatives that any return to

Libya might be greeted by a fanfare, which would be insensitive, was explained. Alobidi gave assurances that this would not happen and that the terms of the PTA would be adhered to in full.[40]

Later that same day there was another meeting with a Spanish lady whose sister had been an air hostess aboard the flight. Another UK relative who she'd got to know over the years accompanied her. She felt frustrated at the lack of voice for the families that had existed throughout all earlier proceedings and had concerns about aspects arising from the trial. Both had worries about the PTA application, specifically, that political and economic factors were unduly coming into play. They were given assurances, however, that the decision would be made on a judicial basis, not any economic or political grounds. She then raised the issue of the Public Interest Immunity (PII), whereby information can be withheld from the court. This was one of the issues that had concerned the UN observer Hans Kochler and it troubled her too. It was explained that it was beyond the power of the Scottish government and the Scottish courts. The PII would have come about through the UK Foreign Office, not the Lord Advocate. The specifics could not be discussed and in any event were not properly known. It was clear that it caused her great anxiety. She also had concerns relating to the security services' involvement, whether MI5, MI6 or the CIA; perhaps as a consequence of the PII. She was unspecific about what aspects concerned her but was obviously worried about it and the effect it may have on both my actions and her quest for justice. It just seemed to be a general fear

---

40 Note of meeting of Justice Secretary with Libyan delegation, 6 July 2009. Published on SG website

that matters to which she was not privy were both happening and of consequence. I told her that of course the security services too were also outside my jurisdiction, but I assured her that the Scottish government would be as open as possible and that the decision would not be subject to their interference. It was all I could do. Those issues were in the main unknown to me but most certainly would not be part of my decision-making.

She was the first person making representations to mention the PII, which nevertheless had been lurking there in the background constantly. I had picked up through various sources what it was supposed to relate to, even though I was also not supposed to know about it. I had just picked it up through contacts and discussion, though equally so had others, including the press. That was frankly a ludicrous situation to face; being Justice Secretary for Scotland, having to deal with the Lockerbie situation and yet being denied information that could be potentially relevant.

What the PII related to was a letter allegedly sent by the King of Jordan to the British Prime Minister John Major not long after the bombing, in which it was indicated that it was the Palestinians who were the perpetrators. In many ways it simply confirmed the unguarded Channon comments to the press corps. It was, though, potentially exculpatory for Megrahi. The UK's position was that this could destabilise the Jordanian royal family and cause disorder in that country given the significant Palestinian presence there. They, therefore, blocked its publication or use.

I could never understand the attitude of the UK government. PII certificates are necessary for all governments but should be used very sparingly. It perhaps should have been available at the trial given its incrimination of others and, indeed, its support for Megrahi's line of defence. Kochler certainly thought so. However, even leaving that aside, the political situation in the Middle East was significantly different in 2009 from a decade before. There had been a succession in Jordan in which the king had been succeeded by his son. In addition, Palestinian ranks were split, with open warfare breaking out between Fatah and Hamas. A letter sent by a deceased king that implicated the Palestinians hardly seemed earth-shattering given what else was happening in the area. The Crown in Scotland did not support the letter's use, though they were always very nervous about reference to it. The British government, however, was entirely intransigent. Later information was to show that there were more contemporary events that were driving their desire for secrecy, but at the time it was one of those situations whereby those in the loop knew but couldn't say and others had suspicions but did not know. The secrecy and use of the PII simply fuelled the conspiracy theories, though it's doubtful whether the information would have been of any significance to the appeal that was ongoing.

The pace was picking up. On 9 July, I listened to the representations of the American victims' families conducted by video conference. I was in Edinburgh, supported by my staff, and there were links to sites in both Washington, DC and New York for the convenience of those in the US. I had always assumed that this would be the hardest meeting, and so it was to prove. Some relatives sat facing the camera with photographs; others held them up to show me the images of their dead loved ones. The grief of all was evident and the simmering rage of some was palpable. After the usual introductions and formalities, Frank Duggan, one of the leading advocates for the American families, expressed his thanks for the opportunity to present their views. Others related their personal testimonies of pain and sorrow. One lady spoke of the loss of her husband, aged just forty, who had been the father of three children aged ten, seven and two years old at the time. She stated that she'd attended 90 per cent of the trial in the Netherlands and that the families had been promised that, if convicted, the accused would serve their sentences in Scotland. Another woman said she'd been just two years old when her father had died on the flight. A further widow told how her husband had been working in Austria in the pursuit of Nazi war criminals and that he'd left two children who were aged just seven and a half and four at the time. An older couple spoke of losing their twin sons on the flight, aged just twenty. The mother spoke of the grief she endured on a daily basis since the events all those years ago. She read a statement out from another relative who could not attend the video conference who also mentioned assurances given at the time that sentences would be served in Scotland. She also added that President Clinton, speaking at the tenth anniversary of the tragedy, had confirmed that as well. And so it continued, with widows and parents all narrating their self-evident sorrow and often continuing anger. They were all adamant that assurances had been given that the sentence would be served in Scotland and were almost uniformly opposed to transfer or release on any grounds.[41]

---

41 Note of meeting of Justice Secretary with Lockerbie victims' relatives, 9 July 2009. Published on SG website

It was a very emotional meeting. The stories we heard were tragic; both the love for the relatives lost and their hatred for the perpetrators of their misery were both visible and audible. Linda Hamilton was visibly distressed and I recall feeling drained by the end. The hardest part of the job of being Justice Secretary is meeting with relatives who have suffered and who have often not even seen justice delivered. I have had to do many such meetings in that role, but this was by far the most difficult.

The next meeting was with the families of some of those who had died in the town of Lockerbie, a salutary reminder of the effect the tragedy had on the community. It was also reflective of the stoic yet dignified actions of the Scottish bereaved. They were gravely wounded, yet were without all-consuming bitterness. The families who attended stated that they had never sought publicity, nor had they tried to comment until now. They did, though, also feel that there were international events at play and that their views might be marginal to the decision as a result. However, they still wanted to let me know their thoughts, as they felt there had been little mention of the town or its dead. They had found some recent publicity distressing and, in particular, comments from a Member of the Scottish Parliament that had suggested Megrahi's innocence. The comments also made disparaging comments about the actions of the Crown, which I thought verged on the defamatory and seemed to have been made for reasons of self-publicity, not for any contribution to the ongoing applications, never mind the ultimate appeal. It seemed, however, that the issue of Megrahi's transfer was becoming a media gravy train and many were latching on to it.

The families were hurt and irked that media reports never seemed to mention the eleven people killed on the ground; a significant loss in such a small, tight-knit community. The focus and publicity was always on those who had travelled in the plane. They related how two houses holding their families had been wiped off the earth when the tragedy occurred. Mother, father and children disappeared from this earth. Poignantly and with deep sadness they told how all that was recovered from the home was the back page of a school jotter and a scrap of a birthday card. Not much at all for a family's life and home. The couple believed the trial of Megrahi to have been fair and didn't wish him to be transferred. They also felt that, as a result of the ongoing coverage, they could never achieve peace or closure. At about the same time as I had been meeting the Scottish victims' relatives, in late July 2009, the Libyan entourage and their Scottish lawyer had met with Scottish government officials and formally lodged Megrahi's application for compassionate release.[42] And so next it was to be the meeting with Megrahi. Ostensibly, it had been scheduled to meet his request under the PTA, but as there was now a live compassionate release application, it would encompass both issues.

The meeting with Megrahi was to be the subject of much controversy and criticism from the political opposition in Scotland. Some of that goes with the responsibility of government and is the duty of opposition. However, the actions of the Labour Party in Scotland in my opinion were both shameful and duplicitous. They chose

---

42 Note of meeting by Scottish government officials with Libyan delegation, 22 July 2009. Published on SG website

to criticise whatever I did and oppose whatever I chose. When asked whether they'd release they would refuse to answer. When their views were requested, all that was received was a diatribe about my actions. Yet all this occurred whilst a Labour government in London consorted with the Libyans and had signed the PTA, clearly desperate for a deal to be struck. Not only did they put narrow party interest before the national interest, but they championed petty point-scoring above the rights of victims and their families. The Conservatives were clearer in their opposition to any release, no doubt fuelled by their being in opposition rather than government, but meanwhile they supported the commercial ventures of their business friends.

There were several reasons for meeting with Megrahi, both legal and practical. The principal one was on the clear basis of legal advice. This was the first prisoner transfer application that had been made by a state on behalf of their citizen rather than by the individual themselves; that legislation had not been set by the Scots, but by the British government. The British Secretary of State for Justice, Jack Straw, had given a commitment that, where applications were not submitted personally by the prisoner, the prisoner had to be given the opportunity to make representations. It was important to ascertain that he really did wish to consider being transferred back to his home country. I was sitting in a quasi-judicial capacity and my decision could be challenged in court, therefore if I had refused to hear from or meet with the applicant given that he'd asked to do so, that most certainly would have been challengeable. Moreover, having afforded a meeting to the victims' relatives, natural justice dictated the same offer be made available to him. An accused is as entitled to a hearing as the accuser, irrespective of how heinous the offence. Despite his crimes, therefore, he was still entitled to a voice. Finally, security practicalities dictated that if he were to be seen, then it should be in the prison in which he was incarcerated rather than in my office. He was in Greenock Prison and I was based seventy miles away in Edinburgh. Even getting Megrahi to hospital for treatment was becoming problematic for police and prison staff. A meeting at St Andrew's House or any other Scottish government offices would have ensured a media convoy, never mind an intolerable level of disruption for those working there.

So it was then that, on 6 August, I met Abdelbaset al-Megrahi in Greenock Prison. Though ostensibly about the prisoner transfer application, there was now an application for compassionate release pending and the clock for both was ticking. Both were on the table and could be commented on. I was supported by my policy adviser Linda Pollock and the Director General. Megrahi's lawyer, Tony Kelly, sat in the corner and only interjected sparingly. I had been told before I went by the SPS that, whilst he was terminally ill, he was not yet visibly a dying man. However, it appeared he had suffered a further relapse that week and what confronted me seemed a tired old man; fifty-six years old but looking a decade more than that. He had a persistent cough and looked like someone suffering from the flu. His English was very good and he was polite, though direct in his remarks. There was no obvious remorse but he was neither threatening nor frightening. He did acknowledge the suffering of victims' families and accepted that many viewed him with hatred; feelings he stressed that he did not reciprocate. He said he felt he had been unjustly convicted and spoke of his appeals and the review by the SCCRC. He spoke of his ill health, that the reports indicated he'd only a short time to live. He said he'd not seen his wife or children since January and had only seen his parents twice since he'd been imprisoned. Chemotherapy would need to commence soon and he felt he needed his family around him for that. He concluded by saying that as he moved towards his final days he wished to be with his family and loved ones.[43]

It was not a lengthy meeting and I recall chatting with the prison governor before it commenced. Both his health and the visits to hospital were becoming more complex for the prison staff. Whilst, like all prisons, there were medical facilities at Greenock, they were limited and obviously not comparable to those of a hospital, or, indeed, a specialist cancer ward. The prison governor explained how, in many ways, Megrahi was a model prisoner. He'd assimilated well and there seemed to be no issues with other inmates. Indeed, he chatted to them about football. He said his prayers, phoned home on a daily basis and he had regular visits from the Libyan Consul, who, interestingly, according to the governor, always deferred to Megrahi. As the governor mused, they were very hierarchical, and I noticed that, too, in their meetings with me. Rank dictated who sat where and who spoke and who didn't. It was clear to the governor that Megrahi was of greater seniority than the consul in Glasgow, indicative of the position he had held in the Libyan security services. As we departed Greenock Prison, TV crews and photographers

---

43 Note of meeting by Justice Secretary with Megrahi, 6 August 2009.
   Published on SG website

descended. Footage appeared on every news channel showing Ian driving and Linda in the front passenger seat. Ian, a very private man, was quite mortified that his picture had gone global and the rest of us ribbed him mercilessly.

That had concluded the formal meetings on the PTA application. No others had been scheduled and my attention would now turn to the decision on both the application for transfer and compassionate release.

The application for compassionate release had been lodged on 24 July. It resulted in almost a parallel set of discussions opening up by officials, with both Megrahi's representatives and the US government in particular. The US Consul General met with Scottish government officials on 4 August to deliver their view on compassionate release and prisoner transfer, which was that they were opposed to both. A copy of the medical advice that had been received through the SPS was also delivered to the US Consulate on 13 August. The British government had all but gone to ground on the matter; other than discussions with officials in the Foreign and Commonwealth Office about the practical consequences of the relations with, and the situation within, Libya in the event of either a release or a refusal.

Other governments and organisations sought to intercede or lobby. The State of Qatar was in touch not simply as a result of its own interests but also on behalf of the Arab League.[44] They were concerned for Megrahi's welfare and eager for his release; they also said how much it would be appreciated by the Arab League and their

---

44 Letter from government of Qatar to Justice Secretary, 17 July 2009.
    Published on SG website

peoples. The Libyan British Business Council also wrote expressing their views, which were strident in their fears for UK/Libyan
relations and doubtless for their own commercial interests.[45] They
were also very eager for Megrahi's release. The letter was signed by
the chairman Lord Trefgarne, who had been flying out to Libya all
those years before on private business jets and who had offered a seat
on the plane to the defence agents. He and Robert Black had been
working for the Libyans both at that time and subsequently.[46] Both
were clearly expressing support for a release. They were, however,
advised that the decision would be made free from any political,
economic or diplomatic interests and politely rebuffed.

There was a further meeting with the Libyan delegation after the
lodging of the application for compassionate release. The previous
meeting had been about the application for prisoner transfer and
preceded any formal application on compassionate grounds. They
had also lodged letters stating that Megrahi would abandon his
appeal if released. It was therefore appropriate to meet with them
yet again. The entourage again swung into St Andrew's House in a
fleet of black limousines. The Minister for Europe, Alobidi, a close
confidant of Gaddafi for many years, was again the lead official, but
once more supported by the phalanx of others. They were again
polite but, as always, rather steely, and I thought there was always
a hint of menace beneath the surface of the delegation and, given
the brutality of the regime, it's little wonder. They again expressed

---

45 Letter from Libyan British Business Council to Justice Secretary, 31 July 2009.
    Published on SG website
46 Letter from Lord Trefgarne to Saif el Islam, 4 June 2007

concern over Megrahi's health and that the treatment for him was inadequate. Assurances regarding his care and welfare were once more given. They raised the issue of the abandonment of the appeal. It was pointed out that no prisoner transfer could take place whilst there were still ongoing proceedings which applied here given that there were still defence and Crown appeals outstanding. The Crown Appeal was that the sentence imposed was too lenient. Regarding the latter, which was moving that the sentence imposed upon Megrahi was too lenient, it was looking rather ridiculous given that he was now terminally ill, but it would doubtless be abandoned if the defence did likewise. Compassionate release was again explained as being predicated on different rules and criteria and I was awaiting the documentation and advice. They were of course well aware of the rules and regulations both through their own legal advisers and the British government. Whilst I did have my own views that the arguments over the Lockerbie bombing would run for ever, irrespective of any court decision, the First Minister was very keen to ensure that the defence appeal continued. The Scottish government had nothing to gain from any abandonment. I advised them of that but made it clear that my decision would not be affected by this either way. The decision on whether to continue or abandon the appeal was to be for Megrahi.

The rules for ministers to follow on compassionate release were contained in legislation and also in prison service guidelines, specifically, Section 3 of the Prisoners and Criminal Proceedings (Scotland) Act 1993. The process is akin to medical parole that exists in many jurisdictions around the world, including the US. Scottish Prison

Service Guidelines had established criteria and they included those suffering from a terminal illness and where death was likely to occur soon. No fixed time limit was set, but a life expectancy of fewer than three months was considered an appropriate period. The guidelines also covered cases of severe incapacity and those where continued imprisonment would, in light of conditions in which the prisoner was being held, endanger or shorten life expectancy.

The application by Megrahi was sent to the SPS. It was unusual in that it had been given directly to government. Normally, it is received and processed by the prison authorities before being submitted to the Justice Department, but remitting the application to the SPS allowed due process to be followed thereafter. The prison governor, social work and medical staff were contacted to provide advice for consideration. The parole board, too, who supervise prisoners released on licence and who also have an input on factors such as the location or release, were duly contacted.

Though no statutory time limit is set for a decision to be taken given the sensitive nature of such applications, they are processed speedily. Importantly, the criteria considered relates to the health of the prisoner, not the nature of the offence committed. If an application is judged not to have met these criteria, the application is simply rejected by officials and does not get put before a minister. All applications submitted to the minister that had first been judged to have met the criteria, both before and since Megrahi's release, had been granted, irrespective of the nature of the offence. At the time of the decision to release him, there had been thirty-nine authorised in total by myself and my predecessors.

Whilst the Prison Service and Justice Department staff were considering the applications and processing the documentation, the media interest was growing and the security net around me continued to tighten. There were not the armed officers that routinely surround UK and US government ministers, but there was a discernible change all the same. The use of a government car, normally restricted to official business, was changed to 24-hour access to try to limit my being unaccompanied. I had already noted that Ian had started locking the doors routinely when I entered the vehicle. He also went on a course that prepared him for the increased threat level, which only resulted in Linda and me asking him to show us ridiculous driving manoeuvres and complaining when he rightly refused. The secured car became the venue for some deeply funny but very black humoured discussions on scenarios that might arise from gun attacks that Ian had been trained in, to helicopter gunships which he said we were on our own with. All helped to reduce the tension; but it was palpable all the same. Ian was kindly and protective, offering to take me to the shops, which I declined, and being annoyed when I walked to meet him once when he was due to take me to the gym. The police had also been notified and regular drive-bys began, not just for me, but for others in my family. Having a police car pass your window on an hourly basis was not something I'd been used to. It was deeply unfair on my wife, from whom I had by this time separated, but who also had to deal with police advisers and regular patrols.

My car was broken into in the parking lot below my flat. The area did have issues with car crime and it was random rather than targeted. I spoke to the young officers who attended, who lamented that there was little that could probably be done. It was an old and modest car and the likelihood of fingerprints from the cheap plastic faacia limited. They filed a report and I arranged for my local garage to take the car away for repair. However, the following morning, when the Chief Superintendent in charge of my security heard about the incident, all hell seemed to break loose. A specialist team in forensic suits descended on the garage to pore over the vehicle. I felt sorry for the garage owner, whom I knew well, and as it transpired nothing further could be found. The security was reassuring in some ways but it could be disconcerting in others, for example when my brother was once viewed very suspiciously by officers as he and I headed back to my flat from a meal in a local restaurant. Funny in many ways, but off-putting for him and others. The security was to be further increased in forthcoming days.

Political life and ministerial business, though, had to continue notwithstanding Megrahi and increased security. Accordingly, I had gone to the Northern Isles in Scotland for a series of meetings with police as well as council and other officials. The islands that make up both the Orkney Isles and the Shetland Isles are off the north coast of Scotland, the latter being a considerable distance out into the North Atlantic; closer almost to Norway than the central belt of mainland Scotland. It's important, though, as Justice Secretary, to remember that you represent all of Scotland, not just the urban areas. They're vibrant communities with distinctive needs as I knew well from my grandparents in the Western Isles. Summer and other recesses are therefore an opportune time to visit and engage with the local community.

Nothing had been scheduled for me relating to Megrahi whilst I was away. Work was all going on by officials in St Andrew's House and elsewhere. However, on 12 August, I was in Orkney when news broke late in the evening that suggested that Megrahi was to be released the following week. No statement had been made by me or any Scottish government official. More importantly, no decision had as yet been made by me, either in respect of prisoner transfer or compassionate release. However, a media frenzy broke. Thankfully, being in Orkney and away from main TV hubs meant I was free from the door-stepping that would normally occur. I had a late-night call with the First Minister given the broadcast headlines but it was agreed no further action was needed at the moment and that the issue was in hand, though the clock was ticking for a decision. The formal documentation and paperwork was still being prepared and the court actions were still outstanding. Not just the decision, but also the timing surrounding its release would be mine. I went to bed knowing I'd be doing an interview with local media on behalf of national broadcasters in the morning, never expecting what was to lie in store.

I'd woken up early and had a shower. I came out to find my mobile phone ringing. With hair dripping and towel wrapped around me, I answered to hear an American voice saying that it was the US State Department on the line and that they'd been given my mobile number by the British Prime Minister's office. They asked if I would take a call from the Secretary of State Hillary Clinton. Just why Gordon Brown's office gave out my mobile number rather than go through more formal channels was never explained. However, all things considered, I was hardly going to refuse the call. But, as it was, the connection could not initially be made. Hillary Clinton was on a plane travelling in Africa and the line was poor. Arrangements were made for a telephone call to take place later that morning. I got dressed and went down to meet Linda and the press officer accompanying us for breakfast. The media was running with the lines of a supposed Lockerbie announcement the following week. I told Linda things had now gone into a different orbit and she'd better let the First Minister's office know that a call was going to take place later that morning with Hillary Clinton.

Normally, taking a call from a foreign dignitary would be done in my or some other government office. However, I was in the Northern Isles and about to embark on a flight from Orkney to Shetland. There was no Scottish government office available; besides, I was scheduled to be at the airport when the call was to come in. It would just have to take place on my mobile phone. Having done the media interviews and other business arranged, we headed to the airport. The call was slightly delayed again due to connection problems. As it was, when it finally came in, I was almost due to board the plane. Linda and I were going through security as she hastily sought to find a private space to take the call. Initially, she located the search room at the airport, which was not much more than a large cupboard.

Hillary Clinton apologised for the difficulties in making contact earlier but explained she was on Air Force Two, the jet provided for the US Vice-President and Secretary of State, and was travelling between Nigeria and Liberia. I said it was a coincidence that I was about to board a plane from Orkney to Shetland. I never bothered, though, explaining the significant difference in scale or stature of Air Force Two and Loganair, who are a small airline flying small planes from, to and between the Scottish Islands.

There were the usual pleasantries and a brief discussion of a mutual acquaintance which I sense surprised her, doubtless not expecting us to have any friends or contacts in common. The Secretary of State was polite and respectful, coming across to me as a most decent lady. She emphasised that she was well aware of Lockerbie, having been a New York senator, where many of the victims had come from, and stated that the US was concerned by the situation. They were opposed to any prisoner transfer arrangement as assurances had been given at the outset regarding imprisonment being in Scotland. With regard to compassionate release, she indicated that there should be clear and independent medical evidence and that the US authorities would wish to see it. I answered that I was happy to arrange this. She also said that if Megrahi were to be released, then they would prefer that he remain in a venue in Scotland. I indicated that I would be willing to speak to the police and others about that; however, there were both logistical and security issues with that, though I undertook to keep the US informed. Though it was a formal call, it did appear that she was simply going through the motions in indicating the official American view.

The call was somewhat complicated by the flight being called as I was still in discussion, and continued as I left the search room and even as I boarded the plane. Linda was frantically trying to ensure privacy as air crew advised of boarding and that mobile phone use was not allowed. She was desperately trying to explain the huge importance of the call, whilst the air steward sought to enforce understandable rules as I stepped on board the plane. It was ongoing in the background as I was speaking and a rather surreal backdrop to the call. Fortunately, the call soon ended and any diplomatic embarrassment was avoided.

Whilst waiting at the airport prior to boarding I had taken a call from Colin Boyd, who had been the Labour Lord Advocate at the time of the trial. I did so out of courtesy. He advised that he'd heard of a possible statement and potentially a decision to release. He wanted to argue against it, which he was perfectly entitled to do given his former role and the potential implications for his reputation. He did, though, appear to me to parrot almost the same lines that the Americans had been using. It seemed as though phones lines were buzzing back and forth across the Atlantic that morning – and not just to me.

The medical information was delivered to the US Consul General later that day. It was important to be as open and frank with the US as possible and time was of the essence. There was a concern that there might be issues with data protection as medical information is private and confidential. However, Megrahi was willing to have the information released and it was duly passed on.

Contact was made with the police regarding his possible release to his home in Newton Mearns. They were deeply sceptical about it. It would require thirty officers simply to search and seal it and another forty-eight to provide security and cover. More would be needed for travel to hospital, which was going to be a regular occurrence. The implications of seeking to turn a suburban residence into secure accommodation were simply not tenable. It wasn't just the security of the premises but the traffic and other implications for the community. That was without even asking the neighbours. Most of them would no doubt have been vehemently opposed and the whole thing would turn out to be a media and security frenzy. The practicalities, therefore, ruled that option out.

Though it was never made public, there was another issue of concern about Megrahi's Scottish residence being used. In an informal chat with a senior officer, he had expressed significant concern that one of the very near neighbours was a major sports commentator for Sky Sports TV. His fear was that Sky News would simply decamp into the adjacent garden for minute-by-minute coverage, and he was probably right. The possibility of live coverage from a house opposite would be too good an opportunity to pass up for a TV channel, but this would have been a nightmare to contemplate for those responsible for security; never mind the local community who would have had to live amidst it.

Other possibilities, such as a hospital or hospice, were considered as alternative locations for release. They were duly investigated; however, none of them were feasible. The only secure hospital in Scotland was for those with a mental illness. That did not apply to Megrahi and, besides, it didn't possess the medical facilities required for his cancer treatment. The hospitals that he was already being treated at were busy and both the security implications and the imposition on other patients made it entirely impracticable. Hospices for the terminally ill and cancer clinics were also considered but they are not secure institutions, and to have Megrahi moved there would have probably meant even more of a police presence than at his home. In any case, I was not going to turn any of those institutions that we are blessed with into prison camps or media hubs with all the hardship and distress such attention would cause.

I was by now in Shetland, even further from the mainland than Orkney. The media speculation was in overdrive and it was probably fortunate to be so far away. After meetings in the main town of Lerwick, we walked back to our hotel past the very busy harbour in Shetland and saw the Scottish government's Fishery Protection ship tied up at the quayside. A small vessel with a gun in its bow, it only seemed to symbolise the puny military prowess of Scotland contrasted with that of Libya, never mind the US. Realisation began to dawn of just how big a league we were now playing in, the potential consequences and a real understanding of just how limited our resources were.

We were a small ship trying to steer a course through turbulent seas and being buffeted by waves from all sides. Whichever way we went we faced hostility. On one side, we had Libya and potentially others in the Arab or even wider Muslim world. Just a few weeks before, UK hostages taken prisoner in Iraq had been murdered. That had followed the execution prior to that of other Western nationals captured in the area. There was hostility to the West and ordinary citizens were becoming targets. Most in North Africa or the wider Arab world neither knew of Scotland nor cared about it. I was aware of the deaths of prison officers that had occurred in Northern Ireland where some had died through terrorist attack. The last thing I wanted was to have Scotland become a place that was demonised and its citizens targeted. I would not allow Scottish oil workers or others, wherever they might be, to face retribution as a consequence of my decision.

On the other side, we faced pressures from the US. They were the most powerful nation in the world and the links with Scotland, both social and economic, were great. I had many friends in the US and had written books on the Scottish diaspora and Scottish societies there. I was aware that my decision could impact on them and my longstanding friendships with them. The US was, also, a country I knew well and visited often, having first travelled there in 1979. I liked the vibrancy of its cities, the beauty of its countryside and the invention and energy in its society. There could potentially be economic issues, whether through the administration directly or simply through public opprobrium, and there were areas of Scottish commercial life that were exposed, not just whisky or tourism. All these factors had to be considered as the maelstrom developed. Although these factors would not affect my decision, I was aware of the potential consequences of my actions.

However, my mind was taken off it that evening. A police inspector had been assigned for our security as we were not due to fly back till the following day and would be staying on the mainland. The story was still running top of the news headlines. He really didn't know what to do with us, so he simply took us out to the pub for a drink and to listen to some fiddle music, for which the island is famous. It seemed a sensible solution from the officer. His improvisation helped ease the pressure. The locals in the pub were very friendly and eager to chat. I suppose we were something of celebrities, with all the news broadcasts now appearing. Moreover, with the remoteness of the island, no one could have got to us and certainly wouldn't have got off, assuming they'd done anything. It was a chance to briefly relax. Yet, it was to be a further lull before another storm.

The media frenzy was relentless and that was without the Clinton phone call being made public at that stage. There were calls for Megrahi's release on compassionate grounds, including from the Church of Scotland, whilst others continued to demand his very death in custody. The papers were having a field day and though this was recess, opposition politicians were relentless in their criticism. Labour members and Tories alike demanded everything from a recall of Parliament to my resignation. What was absent from their comments, however, was what *they* thought should be done. The Labour Party, in particular, was intent on awaiting my decision, then positioning themselves accordingly.

Media officials were being inundated with requests for interviews and information. Others in the Justice Department had to address the urgent request for details and information from governments and agencies alike. A decision had to be made soon as the ninety-day period for consideration of the PTA would be elapsing and, in any event, the frenetic atmosphere was such that it could not be delayed much longer. I was going to have to reflect and decide. In the interim, other work still needed to continue and preparations made for the publicity surrounding the decision.

I knew I was going to have to make my decisions soon and when I did so I would have to make a statement. It would be unlike any previously given by a Scottish minister. For one thing, the news would be global, and it would not be broadcast on Scottish or even just UK networks. Though I was an experienced politician and by then had been a minister for over two years, this was still going to be way beyond anything I had experienced before. Similarly, I had undergone media training before both as a party candidate and as a minister, but this was unique. Accordingly, it was arranged for some specialist training to be given to me for the delivery of the statement and questions that might follow. Officials arranged for Bill McFarlan, a former BBC reporter, who specialised in media training, to provide some tuition. I am hugely obliged to him for his advice and guidance. His professional steer I found invaluable.

Officials had also to commence preparations even though no decision had as yet been taken. Planning for the press conference, for one, needed to begin. Where would it be and who would be there? How would it be announced? If Megrahi was not to be released, then increased security provisions needed to be thought through. Preparations for the safety of Scottish and UK citizens in Libya needed consideration, too. There were many oil and gas workers there and elsewhere in North Africa as well as potential implications for embassy staff. Discussions took place with the FCO to ensure that plans were prepared and that they would be ready to act; including evacuation of embassy staff and civilians if the need were to arise. The FCO were directly involved as they knew the risks and would need to deal with the consequences.

If he was to be released, then the practical arrangements of how he would be removed from the country needed to be considered. The preference was to have him taken from the prison to an airport and depart immediately thereafter on a waiting plane. The last thing anyone wanted was any delay and him remaining in Scotland with all the media frenzy and the security risks that would follow. Once released formally from prison, we would want him out of the country as quickly as possible. Discussions took place with the Libyans to ensure that they would have a jet ready to take him away. They agreed to arrange for a flight to be in London that could then be given very short advance notification to come to Glasgow. It would be there on standby irrespective of the final decision.

Moreover, the Americans had raised concerns regarding how Megrahi would be received if returned to Libya and expressed concerns over a fanfare on his return. The Libyans were advised of this by officials and it had been broached by me in my discussion with them. Assurances were given that any reception would be low-key and respectful to the feelings of the victims' families. These requests were added to by communications, some in much stronger diplomatic language, by the UK and US.

The protocol and paperwork with regard to the compassionate release application was also being followed. I was to receive a formal submission from officials when I returned from the Northern Isles. However, I had been kept appraised as to how the situation was progressing. The medical report was the crucial factor. The reports from the prison governor and social work, whilst important in their own right, would to all intents and purposes be dependent on the medical evidence. The same in many ways applied to the report by the parole board. I had already heard informally through contacts in the SPS that they felt the medical criteria would be met, but I still awaited the formal report. It was evident that the SPS medical officials were seeking advice from specialists treating him regarding the prognosis. All that awaited my return from Shetland.

CHAPTER FOUR

THE DECISION
— MINE AND MINE ALONE

F lying back to Edinburgh from Shetland on the Friday I was conscious that the statement would in all likelihood be the following week. Megrahi's lawyers had just announced that day that they had lodged a formal application with the court to abandon his appeal. That would be heard on Tuesday of that following week. It would be a formality but it required to be duly processed by the Appeal Court and hence the hearing. There was no involvement in either the appeal or the hearing by the Scottish government. It was a decision taken by Megrahi and thereafter for the court to decide.

Meanwhile, the timescale of ninety days for processing the PTA application was nearly up. The media was still a frenzy with claims and counter claims; and calls and demands from all sides for every possible action. The public and press expectation was that a statement would be made that following week. Some suggested Megrahi was getting out the following Wednesday, others that it was the Thursday and some that he wasn't being released at all. The speculation was endless. Arrangements were already being made by officials for a statement that following week, though no formal announcement had been made. Whilst nothing was set in stone there was a momentum growing, given the timescales, that was understandable. I still, though, needed to reach my decision and then the formalities would follow.

Along with the other ongoing discussions and debate this further raised the temperature. Security had been further increased. The hourly police vehicle drive-bys of the office were becoming obvious and disconcerting for staff; and a regular surgery for constituents in my office that Friday afternoon saw a police inspector detailed to sit in the reception area in plain clothes. He later escorted me to an event and I was grateful in many ways simply for his company. There was in fact no need for his protection. Though I was clearly high-profile and recognised by people, no one sought to approach me or seek to discuss the situation. Perhaps an indication that the position I was in was becoming altogether quite lonely.

The time had come for me to make the decision. Firstly, I had to consider the formal submissions and then speak to the First Minister about what I proposed to do. Whilst it would be my decision, I was still a government minister and it would have consequences for him and my Cabinet colleagues. Although neither he nor any other member of the Scottish government ever sought at any stage to interfere in my actions or decision, the solidarity of colleagues who showed support throughout was greatly appreciated. The warmth and sympathy was touching, even if I was subsequently told by Linda that some had refused to travel in the same car as me, fearing for their safety with the heightened security. A solitary journey in more ways than one, the decision was to be mine, and mine alone.

I went to Bute House, the official residence of the First Minister in Edinburgh, that Friday evening for a chat. I informed Alex Salmond of my thinking and what I planned. Given the significance of events, both the Deputy First Minister and the First Minister's senior special adviser were also present; but no officials were there as this was a political rather than governmental meeting. It went on for some time and poor Linda had to wait in an anteroom all that time. There was no opposition to my decision, simply suggestions about timing and handling. They were going to have to deal with the fallout and consequences for the government and party. It was agreed to keep in touch and further calls took place over the weekend as the press speculation reached even new heights, but nothing changed my direction of thought.

I decided to try to be as relaxed as possible throughout this period. I went to a football match with my friend, the former Labour First Minister Henry McLeish, on the Saturday that had been arranged as part of a ministerial visit about tackling knife crime. On the Sunday I played seven-a-side football. The official advice had been not to participate on security grounds, but I simply ignored it. It was something that I had done regularly and the pitch was very close to my home. I really couldn't see any threat other than the risk of a sporting injury. However, I was also conscious that whatever decision I made, life would have to go on. I had been born in the city and had lived in it for many years. It was my home and I was not going to go into hiding. I have always taken the view that people will respect you even if they may disagree with you if you are open, honest and passionate about what you are doing. I could not control the press speculation or the actions of other governments. I was not going to be able to avoid consequences that might follow. All I could do was adhere to the rules and regulations and act as I believed was right. Equally, I was conscious that it was a great privilege to be Justice Secretary. I had come into political life to make Scotland a better place and to seek to do the right thing. This was my moment of truth. I would do what I thought was right and face the consequences afterwards.

And so I came to making my decisions. I was faced with both the applications for prisoner transfer and compassionate release, and I decided to deal with them together. Though submitted at different times, the information and advice on both were now before me and they related to the same individual. Delaying or deferring one or the other simply extended the media frenzy.

I firstly considered the prisoner transfer application. The legislation had been set by the UK government but the paperwork was in order and the criteria met. I had granted prisoner transfer applications before and have done so on many occasions since. Moreover, I have always agreed with the repatriation of prisoners to be nearer their home. Ministers frequently face calls for foreign nationals to be sent home due to the significant costs of incarceration. Many who make such calls, however, howl when our own citizens are repatriated from abroad, despite the hypocrisy in such a position. If foreign prisoners are to be sent back to their own countries, repatriation of our citizens must also be accepted in return.

I also believed that repatriation should occur wherever possible. This was for three reasons. Firstly, the families of criminals have often committed no crime and should not be punished. They have rights that should be considered, whether they be children, spouses or other relatives, and allowing them to be closer and to have more contact is therefore right and proper, whatever the action of the offender. Secondly, this contact helps with rehabilitation. Most prisoners are going to be released at some stage and having them maintain contact with family and friends assists in trying to ensure they do not reoffend on release. There is substantial evidence to support this theory. Finally, I recall meeting Gerry Conlon, who had been wrongfully imprisoned for fourteen years as one of the Guildford Four, accused of a bombing atrocity perpetrated by the IRA, which resulted in innocent Irish people, including himself, being wrongly convicted. His father was also wrongfully imprisoned and tragically died whilst in custody. His detailing of the trauma his mother in Belfast endured struggling to keep in touch with a husband and son in different jails in England was heartfelt. Prisoners need to face the consequences of their actions, but imprisonment should be humane and wherever possible near to their home. Those were also points made by President Nelson Mandela when he had commented on the situation. This, then, was the position I usually took on prisoner transfers generally.

However, this situation was different from the usual ones. Specific assurances and guarantees had been given that any sentence imposed would be served in Scotland. These had been made at the outset of the negotiations over the trial at Camp Zeist. The families of the victims were adamant that they had been assured that it would be the case. The Libyans acknowledged that but simply stated that the situation had changed. The people who could say with certainty were within the UK government. After all, they had entered into the negotiations and treaty with the Libyans. They, though, refused to comment despite requests by me for information and clarification. That I very much regretted. However, the US was explicit in asserting that assurances of imprisonment in Scotland had been given. Not just the Secretary of State Hillary Clinton but also the US Attorney General at the time of the negotiations, Eric Holder, were clear on that. Moreover, he had been the Deputy US Attorney General at the time of the negotiations and was doubtless privy to information and discussions that took place. UN documentation also indicated that. The letters, communications and other indications were all suggestive of a clear understanding that if convicted the accused would serve their sentence in Scotland.

On that basis, I was satisfied that specific assurances had been given at the time of the trial being set that any period of imprisonment imposed would be served in Scotland. That overruled the normal considerations that would apply. On that basis, therefore, I decided to reject the prisoner transfer application.

I then turned to consider the application for compassionate release. The official advice detailed the legislative basis and the guidelines for me to follow.[47] Specifically, that it may be considered when a life expectancy of three months or less applied. It also referred to the evidence that had been gathered or submitted from both

47 Advice to Justice Secretary on Megrahi Application for Compassionate Release, 14 August 2009. Published on SG website

individuals and governments. The families of victims from the UK were generally supportive of compassionate release, whilst those from the US were strongly against. The Libyan government and Qatar, on behalf of the Arab League, were in favour and the US government was against. Finally, it contained the documentation that needed to be obtained, including medical advice as well as reports from the prison governor, social work unit and the parole board.

The principal document was obviously the medical report. It came from Andrew Fraser, the Director of Health and Care at the SPS. He was a man I knew and both liked and trusted. He was highly qualified medically but he had also taken significant advice from specialist clinicians and in particular those treating Megrahi, of which there were several, and at more than one hospital. The report obviously caveated that prognosis in any such case is complex and fraught. Being precise in any such instance is extremely difficult. It detailed the deterioration that had occurred over past weeks as well as the psychological impact it was having on him. It then went on to say:

> In the opinion of his ——————— who has dealt with him prior to, during and following the diagnosis of metastatic cancer, and having seen him during each of those stages, his clinical condition has declined significantly over the last week (period 26 July–3 August). The clinical assessment, therefore, is that a three-month prognosis is now a reasonable estimate for this patient.

It went on to further detail that early release should be considered for the following reasons:

Mr Megrahi is suffering from terminal cancer. The rationale for treatment is symptom control and both he and his family are aware cure is not an option. He has, since first consulting, reported a feeling of isolation – cultural, religious, social and language. He has a strong sense of family duty. The diagnosis of a terminal condition had heightened his sense of isolation and undoubtedly has substantial psychological impact. Mr Megrahi himself has a strong belief of the physical state impacting on the psychological and vice versa. He simply wishes to return home to be with his family, including his elderly mother.

In addition to considering the requirements of the patient, we had also discussed consideration of the family. His return to Libya would, we feel, not only benefit the patient, but would also be advantageous for the family. Mr Megrahi has several children of varying age. If he was returned home, his family could become more involved in his health-care needs. We would anticipate this would benefit them, not only in the short term, but also when considering any potential longer-term psychological impact.

Whilst his condition does not restrict or remove Mr Megrahi's ability to carry out any particular tasks, we do not believe he would represent a risk to himself or anyone else.

We would anticipate a continued decline in his physical condition and increased dependence on external help. We understand plans for transfer of care to Libyan health services have been made (although we are not aware of the specific details).[48]

---

48 Report by the Medical Officer, 10 August 2009. Published on SG website

The report from the prison social work unit was short and understandably so. Both it and the report from the prison governor were in a questionnaire format similar to applications for compassionate release. In the normal course of events, a Home Background Report would have been undertaken by the social worker, assessing the suitability of where the prisoner would be going, or contact made with the medical institution that would be caring for them. Almost invariably this would be somewhere in Scotland, though, on occasion, elsewhere in the UK. In this case, the prisoner would be returning to a foreign land and one with which contact had rarely been had. A full assessment was clearly not possible in these circumstances and therefore it was simply a statement of his current situation and ill health.[49]

The prison governor's report detailed Megrahi's prison history and his behaviour whilst incarcerated. I had met the governor on several occasions. He was experienced and very able, having been in charge of many institutions during his career. A kindly man but aware of the need to be both firm and suspicious of many inmates, his report commented on Megrahi's time spent in prison, during which there had been no significant issues. It commented on the risk of reoffending if released early, which, again, was not really applicable. There had never been any thought or suggestion that he would reoffend or pose a risk to the public, the reason being no doubt that he was terminally ill. In any event, all the information and evidence were that his crimes had been committed as part of his duties for the Libyan state

---

49 Report by Prison Social Work Unit, 4 August 2009. Published on SG website

and he was not a danger to the public or likely to take up any formal intelligence role once again. The trial judge report was attached and reference was made to there being no known previous convictions. Finally, it asked whether the prisoner should be released early. On this, the governor said:

> The prognosis for Mr Megrahi is extremely bleak. Clinical advice would confirm that his death is likely to occur within a very short period. At present he is visibly displaying signs of age-ing and pain during normal daily routine. He regularly refers to himself as a dying man and his mood can be described at times as extremely low. Release of Mr Megrahi will offer him and his family the opportunity to spend his remaining time in his country. This will mean he will have access to his close family at a time when his health is deteriorating.[50]

The final piece of documentation was the report from the parole board, whose function in the case of compassionate release is to advise the minister and recommend any conditions they may deem appropriate. Their report concluded:

> The index offence was of enormous gravity and resulted in the deaths of 270 people and to date no acceptance of guilt has been made by Mr al-Megrahi albeit that his first appeal was not upheld. He does not however have any known previous

---

50 Report of Prison Governor, 5 August 2009. Published on SG website

convictions and he has posed no management difficulties in custody. He has been diagnosed with terminal cancer and has not
responded well to treatment with the result that his condition
has deteriorated rapidly in recent times with resultant effects
on his overall wellbeing. He experiences pain and is described
as having aged. His medical status is confirmed by a number
of experienced consultant clinicians and by the palliative care
team at the local hospice. Whilst there can be no absolute certainty as to such matters there can be very little doubt as to the
short life expectancy which is now available to him.

Mr al-Megrahi's family are no longer in Scotland and he is
therefore unable to have any direct contact with them. In the
final weeks of his life it will be important for both his welfare
and that of his wife, children and elderly parents to have time
together to assist the bereavement process. This is also of cultural and religious importance to them.

Given the term of section 3(2) of the Prisoners and Criminal Proceedings (Scotland) Act 1993 the Board is to look at Mr
al-Megrahi's suitability for release on compassionate grounds
only. It was noted that the term 'compassion' was not defined in
the 1993 Act. In view of the serious nature of his medical condition it would be appropriate to advise the Scottish ministers
that he can be considered suitable for compassionate release.

If compassionate release is granted then it is recommended
that the mandatory life conditions are sufficient in this case.[51]

---

51 Report of Parole Board, undated. Published on SG website

That then was the documentation and information laid before me. It was now for me to decide. It was evident from the advice from all agencies involved that Megrahi met the criteria. The advice was as clear and certain as was possible to be in the circumstances and it came from experienced officials and clinicians. It was not for me to second guess or challenge their skills or competency. I held them and still hold them all in the highest regard. No previous application for compassionate release that had met the criteria and that had been duly processed by officials had been refused. Indeed, that is still the situation that applies. All acted professionally and appropriately. However, as with the prisoner transfer, this was no ordinary case and additional considerations had to be given to the application.

As the parole board had commented, 270 people had lost their lives. This was the worst terrorist atrocity perpetrated in the UK. It had been an attack on innocent American civilians and devastated a small Scottish town. However, the grounds for compassionate release are upon the health of the prisoner, not the gravity of the offence. Criminals that had committed heinous crimes had been released before and doubtless will be again. It was not for a minister to judge simply on the nature of the offence, therefore. The parole board had correctly commented that there was no acknowledgment of guilt by Megrahi and as a result there was no expression of sorrow or remorse for what he had done. However, that again was not a set criterion for release. Others who have been in denial or simply refused to atone have also been released. Simply because he failed to show any compassion to the victims did not mean that we should not show compassion to him. That compassion applied not only to the individual, but also to their friends and family who have committed no crime. A criminal, no matter how depraved, is still someone's son or daughter, mother or father, and those relatives should have the opportunity to say their goodbyes and make peace with their loved one before death. Finally, I have always believed that there should be some dignity allowed in death. A prison cell was not an appropriate place to die, nor, indeed, a hospital in a foreign land far from friends and family.

He was terminally ill and no sentence that could be imposed by a Scottish court was more severe than that. I felt he should be allowed to die in his own land. Those aboard flight 103 had not been given that right or compassion; however, I had been brought up to believe not in an eye for an eye, but to do unto others as you would wish done unto to yourself. That there was a New Testament as well as an Old Testament, after all, and they should be read together. Just because others behaved abominably and appallingly did not mean we had to reciprocate. To do so would be to abandon the beliefs upon which our society is based and lower ourselves to the level we so rightly condemned in the actions of others. I believed those were the values that we held as a people and by which we sought to live and adhere to in our land. On that basis, I decided to authorise his release.

I knew it was going to be controversial and I realised that it was going to be a global story. This was no ordinary decision but one that had international significance and state interests at its heart. The powers of the government I was a member of were limited in comparison with many of those who were seeking to pressurise or persuade us. There was a great deal at stake here not just for me but for those who worked for me and others to whom I was responsible. I remember wondering whether I should make out a handwritten will. There had been the odd threat to life made by cranks, which were invariably investigated but routinely dismissed. However, I appreciated the stakes had been raised considerably and the atmosphere around me was growing tenser. My life in many ways would change irrevocably; for better or ill I knew not, but change it would. I was to be eternally grateful for the support of my staff and officials. Linda Hamilton and Linda Pollock were unstinting in their efforts and Karen Newton and Ian Inglis selfless in their service. They were the anchors to which I was attached as the turbulence raged. There was some further discussion as to whether the decision could be deferred for another few days or even a week or so. I thought that it wasn't feasible. Events were in motion and momentum was growing. The level of expectation was such that it would result in criticism from all sides. Politicians and press were demanding action. The decision would have to be taken that week. However, even though I had decided what my decision was going to be, there was still considerable work to be done.

First of all, a statement had to be prepared. The basis of the decision was contained in the documents that had been placed before me, and so I simply had to detail my logic and reasoning on the matter, as well as expressing any other comments I felt appropriate to make in the circumstances. The practicalities for the statement such as the media arrangements and other formalities were sorted out by my staff, but many organisations and individuals still needed to be told directly by me out of courtesy. The police would have to ensure the transfer of Megrahi to an airport and so I spoke to the Chief and Deputy Chief Constable of Strathclyde Constabulary, who would be responsible for the arrangements. The logistics would have to be considered carefully as the dangers were significantly greater than any normal high-risk prisoner transfer, and there was the obvious media presence to think of too. Given the terrorist threat, a special prison van capable of enduring roadside improvised explosive devices had to be obtained and as such a vehicle was not available in Scotland, one needed to be brought in specially. Again, given the risks involved for both Megrahi and his escort, body armour for their protection would have to be worn as they exited the prison van and entered the plane. That, too, was not standard attire for Scottish Prison Service escorts and again had to be obtained. The Libyans needed to be notified, too, to have a plane provisionally arranged to collect him if a release was to be authorised, as they would be responsible for getting him back to his own country.

Most speeches for government ministers are written by officials. This, though, was significantly different and not simply due to the tragic events of Lockerbie. It was, after all, my decision, rather than government policy and, more importantly, it was to be my neck on the line. I therefore decided to write it myself, which I did by dictating it to one of the senior officials, who then typed it up. A speech as much as a formal statement, it detailed my investigations and provided an explanation of my reasoning. Others with an interest, such as the Lord Advocate, needed to be allowed to make any comments they felt appropriate given the significance of it for them. However, other than a few suggested changes or remarks, the speech remained much as dictated by me. Everything was now prepared. Arrangements were made. The speech was written and staff were ready. The afternoon of Thursday 20 August was scheduled. All that was needed was the final sign-off by me. That would trigger the issuing of the call notice to the media and the notification to all agencies involved that the release was happening.

However, with all the speculation mounting, pressure from the United States was also escalating. Letters were being sent by senators and the media was running with their demands. Late in the afternoon on Wednesday, the very eve of the statement, notification was received that officials from the White House wished to make further representations. I accordingly took a call from John Brennan, now Director of the CIA but then the assistant to the President for Homeland Security. He told me that he had been speaking to the President that morning and that he wanted to pass on their views. I said I was aware of their concerns on the prisoner transfer and he thanked us for passing on the medical information regarding the compassionate release. He asked whether the possibility of Megrahi being released to reside somewhere else other than being returned to Libya was being considered, I said it had been but was difficult given the security implications. Lastly, they worried about the time-scale and sought a delay beyond 1 September, which was the fortieth anniversary of the Libyan Revolution. They thought the release of Megrahi could be used by the Libyan regime for their own propaganda purposes. I explained that that too would be problematic as we were under severe political pressure to act. Opposition politicians were demanding action and threatening the recall of Parliament. He was polite and respectful and I thanked him for his call.

Such a call from the White House could not be ignored and though I was sure that my decision was the correct one, it made me reflect again on the implications it would have not just on Scotland, but the world.

It was an invidious position for one small country with very limited international clout; and also for its government, which had very limited powers. The British government that should also have been representing Scotland's interests was happy to hang the country and the Scottish government out to dry. They wanted a release but wished to avoid the blame for it. No contact was received from them other than work with FCO officials on the practicalities of release. Though the public face of the US administration was that they wanted him to die in a Scottish prison cell, it was clear that they would find compassionate release more palatable. That had always been hinted at and alluded to by US government officials. It tied in, after all, with the security and commercial deals that they themselves were making with Libya and Gaddafi, and had been doing for many years. They now appeared to be simply calling for a delay. There were arguments in favour of that, in particular maintaining good relations with the US. This was a back channel call, however, and the likelihood was we'd be criticised in any event when the release was announced. The arguments against a delay were the issues it might pose for the security of Scottish citizens and others. The Libyans had a plane on standby ready to fly to Scotland and were awaiting a final decision. If there were to be a delay, would the 1 September celebrations that concerned the US become an outpouring of rage against Scotland, with implications for Scots in Libya and elsewhere? Would we need to evacuate our people to save them from any backlash? Could it be done at such short notice?

I reflected and weighed up the arguments for and against, though this was the very eve of what was a very complicated security arrangement that had been coordinated across multiple agencies and countries. To have aborted fewer than twenty-four hours before, whilst possible, would have been complex and difficult. It seemed to me that the situation was tense and a delay would simply make it worse. If it had been a more substantial time delay that had been sought, and at an earlier juncture, there may have been reason to pause. However, this was an eleventh-hour call for a marginal delay, and would cause huge disruption and pose great dangers. Moreover, it was still not going to be met with public approval by the US administration. The risks, therefore, significantly outweighed the benefits.

I decided the die was cast and so, later that evening, I authorised the issuing of the call notice and the preparations for Megrahi's release. I went home to both relax and prepare for my statement the following day. It was going to be a momentous occasion.

THE STATEMENT

I'd gone to the gym the night before to relax. Ian had taken me there and waited to take me home. It did feel a bit like the condemned man awaiting his fate. However, I knew what had to be. I actually slept remarkably well, probably as a result of the exercise. In the morning, I read over the statement to try to get it right in my mind. I also listened to music to try to unwind. I felt calm but focussed. At about noon, Ian collected me to take me to St Andrew's House for a final run-through with officials and advisers before the statement would be made in the press centre there. I recall that Bill McFarlan, the media adviser, said to me as I left the room that this was my chance to stand up for my country and what we believe in, and that I should not kowtow to anyone. His words helped me focus and made me walk straighter, as the significance of it all began to sink in.

The media centre is located in the basement of the building and is limited in space. Arrangements had been made for television to share footage but the number of cameras and press corps was still going to be substantial. I remember running through the statement one final time and then preparing to head down from my office along the back staircases of the building. I was flanked by two special advisers and I could sense the eyes of civil servants watching me. Television sets were being switched on and screens cleared. The statement was being covered live in Scotland and around much of the world.

> I initially went into a holding room to chat with the Director General. I had run through the statement many times by then both in my room and from the set and so I almost knew it word for word. I was ready to go. Walking onto the stage, cameras panned onto me, flashlights went off and reporters primed themselves. The statement took some twenty minutes and was delivered standing

at the lectern that was set up on the stage. This was the statement: It is my privilege to serve as the Cabinet Secretary for Justice in the government of Scotland. It is a post in which I take great pride, but one which carries with it great responsibility. Never, perhaps, more so than with these decisions that I now have to make.

On the evening of 21 December 1988, a heinous crime was perpetrated. It claimed the lives of 270 innocent civilians. Four days before Christmas, men, women and children going about their daily lives were cruelly murdered. They included eleven from one small Scottish town. That town was Lockerbie – a name that will for ever be associated with the worst terrorist atrocity ever committed on UK soil.

A prisoner transfer application has been submitted by the government of Libya seeking the transfer of Mr Abdelbaset Ali Mohmed al-Megrahi, the man convicted of those offences in the Scottish courts. He has also now sought to be released on compassionate grounds due to his prostate cancer that is terminal.

This crime precedes both the election of our government and even the restoration of a Parliament in Scotland. I now find myself having to make these decisions. However, the applications have been lawfully made, and I am obliged to address them. Final advice from my officials was given late on Friday 14 August 2009. I have now had an opportunity to reflect upon this.

Let me be absolutely clear. As Cabinet Secretary for Justice in Scotland it is my responsibility to decide upon these two applications. These are my decisions and my decisions alone.

In considering these applications I have strictly followed due process, including the procedures laid down in the Prisoner Transfer Agreement and in the Scottish Prison Service guidance on compassionate release. I have listened to many representations and received substantial submissions.

Let me be quite clear on matters on which I am certain. The Scottish Police and Prosecution Service undertook a detailed and comprehensive investigation with the assistance of the US and other authorities. I pay tribute to them for the exceptional manner in which they operated in dealing with both the aftermath of the atrocity and the complexity of a worldwide investigation. They are to be commended for their tenacity and skill. When Mr al-Megrahi was brought to justice, it was before a Scottish court sitting in the Netherlands. And I pay tribute to our judges who presided and acted justly.

Mr al-Megrahi was sentenced to life imprisonment for the murder of 270 people. He was given a life sentence and a punishment part of twenty-seven years was fixed. When such an appalling crime is perpetrated it is appropriate that a severe sentence be imposed.

Mr al-Megrahi has since withdrawn his appeal against both conviction and sentence. As I have said consistently throughout, that is a matter for him and the courts. That was his decision. My decisions are predicated on the fact that he was properly investigated, a lawful conviction passed and a life sentence imposed.

I realise that the abandonment of the appeal has caused concern to many. I have indicated that I am grateful to and proud of those who have served in whatever capacity in bringing this case to justice. I accept the conviction and sentence imposed. However, there remain concerns to some on the wider issues of the Lockerbie atrocity.

This is a global issue, and international in its nature. The questions to be asked and answered are beyond the jurisdiction of Scots law and the restricted remit of the Scottish government. If a further inquiry were felt to be appropriate then it should be initiated by those with the required power and authority. The Scottish government would be happy to fully cooperate in such an inquiry.

I now turn to the matters before me that I require to address. An application under the Prisoner Transfer Agreement and an application for compassionate release have been made. I now deal with them in turn.

Firstly, the prisoner transfer agreement.

The Libyan government applied on 5 May 2009 for the transfer of Mr al-Megrahi. Prisoner Transfer Agreements are negotiated by the United Kingdom government.

Throughout the negotiations and at the time of the signing of the PTA with Libya, the Scottish government's opposition was made clear. It was pointed out that the Scottish Prison Service had only one Libyan prisoner in custody. Notwithstanding that, the UK government failed to secure, as requested by the Scottish government, an exclusion from the PTA for anyone involved in the Lockerbie Air Disaster. As a consequence, Mr al-Megrahi is eligible for consideration for transfer in terms of the agreement entered into by the governments of the United Kingdom and Libya.

I received numerous letters and representations, and recognised that a decision on transfer would be of personal significance to those whose lives have been affected. Accordingly, I decided to meet with groups and individuals with a relevant interest.

I met with the families of victims: those from the United Kingdom who had relatives on board the flight, as well as those whose kinfolk were murdered in their homes in Lockerbie; a lady from Spain whose sister was a member of the cabin crew; and I held a video conference with families from the United States. I am grateful to each and every one of them for their fortitude on a matter which I know is still a source of great pain.

I also spoke to the United States Secretary of State, Hillary Clinton, and the United States Attorney General, Eric Holder. I met Minister Alobidi and his delegation from the Libyan government to hear their reasons for applying for transfer, and to present to them the objections that had been raised to their application.

I have noted and considered all the points presented, and also relevant written representations I received.

Prior to ratification of the Prisoner Transfer Agreement, it was scrutinised by the Westminster Joint Committee on Human Rights, to which Jack Straw, UK Secretary of State for Justice, gave a commitment that in cases where applications were not submitted personally by the prisoner, the prisoner must be given the opportunity to make representations.

Mr al-Megrahi had the opportunity to make representations, and he chose to do so in person. Therefore I was duty-bound to receive his representations. I accordingly met him.

It was clear that both the United States government and the American families objected to a prisoner transfer. They did so on the basis of agreements they said had been made, prior to trial, regarding the place of imprisonment of anyone convicted.

The United States Attorney General, Eric Holder, was in fact Deputy Attorney General to Janet Reno at the time of the pre-trial negotiations. He was adamant that assurances had been given to the United States government that any person convicted would serve his sentence in Scotland. Many of the American families spoke of the comfort that they placed upon these assurances over the past ten years. That clear understanding was reiterated to me by the US Secretary of State Hillary Clinton.

I sought the views of the United Kingdom government. I offered them the right to make representations or provide information. They declined to do so. They simply informed me that they saw no legal barrier to transfer and that they gave no assurances to the US government at the time. They have declined to offer a full explanation as to what was discussed during this time, or to provide any information to substantiate their view. I find that highly regrettable.

I therefore do not know what the exact nature of those discussions was, nor what may have been agreed between governments. However, I am certain of the clear understanding of the American families and the American government.

Therefore it appears to me that the American families and government either had an expectation, or were led to believe, that there would be no prisoner transfer and the sentence would be served in Scotland.

It is for that reason that the Libyan government's application for prisoner transfer for Abdelbaset Ali Mohmed al-Megrahi I accordingly reject.

I now turn to the issue of compassionate release.

Section three of the Prisoners and Criminal Proceedings (Scotland) Act 1993 gives the Scottish ministers the power to release prisoners on licence on compassionate grounds.

The Act requires that ministers are satisfied that there are compassionate grounds justifying the release of a person serving a sentence of imprisonment. Although the Act does not specify what the grounds for compassionate release are, guidance from the Scottish Prison Service, who assess applications, suggests that it may be considered where a prisoner is suffering from a terminal illness and death is likely to occur soon. There are no fixed time limits but life expectancy of less than three months may be considered an appropriate period. The guidance makes it clear that all prisoners, irrespective of sentence length, are eligible to be considered for compassionate release. That guidance dates from 2005.

On 24 July 2009 I received an application from Mr al-Megrahi for compassionate release. He was diagnosed with terminal prostate cancer in September 2008. I have been regularly updated as to the progression of his illness. I have received numerous comprehensive medical reports including the opinions of consultants who have been treating him. It is quite clear to the medical experts that he has a terminal illness, and indeed that there has recently been a significant deterioration in his health.

In order to consider the application for compassionate release, I was provided with reports and recommendations by the governor of Greenock Prison, the doctors and prison social work staff. Also, as laid out in statute, I have consulted the parole board. This is the normal process for consideration of an application for compassionate release and my decision is in accordance with all the advice given to me.

It is the opinion of his Scottish Prison Service doctors who have dealt with him prior to, during and following the diagnosis of prostate cancer, and having seen him during each of these stages, that his clinical condition has declined significantly. Assessment by a range of specialists has reached the firm consensus that his disease is, after several different trials of treatment, 'hormone resistant' – that is resistant to any treatment options of known effectiveness. Consensus on prognosis therefore has moved to the lower end of expectations.

Mr al-Megrahi was examined by Scottish Prison Service doctors on 3 August. A report dated 10 August from the Director of Health and Care for the Scottish Prison Service indicates that a three-month prognosis is now a reasonable estimate. The advice they have provided is based not only on their own physical examination but draws on the opinion of other specialists and consultants who have been involved in his care and treatment. He may die sooner, he may live longer – I can only base my decision on the medical advice I have before me. That medical advice has been made available to the United States government at their request and has been published on grounds of public interest.

It has been suggested that Mr al-Megrahi could be released from prison to reside elsewhere in Scotland. Clear advice from senior police officers is that the security implications of such a move would be severe. I have therefore ruled that out as an option.

Having met the criteria, it therefore falls to me to decide whether Mr al-Megrahi should be released on compassionate grounds. I am conscious that there are deeply held feelings, and that many will disagree whatever my decision. However a decision has to be made.

Scotland will for ever remember the crime that has been perpetrated against our people and those from many other lands. The pain and suffering will remain for ever. Some hurt can never heal. Some scars can never fade. Those who have been bereaved cannot be expected to forget, let alone forgive. Their pain runs deep and the wounds remain.

However, Mr al-Megrahi now faces a sentence imposed by a higher power. It is one that no court, in any jurisdiction, in any land, could revoke or overrule. It is terminal, final and irrevocable. He is going to die.

In Scotland, we are a people who pride ourselves on our humanity. It is viewed as a defining characteristic of Scotland

and the Scottish people. The perpetration of an atrocity and outrage cannot and should not be a basis for losing sight of who we are, the values we seek to uphold, and the faith and beliefs by which we seek to live.

Mr al-Megrahi did not show his victims any comfort or compassion. They were not allowed to return to the bosom of their families to see out their lives, let alone their dying days. No compassion was shown by him to them.

But, that alone is not a reason for us to deny compassion to him and his family in his final days.

Our justice system demands that judgment be imposed but compassion be available. Our beliefs dictate that justice be served, but mercy be shown. Compassion and mercy are about upholding the beliefs that we seek to live by, remaining true to our values as a people. No matter the severity of the provocation or the atrocity perpetrated.

For these reasons – and these reasons alone – it is my decision that Mr Abdelbaset Ali Mohmed al-Megrahi, convicted in 2001 for the Lockerbie bombing, now terminally ill with prostate cancer, be released on compassionate grounds and allowed to return to Libya to die.

There had been a discussion with officials as to whether questions should be taken. However, it seemed to me important not just what I said but that I be prepared to answer for my decision. The room was packed, though there were fewer questions than I had been expecting. None were complex or difficult. I then left the stage and returned to the holding room. There was a brief chance to relax and grab a coffee before going out again for TV and radio interviews. The most aggressive in tone were those with American journalists. The questioners could not comprehend why Megrahi would not be left to die in a Scottish prison cell. I tried to answer as politely as possible despite quite strident stances being taken. After over five hours of media interviews I finally was taken home by Ian.

I had received a message from Karen coming out of the interviews saying that police would be coming to my flat but there was nothing to be alarmed about. It transpired that plain clothes officers in an unmarked car had been watching my flat whilst I was giving my statement. To their consternation, two men had attempted to break into the common stair before their very eyes. They immediately apprehended them. It seems that it was purely coincidental and related to an attempted theft and nothing more sinister. However, senior officers decided that additional security might be required and police staff came to install a panic alarm linked directly to a control room. It was to remain for some time.

As I was delivering my statement, Megrahi was already en route to the airport and the spotlight began to move to him. It had been coordinated beforehand that as I rose to speak he would be ready and primed to be put in transit. He, along with others, was given very brief prior notification of the decision. The eventualities had been planned and prepared for. Megrahi packed what few possessions he had and the Scottish Police and Prison Service prepared to move the convoy that would take him to the airport. The Libyan flight headed north from London to collect him. It had been arranged with the Libyans that they would have a plane available irrespective of the decision. If it was a refusal, the flight would be aborted. If it was granted, it would head for Glasgow Airport. Similar courtesy calls were made by Scottish government officials to victims and states who had an interest.

The security entourage was already preparing to head from Greenock Prison to Glasgow Airport as I started to detail my reasoning. Cameras followed the departure from the prison gates and the arrival on the airport tarmac. The world watched the exiting of Megrahi from the prison van to the waiting steps, for him to climb aboard the aeroplane. He was escorted by prison staff in body armour, which he was also wearing. Armed police were in close proximity throughout. No risks were going to be entailed regarding his safety whilst in his final moments in Scotland. He was met by waiting Libyan officials at the top of the steps. The doors closed and the plane departed. The Director of Communications at the SPS recalled that he'd been so engrossed in obtaining the protective vests for prisoner and staff that he'd forgotten to get his on. Accordingly, he was the only person on the airport runway without protective attire. The plane took off from Scotland and headed for Tripoli. There was relief all round that he was safely gone. But, though Megrahi had left Scotland, the reverberations here had only just begun.

CHAPTER FIVE

THE FALLOUT

That evening I was unwinding back in the flat with friends and family who had come round. It had been and still was a tense time. It's at times like that when you realise just who your true friends are. Their company was not just an expression of friendship but solidarity; and it was much appreciated by me.

The BlackBerry was beginning to go into overdrive. Emails were arriving at an incredible rate. There were too many to read every one, besides which I was really too tired to care. Some were from Scots and those south of the border expressing their support for my stance. Others, many of which were from the US, were condemnatory, and often threatening and abusive.

The television was on, and the news was still wall-to-wall coverage of Megrahi. Footage of his arrival in Tripoli began to be broadcast, which showed throngs of people and joyous crowds assembled to meet him at the airport. Scottish flags were being waved by many. Saif Gaddafi, one of Colonel Gaddafi's sons, met the plane. It appeared to be a hero's welcome – exactly what we had been assured by the

Libyans would *not* happen. They had been specifically asked by us to ensure that any reception would be low-key and respectful to the victims; and they had assured us it would be. It was obvious, though, that this spelt trouble. However, as I needed to rest, that was to be for another day. It would be years later before I would discover what had really happened and how the 'hero's reception' was not what it seemed.

The decision was always going to be attacked one way or other, but the hero's reception, as it had seemed at the time, caused additional problems and criticism. The focus and news agenda had now moved on from the compassionate release of a terminally ill man to the celebration of the return of a convicted bomber. It resulted in significant condemnation from both the British and American governments as well politicians from around the political spectrum. President Obama's Chief Spokesman described it as 'outrageous and disgusting'.[52] Downing Street stated that Gordon Brown had appealed to the Libyans not to give Megrahi a hero's welcome on his return. The Foreign Office even stated that they were reviewing a plan for Prince Andrew to attend the fortieth anniversary celebrations[53] – a fact they hadn't mentioned before, but illuminating given his significant role as a trade envoy for the UK.

The Scottish flags at the airport were also an unwelcome surprise. They had not been supplied by the Scottish government and were certainly not routinely available in Libya. Moreover, they could not have gone in on the plane that had collected him, as they were being

---

52   *Daily Telegraph*, 21 August 2009
53   Ibid.

waved as it landed. Just who had supplied them has never been detailed, but dirty tricks were feared.

As it turned out, not all was as it seemed on the TV screens, and the widely condemned 'hero's reception' was far from that. There were no huge crowds giving a rapturous reception at the airport. Instead, there was a reception at the airport of 100 young people, though they did have Scottish flags. Saif Gaddafi held a press conference at which he thanked the Scottish and UK governments. However, any plans of a larger crowd had ceased following President Obama's warnings. The US had been clear that there would be significant consequences if there was a fanfare at the airport and an overt display by the regime.[54]

However, there was a separate and much larger rally going on in Green Square, Tripoli at the time. It was entirely unrelated to Megrahi's release and, indeed, many at that event were oblivious to his arrival in Libya. The event was not even covered live on Libyan television.

Those two events were later configured on TV reporting to give the impression of him being met by cheering crowds at the airport. The imagery was such that the very large crowd in the square appeared to be celebrating Megrahi's return as the plane landed at the airport, which they were not. However, the footage made it look otherwise.

The US embassy in Tripoli had sent cables that indicated that the reception was 'low-key' and had 'technically' stuck to the agreement,[55] and some others, such as retired diplomats, also suggested that

---

54 Chorin, *Exit the Colonel*, p. 157
55 Ibid.

the reception was in fact nothing exceptional. However, they were overshadowed by the extensive coverage that appeared to show the very opposite. People's eyes could not be deceiving them, after all. The evidence of a celebration was there for all to see. How that footage had been constructed, why it was done and who was responsible for it, is not known. Presumably, it was created by Libyan TV, encouraged by Gaddafi, in an attempt to show the regime in a favourable light. As the American cables disclosed, the Libyans seemed to be trying to 'manage the optics' for two distinct audiences, but they did adhere to the agreement.[56]

The US and UK governments, despite having clear evidence from their own representatives to the contrary, were relentless in their condemnation. After all, UK and US officials were at the airport and saw for themselves what the true nature of the reception was and had advised their respective governments in cables. Yet those governments allowed a lie to develop fuelled in no small measure by them to suit their political agenda. The damage was done. No clarification was made by UK or US authorities and an acceptance developed of a scandalous breach of trust by the Libyans and condemnation of the Scottish government for their decision and naivety. The Scottish government, therefore, was to be pilloried for allowing a hero's reception, when the accusers well knew there had been none. With the Scottish government having no staff or sources on the ground, it was a perception even I believed for quite some time, until the truth finally emerged.

---

56 Ibid.

The criticism continued to mount. Having made the decision, though, it was now time for me to step back a bit and allow others to step forward to defend me. Principally, that would be the First Minister. Though it had been my decision, I was a member of his government and he was accountable for me and my actions. I had said before that I would be willing to resign following the decision to deflect criticism from him and the collective government. It seemed, though, that the desire of the opposition in Scotland was to bring down the entire government, not just one minister. Accordingly, the need to do so never arose and I was neither asked for nor tendered my resignation. It was always known, however, that I would do so if it was needed. My loyalty was to the collective SNP government in which I was honoured to serve. That collective loyalty was reciprocated by the First Minister, who very ably and stoutly defended me throughout and I am extremely grateful for that support not just at the time but over years subsequently. The same applied to all my Cabinet colleagues and the entire party. Whether they all agreed with me, I know not, but they stood by me and I am for ever indebted to them for that.

The following day the First Minister was publicly defending my decision. A bit of a tag team developed where I would comment or respond one day and he would appear and speak the next. The condemnation from the US was running widely in the press and media, and Scottish politicians were jumping on to the bandwagon. Even the Director of the FBI sought to get in on the act. Very shortly after the decision, Robert Muller's office contacted Lothian and Borders Police late one evening demanding my home address to have a letter delivered to me personally. The police in turn contacted the Scottish government. It was contrary to all inter-governmental protocols. Linda refused to do so and advised that it could be delivered to St Andrew's House in the usual fashion or else emailed. She didn't trouble me overnight but told me the following day. I always wondered whether the police had sent an armed response vehicle to watch my flat whilst I slept. I was grateful to Linda for her handling of the situation. She defused what might have been a diplomatic incident and allowed me an undisturbed sleep.

Robert Muller's actions were not surprising. A few years later he came to Edinburgh to meet with the Lord Advocate to discuss the ongoing investigations in Libya into Lockerbie. Before he even arrived at the Crown Office, he insisted on it being swept for bugs and other covert devices. I remember wondering whether that meant he felt the Crown would spy on him or our security was so lax that it could not be trusted. Apparently this is standard procedure, however, and is insisted upon everywhere he goes. Either way, it was insulting given that both he and the Crown were jointly involved in investigations into Lockerbie. However, the story about his letter ran significantly in the press. Now, it was not just the President of the United States who had condemned the release, but the Director of the FBI who was criticising me.

The British government, whilst not explicitly condemning the decision, were very keen to heap the opprobrium for it onto the Scottish government. The Foreign Secretary David Miliband had condemned the so-called celebrations for Megrahi's return, despite knowing what had really happened. They flagrantly denied allegations of commercial interests or any involvement with Libya, despite this being the case. However, their position began to unravel. The Scottish government had always wanted to be as open as possible, and to counteract criticism it had always been the intention to publicise as much information as possible. This forced the UK government to agree to do likewise. This position has, however, never been accepted by the US. As with the International Criminal Court, the US sadly often adopts a position of seeking to enforce standards on others that it will not accept or abide by itself.

However, from the information that was published early on by UK Labour governments, their hypocritical position on the release began to be exposed. A letter from Ivan Lewis, UK Minister of State for Foreign and Commonwealth Affairs, on 3 August was clear and unequivocal in its desire for prisoner transfer.[57] Moreover, communications also disclosed that Bill Rammell, who had been a Foreign Office Minister prior to Ivan Lewis's appointment in June 2009, had told the Libyans in February that neither the Prime Minister nor the Foreign Secretary wanted to see Megrahi die in a Scottish prison cell. The correspondence from Jack Straw also showed the underlying commercial interests behind the UK government position. He was quoted as stating that excluding Megrahi from the PTA would 'risk damaging our wide-ranging and beneficial relationship with Libya'.

The deals in the desert continued to be denied but were becoming evident for all to see. Further information on commercial and other deals came to light over coming weeks. It even transpired that

---

57   Letter from Ivan Lewis, 3 August 2009. Published on Foreign Office website

the Police Service of Northern Ireland (PSNI), with the support of the UK government, had been involved in providing training for the police service of Gaddafi's regime.[58] Given the shooting of PC Yvonne Fletcher by the Libyans, that was to look remarkably callous. The hypocrisy of politicians, and especially those in the Labour Party, was shameless. Notwithstanding what Labour in the UK had been pushing for in private, Labour in Scotland was strident in their public condemnation of the release. They knew what had been going on and were well aware of their London colleagues' desires. Gordon Brown, after all, represented a Scottish constituency. But this did not stop their Scottish colleagues expressing faux outrage and horror at Megrahi's release. They piled on the pressure in the Scottish Parliament and the Scottish press.

Other parties behaved equally badly. I watched with some incredulity the Tory peer Lord Carmylie condemn me in an interview. He, as Peter Fraser, had been the Lord Advocate at the time of the prosecution in Camp Zeist. He sat in the same Tory group in the House of Lords as Lord Trefgarne, who'd been pushing for a release long before I was involved. Moreover, I recalled a convivial chat I had with a very senior judge who I knew well shortly before my statement after a ministerial meeting had concluded. I had privately advised of my intentions, given the significance of it for the judiciary in Scotland. He related how, as a young advocate, he'd been involved in the Lockerbie Fatal Accident Inquiry. He remembered the then Lord Advocate, Peter Fraser, assuring him that they knew

---

58   Amnesty International UK, 18 September 2009

it was the Palestinians that had done it. Fraser had also criticised the trial but still felt free to join in what was beginning to appear like an open season for attacks upon me.

Thankfully, there was significant support coming in from ordinary people in Scotland, the UK and elsewhere. In the main, this was on the basis of my having expressed my belief in compassion being shown, though others did so because they thought I had stood my ground against pressures from elsewhere. Some gestures were very touching and I was extremely grateful for their kindness and consideration, which helped to sustain my morale before what seemed a never-ending deluge of criticism in the media. Obviously, not all were supportive and many from the US were downright hostile. Linda received an email from someone who threatened to rape her and throw both of us into a vat of acid. I recall one email in which the sender said that they 'prayed to God every day that my family and I died an excruciating death'. I never understood which God he was praying to, but it was certainly not one that I had been brought up to believe in.

The support of the Faith Communities was not only very much appreciated by me on a personal basis but also helpful in mitigating the onslaught. Some of the churches in the US expressed support for the decision, which cannot have been easy for them given the tide of publicity. The Church of Scotland had previously expressed support for Megrahi's release. Cardinal Keith O'Brien of the Catholic Church in Scotland also spoke out in support. He was subsequently embroiled in a personal scandal and stepped down. However, his support was greatly cherished by me and much appreciated. One of the American victim's families retorted that he should 'get back to his knitting'. It was hardly the way to address a religious leader, even if you strongly disagreed with him.

Others also intimated their support for the decision. Former South African President Nelson Mandela had expressed his backing, which resulted in a major Scottish Sunday paper running a banner headline that read: 'Mandela Backs MacAskill Decision'. I have always been a huge admirer of President Mandela, viewing him as one of the greatest men of the twentieth century. I was hugely honoured, even if political advisers were more concerned about the public benefit. A copy of the page was framed and still hangs on the wall in my office.

It was time for a brief holiday to provide some respite from the onslaught. I'd booked a few days in Budapest along with my youngest son, and Ian took us to the airport, where arrangements were made to have us taken through the airline staff security check-in. Waiting to board, my son was greatly impressed by the police officers escorting us, showing their badges and waving us into the first-class lounge, where we were told to sit wherever we liked. We were pre-boarded and placed in the very back seats. However, it was passing through Amsterdam airport that the global significance hit home. The newspaper racks were full of papers and magazines in many languages, all leading with the Megrahi release story and many with front-page pictures of it. Arriving at the hotel, we checked in only to see copies of the *Wall Street Journal* stacked high at reception with a photograph of me on the front page. I recalled thinking that would never happen again. Thankfully, neither the hotel staff nor anyone else made any connection. It was a relaxing four days with my son but I knew that it would be all change when I returned. I may have been off the front pages by then, but the political storm had not abated.

The parliamentary debate took place on 2 September. I had not long returned from the break with my son and Parliament had itself just returned from recess. I was to make a statement and thereafter face questions. Subsequently, there would be a debate in which the First Minister would close for the Scottish government. I decided to simply repeat the statement I had made at the time. Parliament had been in recess and therefore the statement had been at the Scottish government offices. This was now the opportunity to formalise what had occurred, besides which the issue remained exactly the same. In many ways, therefore, the questions and debate were simply political theatre – and so they were to prove. The opposition were relentless in their criticism and condemnation. Labour, in particular, notwithstanding revelations that were disclosing the UK government's hypocrisy. One Labour member broke ranks to offer support. Malcolm Chisholm, who had always been principled, spoke out, and I remain grateful to him for his courage and decency. I dropped him a personal note after the debate to thank him. Other than that, it proceeded on partisan grounds. The First Minister was forceful in his closing remarks, in which he attacked the Labour Party and the evident duplicity of the British Labour government.

In November, a group of US congressmen were in Edinburgh for a major NATO meeting and asked to meet with me. Arrangements were made between my officials and the US Consul General. They asked for information and reasoning, which I was happy to provide and detail. As ever, they were forceful but polite. They had an opportunity to air their grievances and doubtless related it through the media to their constituents back home, though the meeting was low-key and not publicised here. They had the documentation provided to them upon which I had made my decision as well as some updated medical information that had been received from Libya. As ever, it appeared to come down to a cultural divide. Justice as punishment and vengeance rather than reform and rehabilitation; eternal damnation rather than compassion. Speaking to the Consul General afterwards, she was clear that Megrahi was now history as far as the State Department were concerned, though they 'would like him to die soon', as she put it. His death would close the story down, but his early passing was not to be.

Later that month, I appeared before the Scottish Parliament's Justice Committee for yet another gruelling interrogation. Frankly, the issue and the line of questioning had not moved on and the debate went nowhere. The pressure continued both within and without Parliament. There was a scurrilous reference made both in the Scottish press and, indeed, the *Wall Street Journal* to my brother having once worked for BP. That he had but, as they had said, it was years ago. Indeed, he'd moved away from working in oil into renewables. The story was simply a slur trying to imply links between Scotland and BP over the release of Megrahi. I was sorry for my brother and felt guilty for what had happened as a result of me. He is neither involved in politics nor responsible for my actions. Highlighting my brother was unfair on him and irrelevant to the situation. But, it underlined that nothing and no one was off limits.

At the turn of the year, it was down to London to appear before the House of Commons Scottish Affairs Select Committee. The election of an SNP government had seen the end of the days in which Scottish politicians would go to London deferentially. In my opinion it was simply an attempt by Labour MPs to grandstand and seek to belittle not just me but the Scottish Parliament, which many of they and their colleagues held in contempt. Though Megrahi was ostensibly the reason for calling me, in reality it was simply a way for them to try to show their superiority to the devolved administration. There was, therefore, an edge to it, and it was not just me who had been called to appear before them but also the First Minister. Though the tone of the questioning was more aggressive, the questions were, if anything, of a poorer standard than the Scottish ones. Over my years in Parliament I had noted that, whilst Westminster may be bigger, it was not necessarily better; it simply had more members to choose from. It was yet another political charade that I simply had to endure. It was brightened by the police officer who had been sitting in as security and who, whilst escorting me out, remarked in a broad and rather gruff cockney accent that, as I would appreciate, he had no love for terrorists, but he thought I had made a brave and humane decision. It was kind of him and cheered me up after a gruelling session. I always thought his views were more in accord with ordinary Londoners than those who sat in the Halls of Westminster.

In July, the issue, like the weather, heated up. Politicians courting publicity were a significant driver of events and there had been a substantial change in the political landscape in the UK. Mid-term elections were approaching in the US and American politicians, in particular Senator Robert Menendez, were keen to get in on the action. In addition, David Cameron had been elected UK Prime Minister in May 2010 and was going to meet with President Obama for the first time. Added to that cocktail was the environmental disaster involving BP in the Gulf of Mexico in April of that year, where the company become the bête noire of the US. All that together created a maelstrom of attacks from all directions. A Tory MP called for me to apologise for my actions. I noted he was chair of the All Party Parliamentary Group on Libya. Rather shameless given the lobbying that organisation had been doing for commercial deals in Libya, with some on the Gaddafi payroll. Even those stepping down from politics got in on the act. David Miliband, the outgoing UK Foreign Secretary, condemned the release despite clear and published evidence of communications with the Libyans that he did not want Megrahi to die in a Scottish prison cell.

Cameron headed across the Atlantic. The newly installed Prime Minister was very keen to make it clear to the US that the Megrahi release had nothing to do with the incoming Conservative and Liberal Democrat coalition government and that it was all the responsibility of both the outgoing UK Labour administration and the SNP government in Scotland. He was also undoubtedly trying to defuse some of the understandable anger in the US over BP and the oil spill in the Gulf of Mexico. Cameron and Obama were united in stating that they violently disagreed with the release. Stories had begun to appear suggesting that the US had been more comfortable and supportive of compassionate release than prisoner transfer. That was the case, but, clearly, when you are

Commander-in-Chief, you wish to be seen as a warrior and deny any stories that detract from that. The US never commented on the commercial or strategic interests they had or were pursuing with Libya, choosing instead to continue to give the impression that it was a pariah state that they spurned all the whilst keeping silent about the meetings that Obama and his administration had had with the Gaddafi regime.

The US Senate Foreign Relations Committee wanted to convene a hearing into the release of Megrahi and related events. Initially they were writing simply seeking information from the Scottish government. This then changed to demanding the attendance of me and others. They were chaired at that time by Senator John Kerry, though he seemed to defer on this issue to Senator Robert Menendez. They sought to have myself, the SPS Director of Health and Care, and Jack Straw, the former UK Justice Secretary, attend. The story ran big in the media at the time, both in the US and in the UK. Menendez was particularly exercised by the possible links to trade deals with BP. In that he was partly correct but it had been the British not Scottish government who were involved. I did always wonder, though, what he'd have said had Halliburton got the contract. That was never to arise nor, indeed, did any real mention of all the other US corporations that were trading with the regime.

It appeared that there was going to be a Senate hearing, though no date had been set. I responded to this news in media interviews by saying that I had been elected by my constituents in Edinburgh East and Musselburgh and it was to them and the Scottish Parliament that I was accountable, not the United States Senate. I had no intention of going and, in any event, was not compellable by them. The Scottish government and I were happy to cooperate in whatever way we could, but we were not going to be at the beck and call of a few grandstanding US senators. Apparently, there had also been plans to call Tony Blair, but they had been quickly dropped. That was hardly surprising given Blair's undoubted involvement in deals in the desert and other commercial transactions with Libya. Moreover, the UK ambassador was also not to be called, despite being on the scene not just at the time of the release but before, when commercial negotiations were ongoing. There could be some investigation it seemed, but those enquiries would be limited. The USA wanted to pillory the Scottish government and me but not expose their commercial and political deals and discussions with Libya.

The British government and Jack Straw were also not going to attend. It was contrary to international protocol and no doubt they also wouldn't welcome some of the questions that might be asked. BP had been called to attend but was proposing to send someone of fairly junior rank. So, in the absence of any significant witnesses to vent their spleen on, they abandoned the proposed hearing. Communications were, though, received from the Foreign Relations Committee and were all responded to politely and factually.

The efforts by Menendez were cack-handed and ultimately backfired on him and the committee. Some of the letters were ill-temperate, factually inaccurate and diplomatically irresponsible. I even recall one that referred to me as the Commerce Secretary for Justice. It may have been written by a staffer but it displayed a major lack of knowledge and understanding. Menendez himself was later to find himself embroiled in a scandal when in 2015 he was indicted on corruption charges.

The onslaught by the senators did seem to sway public opinion in Scotland, but not as he would have wished it. Scots can be fickle when differentiating between their right to criticise one of their own and protecting one of their own from outside criticism. It may be a small-country trait, but it certainly applies in clannish Scotland and certainly when the criticism is coming from England or the US. Whether they had agreed or disagreed with the decision, Scottish public opinion tended to see the intervention both as wrong and bullying.

Moreover, both the immense power of the United States and the perception of double standards on their part further fuelled this condemnation. I recall receiving an email from a man in England pointing out that when there had been a Coroners' Inquiry in England into the death of a British soldier killed by so called 'friendly' fire, the US had refused not only to attend but to even cooperate. Sympathy swung behind me. Cards and cakes were received in the office from elderly ladies and I remember going out for a meal with a friend one night. The use of a government car had by now been scaled back once again, to ministerial duties only as security lessened. Accordingly, I took a bus along to the centre of town. The driver gave me the thumbs up after checking with some surprise that it was me and the same warm atmosphere was experienced in other venues. My friend was a famous musician and it surprised me to have a higher profile that night than him. I doubted that the American senators could use public transport or get such a warm reception in public venues. The public reception in Scotland remained friendly.

I had to make a further statement in the Scottish Parliament in late February 2012 following the publication of Megrahi's book in conjunction with the author John Ashton. The basis of the book was that he was innocent and not involved in the bombing, and an allusion was also made to the Heathrow break-in. No answers were given with regard to the key areas of suspicion, such as why he had been in Malta or lied about it. The book garnered significant publicity, as any new publication or release on Lockerbie does, but there were also the vested interests of the author and publisher in promoting the book and others in furthering the campaign that Megrahi was innocent. There was little new that came out in the book or media other than a rehash of what had gone before and the same lines from all parties involved.

The focus, though, in the Scottish Parliament, was primarily on whether there had been any pressure put on Megrahi to withdraw his appeal. The book itself stated that he'd signed a provisional withdrawal as early as March 2009, which had not been lodged and, indeed, had been unknown to me. A subsequent news story from a well-connected journalist knowledgeable on the issue suggested it had been motivated by family reasons. I emphasised that it had been his choice and would have made no difference to my decision. It really passed off without any significant difficulty, though, again, it was stressful at the time.

But Megrahi was still alive, having significantly passed the prognosis of three months' life expectancy. His death, which the Consul General had said would close it all down, hadn't happened.

WHY IS HE NOT DEAD YET?

Megrahi living beyond the three-month prognosis became a significant issue. It had been the basis upon which he had been released and opened us up to accusations and ridicule. As each anniversary passed, whether of the atrocity or the release, this pressure was heightened as the news agenda focused back upon the original decision. The ninety days passed in November and was followed by the twenty-first anniversary of the bombing itself the next month. The year 2010 saw the first anniversary of his release and the twenty-second of the bombing. And so it continued until he finally died on 20 May 2012.

Before this, however, such was the intensity of the clamour for his death that I sometimes thought that some saw it as my obligation to go and personally oversee or even deliver his demise. Rumours of his death surfaced and even news broadcasts announcing it had erroneously been made from time to time, but what was never challenged, though, was that he was terminally ill and dying. That was clear and self-evident. Still, however, there remained the question from many: 'Why is he not dead yet?'

Some of the coverage of Megrahi's latter months was particularly ghoulish. Many of the demands for his death came close to an insistence for his execution. Initially, he had gone back to his family and lived quietly, shunning publicity. Photographs and information were limited, though he cooperated as he was required to do with the Scottish authorities. There were occasional difficulties for social work staff monitoring him, given the logistics of contacting him in

Tripoli, but, in the main, he complied, and it was only in the latter stages as civil society in Libya began to break down that contact difficulties began to arise. Even then, however, he sought to liaise and in any event that was at a stage where there was little he could do other than seek to minimise pain and await his death. As he had in many ways been a model prisoner, he was a cooperative probationer, other than the practical difficulties imposed by geography and telecommunications. The conditions imposed upon him, given the location, were the standard ones for all prisoners, and included restrictions on leaving the country or moving house without prior consent. The only issue of any dispute was a request at one stage by the Libyan authorities for him to go to Egypt for treatment for his illness. I considered it long and hard but eventually refused. The nature of the treatment was never fully detailed or clarified and on that basis I decided that the treatment could either be available in Libya or could be brought in for him to receive it there. No further request or clarification was subsequently made, and whether they sent him but kept it secret or made other arrangements I know not. But, there has never been a suggestion from Libya or Egypt that he went and I can only assume alternative arrangements were made or it was never really necessary anyway.

The reports coming through from the social workers were of a man failing but still surviving. From time to time news reporters pursued him. The cancer had spread to other parts of his body but still he hung on tenaciously. Initially, he was shown in a wheelchair looking drawn and wearing a mask, though not, it seemed, at death's door. Later on he opened up his home to show his final plight and what was seen was an old and stricken man being treated by his family. In late August 2011, a CNN news reporter described him as just a shell of a man, surviving on oxygen and an intravenous drip.[59] The focus didn't remain on him for long, though, as it seemed accepted then that it was simply a matter of time before his death and, in any event, the collapse of Libya made following events there dangerous for reporters.

The US Consul General had mentioned at the meeting with congressmen as far back as November 2009 that his death would ease matters. Others had said the same. I decided early on that I would not wish him dead, any more than anyone else. It's not for me to exercise the power of life and death over anyone or for me to seek to do so in any spirit or form. To do so, I felt, would demean me and be contrary to the basis upon which I had made my judgment. If he was exceeding life expectancy it was certainly at the price of quality of life. Indeed, the regular briefings from social work staff did show a continued decline followed by a rapid descent.

He died on 20 May 2012. I was advised by a text message from my private office and the news schedules soon began to roll with it. Some of the comments that came in from a few American relatives were quite brutal, expressing hope he'd had a slow and lingering death. Though I confess to having been frustrated on occasion that the issue was still on-going, I stood by my pledge not to wish anyone dead.

The question still often asked, though, was why did he live so long after his release? The medical advice available at the time was

---

59 *Daily Mail*, 30 August 2012

given in good faith, and was provided not just on the prognosis of the Director of Health and Care at the SPS, an eminent clinician in his own right, but after he'd taken considerable evidence from specialist consultants involved in the care and treatment of Megrahi. There was no interference by the Scottish government or any other authority with their medical determination. It was a clinical decision alone. It was not for me to second guess or challenge a specialist report on an area in which I have no expertise. The diagnosis was clearly shown to be incorrect, but that does not make the basis upon which they granted it wrong. They had caveated in the report that advising on life expectancy is notoriously fraught, especially in cancer cases. That was something in which they had the support of the medical profession, though many grandstanding politicians seemed to suggest that accuracy could be pinpointed to the very day, if not hour. There are two reasons why I think doctors were right in their initial prognosis but it turned out to be wrong in practice.

Firstly, Megrahi was testimony to the power of the human spirit. As the prison governor's report detailed, whilst incarcerated in Scotland his mood could be very low. He was in a prison in a foreign land and separated from his family. He knew he was dying and had little to live for. He had already refused some treatment that had been offered. The likelihood is that he would have refused more. He'd simply have turned his face to the prison's walls and sought relief in death; which in all likelihood would have come upon him very soon.

As it was, he was returned home to his family. That, I believe, gave him the will to live. He had been separated from them for many years and no doubt wished to make up for lost time; and time that was shortening fast. One can only imagine that there were family events and anniversaries that he would have wished to live to see and be a part of. He went home to die but found the spirit to live, for a while longer at least. Secondly, though, there was the medical treatment that was available in Libya but not in Scotland, about which rumours began to emanate, with articles also appearing in newspapers, as the second anniversary of his release in 2011 approached.[60] They concerned a so-called wonder drug he was receiving in Libya. It was in fact Abiraterone, a hormone-based therapy drug. It had ironically been discovered by British scientists at the Cancer Research Institute in London but was not freely available in Scotland through the NHS. It had extended life expectancy in clinical trials in England and was on the market privately through pharmaceutical companies. However, its cost was significant, at around £3,000 per month, and its use had therefore not been sanctioned by health authorities in Scotland. But it seems to have been one of the factors that extended Megrahi's days. Blood transfusions and other medical treatments were also provided. Until the final collapse of a functioning state, the Libyans were prepared to pay for the best treatment available from wherever and provide it for him. In Scotland, not only would his spirit have flagged, therefore, but the life-extending drug would not have been prescribed. It is my belief that it was due to the strength of the human spirit and the wonders of modern medical science that combined to extend his life significantly.

---

60 *Daily Telegraph*, 19 August 2011

The doctors and consultants were therefore right in their initial prognosis on life expectancy; it was his circumstances thereafter that changed. They acted professionally and appropriately throughout and have been, in my opinion, unfairly maligned.

From the very outset, the Scottish government decided to be as open as possible on its actions and to publish as much as practicable. With nothing to gain but a lot to lose, being as transparent as possible was the best defence to accusations which might arise. That was how it was to be and how, indeed, it has remained. A timeline was provided and papers, documentation and submissions published. The meetings held with victims' families were detailed and made publicly accessible. The information that was the basis of the decision to release has been published. Some names have had to be redacted, for example in the medical reports, to preserve the anonymity, but apart from that, everything has been published in its entirety. Some medical information was difficult to release initially due to confidentiality rules, but these were overcome and, other than some minor redactions of individuals' names, was also made fully available.

The UK agreed to the publication of the correspondence with the Scottish government. The State of Qatar also authorised the release of correspondence. Libya did likewise with their meetings. However, the US adopted its standard policy of refusing to allow for the release of diplomatic correspondence or communication. Much in relation to commercial and strategic deals has subsequently come out through WikiLeaks or other non-governmental sources. It was similar in some ways with the UK government. The correspondence between them and the Scottish government at the time of release was published. Moreover, there was a review of the Megrahi issue by the Cabinet Office when the new coalition government came to power in 2010. It indicated that BP's interests had been pivotal to the former Labour government's actions and that they had done all they could to try to secure Megrahi's release. It also found that the Scottish government had not been a party to that. However, other issues relating to the commercial deals and the role of MI6 were either not considered or remained classified – as they do to this day.

There was one area about which the Scottish government were still anxious to publish information, but were constrained by legislation. That was the decision of the Scottish Criminal Case Review Commission (SCCRC), who had referred the case back to the High Court for a further appeal back in June 2007. They had formed a view that, after extensive investigation of witnesses and the examination of further evidence, there was an arguable case for the conviction to be reconsidered. That had been released to the press together with a synopsis of the basis of their decision. However, the full extent of their research and evidence, which was substantial, was precluded from publication. That appeared at odds with other jurisdictions but the issue had never arisen before.

The preclusion of publication was the result of legislation establishing the organisation, which did not allow for the publication of the evidence in the event of abandonment of an appeal. With the appeal having been dropped, there was now neither a court hearing to consider their concerns nor an opportunity to consider the basis of why they had had them. The submissions and statements they had obtained were substantial. The situation was in limbo. Whilst the

Scottish government had no objections to the publication of the documentation, the SCCRC were precluded from doing so by the existing law. The UK government would have to assist in the legislation as it affected them as well. The Crown also had some minor concerns. It accordingly took some time to overcome as specific legislation was required and discussions were needed with both UK counterparts and other interested parties. It was complex given the volume of evidence they'd obtained and the number of people they had interviewed; and often awkward to achieve with cross-border discussion and official reluctance. However, legislation was finally delivered in 2012 when, other than where an individual's personal safety could be threatened, the statements and documents were made available in full.

There was to be nothing startling or revelatory in the documents released. Much had already been within public knowledge but there was a principle of openness and transparency to be kept. Moreover, it was felt the formal documentation was a relevant factor and should be available for all who may wish to see it. To have failed to disclose it would simply have fuelled further conspiracy theories or given credence to claims of an institutional cover-up. From discussions with individuals on the commission, it seemed that they were satisfied that there were issues relating to the conviction that caused them concern and made the conviction potentially unsafe. Foremost amongst them was the evidence of Gauci, which was the basis of much of their submission. Though there were some other concerns, it was evident that it was that aspect of the evidence that concerned them most. It wasn't simply the limited identification by him of Megrahi, which was weak at the very best and only made after a significant passage of time, there was also the convoluted way in which it had been concluded that 7 December must have been the date of purchase. Perhaps most compelling of all was the payment made to Gauci for his evidence. Whilst no aspersions were cast on him as an individual, it certainly raised doubts about the evidence, given its already weak nature. Removing Gauci from the prosecution case almost certainly would have resulted in an acquittal since he provided the only direct link to Megrahi.

The calls for an inquiry into Lockerbie continued, from both relatives and politicians. Dr Jim Swire, in particular, was keen, along with others who believed in Megrahi's innocence; though others who thought him guilty were also equally eager to have a full and open investigation into the event. I have always been supportive of the position of the Scottish government, which is that there should be one, but at a jurisdictional level and with the powers that could deliver a successful outcome. Calls for an inquiry to be instigated by the Scottish government, however, were pointless. The reach of the Scottish courts does not extend outside this land and many if not most of the relevant witnesses could not be compelled to give evidence by a Scottish tribunal. Any Scottish inquiry would be restricted to a rerun at best of what information was already available and would not be able to access individuals or evidence from elsewhere that might be highly pertinent. Given that this involved state interests and individuals around the globe, an inquiry would have to be international both in its authority and reach. The power to seek information from governments or agencies would be needed and the authority to have witnesses brought from wherever they lived would also be essential. For that reason, the UN or some other internationally agreed tribunal was required. Sadly, it has neither been sought nor established by the international powers that be.

It was suggested that Megrahi's family would seek to resuscitate the appeal. It is legally possible for those with a close interest in a case to make a further application for review and subsequently for appeal. That would certainly apply to his family and those campaigning for Megrahi's innocence were advised of that. There were constant suggestions by those campaigning for his release that it was going to happen but it never did. Perhaps it was due to the situation in Libya or because of other issues, but the family seemed to drop all interest in further legal actions. That gave credence to what the former governor of Greenock Prison told me many years after the release: that it was Megrahi's family who wanted him to drop the appeal. Attempts were subsequently made to try to reinstate the appeal through the families of some of the victims. Dr Jim Swire and Rev. John Mosey were principal in that. The SCCRC sought clarification from the Scottish courts as to whether victims' relatives could be classified as having a legitimate interest in re-raising an abandoned appeal on behalf of an accused, and the request was rejected by the Scottish courts in 2015.

The police and prosecution services still retained an open file on Lockerbie. The FBI and US Department of Justice did likewise. After all, though they were certain they'd got the right man, it was always accepted that he had not acted alone. Police and prosecutors had maintained links with the Libyan authorities ever since Camp Zeist, but little progress had been made or was anticipated. Hopes rose, however, when the Gaddafi regime was toppled. There appeared the opportunity of gaining access to information about what had happened at Lockerbie and to finally unravel more of the mystery of the affair. The new authorities appeared initially willing to be open and cooperative. They even acknowledged the former regime's complicity in the atrocity. The defecting Libyan Justice Secretary stated that Gaddafi had been behind the bombing[61] and subsequent discussions that were had with the new interim government alluded to Megrahi being involved, but at a lower level than had been portrayed.

In late August 2011, it was arranged for me to put in a call to a representative of the National Transitional Council (NTC) in Benghazi, who were in control of that part of the country as the civil war raged and the Gaddafi regime tottered. The purpose was to make contact regarding both Megrahi and more general information relating to Lockerbie. The call was altogether rather bizarre. The spokesperson knew who Megrahi was, but cared little about either Scotland's interest in particular or the Lockerbie bombing in general. Understandably, their priority was humanitarian aid and the preservation of law and order in a failing state. They indicated that they'd sealed the Justice Department and were seeking to guard it. There had been talk of Megrahi being extradited or even taken to the US and they indicated that that would not happen. It must have seemed almost a nuisance call to them as devastation and destruction surrounded them. However, the file remained open and hopes were still high.

---

61 *Daily Mail*, 24 February 2011

The Lord Advocate and the Director of the FBI went to Tripoli for discussions in the spring of 2012. Further visits by police and prosecutors working on the case followed. The Libyans offered to reciprocate with senior prosecutors coming over to Scotland. The Libyan ambassador said they'd provide all the files but that it may take some time. However, as with events in Libya, hope appeared to be fading as the country collapsed into internecine warfare. The new Libyan government officials began to worry about public opinion back home. Libyans felt raw about the compensation they had paid whilst suffering themselves and further investigations seemed to run the risk of a public backlash. Muammar Gaddafi was killed. Others, including his son, Saif Gaddafi, and Abdullah Sanussi, fled but were captured and sentenced to death. It appeared many in Libya simply wanted to draw a line under the Lockerbie bombing and its aftermath and move on with more pressing issues. Several years on from that initial optimism, little has been recovered to show for it. As a result, much of the Lockerbie story remains untold.

Amidst all this world of secrecy, snippets did still come to light both in the initial weeks after Megrahi's release and in the years to follow. That was always bound to happen but they were interesting all the same. Some were of greater relevance than others but they all helped to paint a picture. It was clear that the release was just one chapter in a much larger story; and one in which Megrahi was just one of many players.

In August 2010, I attended a festival in Edinburgh at which the principal speaker was Azeem Ibrahim, who established and runs the Scottish Institute, a think tank in many ways, but which has significant contacts with the US and political interests there. He advised that he'd be doing his best to protect Scotland's reputation from invective from some quarters in the US. The concerns over a backlash that might have a significant and damaging effect were understandable, if ultimately to be proved groundless. He then added that it was well known in influential political and Pentagon circles that the Iranians had offered up a bounty of $10 million after the downing of the airliner by USS *Vincennes* in July 1988. Though nothing new in that snippet, it was illuminating in being a factor known by many in the US, but rarely mentioned here.

That same month, the UK government got wind that *The Herald*, a leading Scottish newspaper, had picked up the story of the letter sent from the King of Jordan to John Major implicating the PFLP-GC in the bombing. This had been the subject of the proposed PII. They were threatening to interdict (the Scottish term for an injunction). It did not in fact transpire as though a journalist had the story, it had not been filed for publishing. The threats from the UK government caused some consternation at the paper, however, where many had been oblivious to the story unearthed by their reporter. The paper, therefore, did not run with it at that stage.

In April 2012, I took a call from Alastair Burt, a Foreign Office Minister, who was heading to Tripoli. It was a courtesy call to explain that the UK government was very concerned that *The Herald* had been going to run a story on the PII relating to the letter. If need be, they were once again going to interdict if it was required. I advised that the Scottish government sought for as much openness as possible and wished similarly for information that was relevant to be in the public domain. Moreover, I pointed out that this was also in the midst of the Arab Spring. The UK government, though, was not for shifting and it seemed they had spiked the story, at least for a while, with their threats to the paper.

Later that month, I had a coffee with a journalist from *The Herald* who told me that the FCO had put the paper under severe pressure, threatening even to pull a full day's edition. That was an action unheard of in my lifetime in Scotland. The paper, it seemed, had been considering doing a story but only one that was fairly muted. The underlying reason for the UK government's nervousness did not now relate to Lockerbie but instead to attempts to have Abu Qatada, a radical Muslim cleric, deported to Jordan. The courts had intervened in his proposed deportation but the UK government was still anxious to have him removed, viewing him as both dangerous and disruptive. His argument for avoiding deportation related to its impact on his human rights if he were to be returned. The situation was fraught regarding whether it was safe for him to go to Jordan. Unfavourable publicity might jeopardise the willingness of the Jordanian authorities to accept an individual that the UK clearly wanted removed from their shores. The FCO appeared to be conceding that some publication would be necessary and had agreed with the paper the lines that could be taken. Alastair Burt again telephoned me to tell me that they were worried about it breaking in some uncontrolled way in the press.

The Herald eventually ran the story a few months later. The story, when it came, though, was muted and referred to evidence implicating the PFLP-GC and that the UK government had threatened to take action against the paper. There was no mention either of the specific letter by the King of Jordan to John Major or even of that country. Megrahi was by now dead but they were looking heavy-handed and the story in some shape or form was beginning to get out. However, the Abu Qatada issue was still obviously too much in the fore to mention Jordan, even if the letter related to Megrahi and Lockerbie.

About the same time, I also heard a rather ironic story. It seemed that both Megrahi's doctor and nurse who were treating him in Libya in his final days were Scottish. One was from Lanarkshire and the other from Ayrshire. Understandable, in some ways, as Scotland, with so many great medical training institutions, provides graduates in abundance. Moreover, the opportunities for money to be made in Libya apply to medicine as with oil and other industries. However, as they say, you couldn't make it up!

Finally, in October 2011, a close friend of mine who was in a very senior position relating to prison healthcare was at an international conference in Venice. It was attended by other top practitioners in the prison health sector from around the world. One of the other delegates was an official with a very high position indeed in the Tunisian Prison Service, who had been in post for some time under both new and old regimes. He was also linked with the military, holding a very senior rank in the army. Discussing Lockerbie, he claimed to know who had been responsible for it. He agreed to write the name on a piece of paper and give it to my friend. The name he wrote down was Ahmed Jibril – founder and leader of the PFLP-GC.

BLAIR AND BUSH DO A DEAL WITH THE DEVIL

Much had been hidden or cloaked in secrecy. However, as ever, the truth began to seep out through leaks, disclosures and investigations that showed the clandestine world that had existed for almost a decade, as the UK and the US had courted Libya. It painted a vastly different picture than had been done so by them at the time of Megrahi's release and one that they had kept from public view. It involved the security services as much as business. It was trade and commerce for weapons and prisoners. Blair and Bush had entered into a deal with the devil – a Faustian pact with Gaddafi.

They were not alone, though, in their consorting with Gaddafi, as both Italy's Prime Minister Silvio Berlusconi and the French President also had close links with him. However, Blair, in particular, had a specific interest that continued even after he demitted office as UK Prime Minister, with commercial visits continuing to Libya until the virtual collapse of the regime.[62] The spectre of deals in the desert hung over discussions between the UK and Libya. They referred to meetings by UK PM Tony Blair with Gaddafi in both 2004 and 2007, when he travelled to North Africa to shake the hands of the Libyan despot and sign commercial deals. Similar accusations of trade and military interests applied to the US. However, the references were unspecific and remained unsubstantiated in many ways.

They were not to come out until after the release of Megrahi. In the interim, the UK and US administrations maintained their faux

---

62 Chorin, *Exit the Colonel*, p. 136–7

outrage about the release of a mass murderer and giving succour to a dreadful regime. Whilst all along they consorted with Gaddafi, gaining commercial deals, supplying weapons and even rendering Libyan dissidents back to him for torture. The BP deal, it transpired, was but one part of a much larger picture. The commercial and strategic links were significant and had been ongoing for years before the BP negotiations. Blair and Bush were as complicit in this as they were in the disastrous war in Iraq. Some information came out with the change of administration in the UK and others with the fall of the regime in Tripoli. Details have since emerged both in a book by one of the US diplomats who served in Tripoli between 2004 and 2006[63] and also in a report by Human Rights Watch (HRW).[64] Amnesty International also highlighted the training of the Libyan Police under Gaddafi by the PSNI and other UK police forces in 2011.[65]

Overtures towards Libya began following the trial at Camp Zeist and the payment of compensation to the victims' families in 2003. US approaches to bring the rogue state back into the fold had commenced under President Clinton, with Secretary of State Madeleine Albright authorising secret meetings several years before.[66] The thawing in relations had continued under George Bush, who refrained from including Libya in his 'Axis of Evil' speech in 2002 when Iran, North Korea and Iraq were specifically mentioned. In White House parlance they moved from a 'rogue state' to a 'state of concern'.[67]

---

63 Ibid.
64 'Delivered into Enemy Hands', Human Rights Watch, 5 September 2012
65 Amnesty International UK, 18 September 2009
66 Chorin, *Exit the Colonel*, p. 65
67 Ibid., p. 68

In May 2006, Libya would finally be removed from the US list of state sponsors of terrorism. That continued under the Obama administration which took office in 2009. In the spring of that year, in the run-up to Megrahi's release, Hillary Clinton met with one of Gaddafi's sons, Mu'tassim, at the State Department. She said after the meeting that 'we deeply value the relationship between the United States and Libya'. She went on to add: 'We have many opportunities to deepen and broaden our cooperation, and I'm very much looking forward to building on this relationship.'[68] And so it was to be. Even President Obama got in on the act, shaking Gaddafi's hand a few months later on 9 July at a G8 summit in Italy.[69] That was only weeks before the release of Megrahi was to cause such a storm and bring condemnation from the US. Libya was being courted, but that was not their public stance.

As a consequence of these and other actions, sanctions were lifted and Libya was opened up for trade and commercial deals. The lifting was to be of benefit for many multinational companies. There was some jealousy, it seems, in American circles that European companies were already trading extensively and no doubt profitably in Libya, with the Italians and French to the fore and the UK scrambling to keep up. Numerous other countries from around the globe were also venturing in and American firms wished to get their share of the action and profits. Many companies were actively lobbying the White House and the State Department eager to get access for business. Many, though not all, were oil companies. Assets had been

68 Ibid., p. 160
69 Ibid.

nationalised by Gaddafi many years before in that sector and the possibility arose not just for new business to be gained but for the restitution of assets that had been expropriated. Also, new oil licences were being granted by Libya in 2005 for exploration and production sharing. That was of interest to US companies. Occidental, Amerada Hess and Chevron Texaco were all successful along with their business partners in obtaining licences. Such was the scramble, the then CEO of Occidental even flew in personally to meet with Gaddafi. Other licences went to firms from around the world, but none from Europe. However, the Europeans were to get their share in a later release of licences as the Libyans sought to play one economic bloc off against the other.[70]

However, commerce and trade weren't the only driver for the US seeking a rapprochement. There was the strategic and military desire to tackle the rise of Islamic extremism. Gaddafi could provide intelligence and also take action against some of the terrorist groups both within Libya itself and without in the wider African and Arab world. The Libyan Islamic Fighting Group (LIFG) was one of the principal opposition groups in Libya. Links had been made by American intelligence between a member of the LIFG and bombings carried out on US embassies in Tanzania and Kenya.[71] Other members had joined with Al Qaeda and had been fighting in Afghanistan. The ostensible reason it was suggested was to have Gaddafi abandon weapons of mass destruction. However, it appears that there, as with Iraq, he had neither possessed them nor had the capacity to create them.

---

70 Ibid., p. 98
71 Ibid., p. 63

It was, though, a good cover for the covert war. Post 9/11 and with the consequences of the wars in Iraq and Afghanistan, allies were needed everywhere, even amongst former enemies. And Gaddafi was to be one of them in tackling Islamic extremism.

There were to be significant benefits for Gaddafi himself and his regime. The country had been hurting under sanctions that affected not just the economy but daily life. Ordinary citizens benefited from a boost to the economy and the availability of medical and consumer goods, previously restricted. The Gaddafi regime, though, also benefited from military hardware provided and training given for his forces. Much of the weapon sales and military advice was for counter insurgency and capable of dealing with internal repression. The regime was being supported against its internal opponents by the West. But, there was to be more than just arms and training given to Gaddafi.

There was to be the return of dissidents opposed to his regime – irrespective of whether they wished to go back or not. The Libyan regime had been brutal to those who opposed it. That applied irrespective of the basis of their opposition; whether democratic or Islamist, tribal or national. Many had died and many more had been brutally tortured. Massacres had taken place. Gaddafi was rightly labelled a despot by the UK and US. Many had fled to other countries around the world. They were now put in danger as the UK and US conspired to return them to Gaddafi's clutches.

In February 2004, the US began to officially return to Libya. Most European embassies had returned a few years prior to that. The ban on US citizens travelling to the country was lifted with the encouragement of the oil companies. In July 2004, a Diplomatic Mission was opened and at roughly the same time the CIA opened an office.[72] They were not alone in their wooing of Libya. On 25 March 2004, Tony Blair visited Libya. The HRW report disclosed that

> he and Gaddafi formally mended relations between the two countries and discussed their common cause in counter-terrorism operations. On the same day, Anglo-Dutch oil giant Shell announced it had signed a deal worth up to £550 million (approximately $1 billion US) for gas exploration rights off the Libyan coast.[73]

As stated it wasn't just commerce but prisoners that were involved. Rendition flights of Libyan dissidents back into the clutches of Gaddafi were equally part of it. The CIA and MI6 were complicit in that. Torture followed and the security services of the UK and US were complicit. A prisoner, Al Saadi, was rendered within days of the Blair visit as the UK and US security services conspired to return him to Libya.[74]

Blair went to Libya again in May 2007 to see Gaddafi and was this time accompanied by the CEO of BP and other corporate leaders. The BP interest was the deal that Jack Straw had been anxious to promote and related to two onshore and one offshore fields. The trade, though, did not end with that arrangement. In 2008, the UK Trade and Industry Defence and Security Organisation secured a deal for its member company General Dynamics worth $165 million. Part of

---

72 'Delivered into Enemy Hands', Human Rights Watch, p. 16
73 Ibid., p. 7
74 Ibid.

the deal, it's reported, was to train the Khamis Brigade who were a 10,000-man unit dedicated to the personal protection of Gaddafi.[75] The PSNI and other UK forces, as Amnesty International detailed, had also been over training the Libyan police, who were pivotal in the propping up of the regime. The PSNI and their predecessors in the RUC are probably the most experienced police service in the whole of Western Europe in dealing with counter insurgency. Their experience with Republican and Loyalist paramilitaries in Northern Ireland throughout the Troubles has given them an expertise and experience few can match. It was no doubt by design rather than accident that their experience was sought by the Libyans. This came to light in the Amnesty report published just weeks after my decision to release Megrahi. It had been ongoing whilst the UK had fulminated over my decision to release him but was largely ignored by the media in the UK.

Britain was not alone either; an arms industry expert reckoned that between 2006 and 2009 EU governments authorised sales amounting to over $1 billion. The US didn't seem to supply Gaddafi with military hardware but others such as the Russians and Chinese did.

The trade went both ways. Upon the lifting of the EU arms embargo, the Gaddafi regime itself went on a spending spree, in particular on small arms and other military hardware capable of dealing with civil disorder and insurrection. Britain, France and Italy were amongst the sellers of the weaponry, though many others also joined in. It continued until the beginning of the end days for the

---

75 Chorin, *Exit the Colonel*, p. 136

regime, in early 2011. Gaddafi thus both expanded and replenished the arsenal that kept him in power.

The Gaddafi family also benefited, on a personal basis, in many other ways. Saif Gaddafi bought a mansion in Hampstead, London for £10 million in July 2009, a month before the outrage over the release of Megrahi.[76] It was he who had welcomed Megrahi back when at the airport in Tripoli but it seemed he was equally welcome in London. Saif Gaddafi also entered into a relationship with the London School of Economics, which was to cause that institution some embarrassment in due course.

HRW highlighted the other payback the Libyan regime received in the return of dissidents. Some were even despatched back from Guantanamo or Bagram where they'd been detained. They were returned under duress and were met not with garlands of flowers but torture and ill treatment. Most would return to the notorious Abu Selim prison that had been the site of a massacre of 1,200 inmates in the space of a few hours by the regime in 1996. It had received little international attention but held horrific memories for Libyans and especially those opposed to the regime. One prisoner rendered, Al Libi, died in custody in May 2009. Apparently committing suicide, though no independent investigation was ever carried out.[77]

The HRW report primarily detailed the involvement of the US and the CIA in the rendition, though the UK and MI6 were also actively involved. As the report disclosed it was 'an important chapter in the larger story of the secret and abusive US detention programme

---

76 Ibid., p. 158
77 'Delivered into Enemy Hands', Human Rights Watch, p. 74

established under the government of George W. Bush after the 9/11 attacks, and the rendition of individuals to countries with known records of torture'.[78] The investigations following the collapse of the Gaddafi regime detailed the 'degree of involvement of the United States government under the Bush Administration in the arrest of opponents of the former Libyan Leader, Muammar Gaddafi, living abroad, the subsequent torture and other ill-treatment of many of them in US custody, and their forced transfer back to Libya'.[79] The report was to expose waterboarding and other practices as well as unlawful rendition. These were clear human rights abuses compounded by the torture they faced on their return. Most had fled the country in the 1980s and many had gone to Afghanistan. A large number were members of the LIFG, ironically later to be supported by the West as they sought to overthrow the regime. They paid the price for the Bush and Blair deal with Gaddafi.

The HRW report detailed communications between Moussa Koussa's office and both the CIA and MI6 concerning the transferring of dissidents back to the regime. They had received reports in 2006 and 2007 that several Libyans who had been in American custody had been transferred back. They were not alone and the later HRW report narrates many who suffered likewise through MI6 and CIA collusion with the Libyan regime. The security services dealt with Moussa Koussa personally on many occasions. The irony being that he had been implicated as having a senior role in the Lockerbie bombing, but was to be their main link to the regime on rendition.

---

78 Ibid., p. 2
79 Ibid.

Koussa went to see another rendition victim, Mustafa Salim Ali el-Madaghi. The victim told HRW that 'He asked me: "Do you know who brought you here?" I didn't want to say anything. He said, "The Americans brought you here. It's all over now. There is cooperation between us and the Americans." I was sure that was the case, but he just confirmed it for me.'[80]

Koussa was to defect as the Gaddafi regime fell apart and was spirited away by MI6 to London. Rumours abounded that he'd been a double agent assisting the United States for some time providing knowledge and information that appeared important in closing down an Al Qaeda network operating in Dubai and Malaysia.[81] When that relationship had commenced is not known. He had been a master's graduate from an American university but subsequently become a major player in the Gaddafi regime. Notwithstanding that HRW discovered that he'd developed not just a close link with the CIA but with MI6, it appears that the head of the Middle East North Africa Division of the latter had even sent him a handwritten note stating how he'd missed his company at a Christmas lunch. Little wonder they got him out of the chaos and disorder that was developing in the country.

One case in particular became high profile. Abdul Hakim Belhadj had left Libya in 1988 and gone into exile. He became the leader of the LIFG and at one stage was in Afghanistan. He subsequently left there and was drifting around the world seeking asylum. Whilst in China with his pregnant Moroccan wife he decided to try to seek asylum in London. The Chinese authorities sent him to Kuala

---

80 Ibid., p. 50
81 Chorin, *Exit the Colonel*, p. 144

Lumpur in Malaysia. It was then suggested that he could travel to the UK but only by going through Bangkok in Thailand. When he arrived there he and his pregnant wife were handcuffed and blind-folded and rendered to Libya in March 2004.[82] Days after that, Blair had met with Gaddafi for the deal in the desert, an oil deal for Shell was then concluded and a further prisoner was rendered to Libya.[83]

The documents obtained by HRW showed the involvement of both the CIA and MI6 in that rendition and their cooperation with Libyan security services. One fax detailed the CIA thanking the Libyan security services for the hospitality shown to their officers when they had been over. Another requested that a Libyan security officer accompany them on the flight from Kuala Lumpur. MI6 were equally conniving with the Libyan security services. Belhadj was imprisoned on his return and he was sentenced to death. He remained there until his release in early 2010 as Gaddafi sought to try to make overtures to dissidents, as opposition to the regime mounted. Belhadj sought to pursue court actions in the UK, including seeking to sue Jack Straw, the then Foreign Secretary. Formal inquiries were also established. The current investigations seem to have petered out as secrecy still prevails and many have refused to cooperate with what they fear is a whitewash. But, the issue of collusion by the UK with Gaddafi's henchmen was clear and documented.

As mentioned earlier, another Libyan national, Sami Mostafa al-Saadi, was rendered from Hong Kong to Libya with the active involvement of the UK and US. It seems to have been initiated by

---

82 'Delivered into Enemy Hands', Human Rights Watch, p. 57
83 Ibid., p. 63

MI6 but the ultimate transportation carried out by the CIA. Those organisations were working closely together and also with the Libyan government. He was to arrive in Libya just a few days after Blair's historic visit in March 2004 but not in comfort or under his own free will. He, too, has sought to pursue claims against the British authorities.

All this disclosed a history of attempts to bring the Gaddafi regime back into the fold that had been ongoing for a decade or more. The BP deal was not a one-off transaction but part of many commercial links with Libya, not just British and American, both before and after the release of Megrahi.

It was accepted Megrahi hadn't acted alone. He didn't do it for his own cause or personal benefit. He was a relatively senior Libyan agent but still junior in rank to Senussi, Koussa and ultimately Gaddafi. If he had acted, it would have been on their authority and under their direction; such was the nature of the Libyan state. If he was involved in the bombing, then they must have known and would have ordered and instructed him to do it. This was state-sponsored terrorism.

It's not just the evidence before the court that implicated Libya. Gaddafi himself accepted culpability by the Libyan regime. That wasn't just the signing of the UN treaty or the payment of compensation to victims, it was also by his own admission. In an interview with the *Washington Times* in July 2003, he accepted his country's guilt for the downing of Pan Am flight 103. He explained it had

originally been an Iranian retaliatory terrorist attack for the downing by the US Navy of a peaceful Iran Air Airbus on its daily run across the Strait of Hormuz. Nobody in our part of the world believed the US government when it said it was an accidental occurrence. So the Iranians subcontracted part of the job to a Syrian intelligence service, which in turn asked the Libyan Mukhabarat to handle part of the assignment. That is the way these things were planned in those days. If we had initiated the plot, we would have made sure the accusing finger was pointed in the other direction and we would have picked Cyprus, not Malta, where some of the organisation was done. The others picked Malta presumably to frame us.[84]

Nor was it just the Gaddafi regime that accepted Libyan responsibility for it. Following the fall of the regime, the NTC stated publicly that Gaddafi had personally ordered it. In February 2011, Mustafa Abdel-Jalil, who had been Justice Minister under Gaddafi, had defected and been appointed head of the NTC. He stated: 'Gaddafi gave the order about Lockerbie' when interviewed by a Swedish paper. He said that he had proof that Gaddafi had personally ordered Megrahi to commit the crime. The NTC never sought to deny state involvement, simply seeking to pass the responsibility to their former despotic leader. They also made the point that Libyans had already suffered and paid for it through sanctions and compensation.[85] Discussions since, between law enforcement and the new Libyan authorities and prosecutors, have confirmed that involvement.

---

84 'Gadhafi's secret message', *Washington Times*, 2 January 2004
85 BBC, 23 February 2011

With Libyan involvement, then, it meant it went right to the very top. This would not have been done by a Libyan agent without direction from above. Libya was a totalitarian state. Lesser decisions than bombing a plane required to be authorised. A decision such as this without consent would have seen action taken against the perpetrator. Many had suffered death and torture for considerably less. Loyalty, though, was shown to those who served Gaddafi. The regime, after all, sought to look after Megrahi's welfare and ultimately bring him home. It fitted the actions of the regime over the forty years of Gaddafi's rule. Murder and terror were part of his regime's very DNA. He would have known and approved it. Lockerbie was just one of many terrorist actions that the Libyan regime under Gaddafi carried out.

But, Gaddafi was not alone. He had his acolytes and aides. Whilst Gaddafi might sign it off, others would do the dirty work. One of the principal players was Abdullah Senussi. He was not only head of internal intelligence but close to Gaddafi. In addition to the tribal loyalties, there were family ties, as he was married to Gaddafi's sister in-law. He was pivotal. Indeed, he was convicted in absentia of involvement in the bombing of the UTA airliner in Niger the year after Lockerbie. He was a man with few compunctions and little mercy. He had authorised the brutal slaying of 1,200 prisoners at Abu Selim prison in 1996. Others over many years were to suffer because of him, as his ruthless prosecution of dissidents showed. He was a friend of Megrahi's and no actions by Megrahi would have been without his orders or consent.

Others, too, would have had to have been in the know and given instructions or provided assistance. Moussa Koussa was also a very close confidante of the Libyan leader. He later became head of external security in 1994 until 2009 when he became Foreign Minister. At the time of the Lockerbie bombing, he headed up an organisation known as The World Centre to promote the Libyan regime's views but which was viewed in the West as the source of training and funding for revolutionary groups. He was also a close confidante of Gaddafi and would have been critical even before his formal security roles. That triumvirate would have been amongst the principal conductors of the Libyan actions.

However, though Libya was pivotal, it was not alone. As a former senior police officer once said to me, it was a coalition of the willing.

So what happened? The atmosphere between the West and Middle Eastern states including Iran, Libya and client organisations was poisonous by the summer of 1998. When in July of that year the USS *Vincennes* brought down an Iranian plane flying across the Strait of Hormuz killing all aboard it grew significantly more venomous. The United States neither sought to atone nor apologise for it. That caused anger and outrage not just in Iran but in the wider Muslim and Arab world. It built upon the foundations of distrust and hostility that had grown up over many years and in the main were rooted in problems in the Middle East. Whether the US being contrite would have changed the course of history can only be speculated on. Certainly, it would have done no harm and may have assuaged more moderate elements, but whether it would have resulted in vengeance not being sought by other more militant groups is far harder to say. The bitterness and hostility was longstanding and the belief of an eye for an eye existed on all sides irrespective of their faith. Both sides had a tendency to seek to be avenged for wrongs done or actions taken against them. But, what it did do was result in Iran putting up a bounty of $10 million to bring down an American airliner as revenge. That was confirmed by security and Pentagon sources as well as in the Middle East. Iran put up the money, but who would do it?

Enter the PFLP-GC. They certainly had the capacity and the will to do it. They also had the personnel and the expertise, as past atrocities confirmed. Their leader, Ahmed Jibril, has been identified by several sources as pivotal to the atrocity. He's been described as being present at meetings with senior government figures in Iran and is identified by many in the Middle East as being the pivotal figure. The PFLP-GC would be assisted by others. That, too, was normal. Hence, Gaddafi's mention of the Syrian Security Services' initial involvement. Carrying out such actions involved many states and organisations working together and sharing skills and expertise. Past atrocities testified to that cooperation.

The PFLP-GC had worked closely in the past with both the Syrians and the Libyans. The Syrians had supported and been pivotal in its establishment when it had been set up as a splinter group from another Palestinian organisation in the late 1960s. Meanwhile, many of them had served with Libya in Chad and been involved in other military or combat zones. The Libyans were used to cooperating with other groups either to promote or support terrorism. It was part of their modus operandi, whether that be directly involved or through supporting others. The PFLP-GC was to carry it out, supported in the shadows by both the Syrian and Libyan security services. Hence the initial suspicions that fell on the Palestinians and the PFLP-GC in particular.

They set to work on their planning to perpetrate it, acquiring flight timetables and even Pan Am luggage labels for the aircraft. Radio cassettes and timers were acquired for the bomb. The Western intelligence services knew that something was brewing and were on their guard and on high alert. A plane was being targeted and terrorists intent on carrying it out were on the loose. There was considerable fear and alarm. In October of that year, good work by the German police saw a significant PFLP-GC cell detained and broken near Frankfurt in Germany. But that success did not stop the alarm bells ringing. They'd stopped one cell, but there would be others out there, willing and eager to carry on where the others had failed. The security services knew that – hence the Helsinki warning given shortly before Pan Am 103 was downed. The PFLP-GC, though, was badly incapacitated and looked for help. They needed assistance, having lost both men and materiel. That call for help was answered by the Libyans, who already knew of the plans. They were already involved in the supply of timers and other support.

The Libyans picked it up from there. Gaddafi himself stated that they hadn't initiated it. They came in to assist the PFLP-GC. They had experience in bombings in the past and working with the PFLP-GC. They'd already have been sighted on the plan. It was now reaching a new and deadly stage. Malta was to be the setting for it. Gaddafi regretted having the island used for the loading of the bomb, suggesting that if Libya had initiated it then another country would have been selected. Plans were probably so far advanced, however, that to change would be to abort. But, for whatever reason, though, Malta it was to be and steps were taken to prepare.

The clothes were acquired in Malta, though not by Megrahi. The identification is suspect. The attempts to make the purchase fit the two possible dates when Megrahi was there are problematic indeed. The final selection of 7 December to tie in with the big European football fixture fails to take account of the meteorological evidence of there being no rain. Given the importance placed on Gauci recalling an umbrella having been bought, all that seems rather implausible. They were, though, certainly bought at Tony Gauci's family shop in Sliema and by a Libyan. The shop, after all, was only a short distance from the Libyan People's Bureau. It was off the main shopping streets and a big sale would resonate with any shopkeeper; especially one that was strange with little interest being shown by the purchaser.

But, if Megrahi didn't buy the clothes, he was certainly involved. He had held a senior post in the Libyan Security Service as head of airline security which mirrored his job with Libyan Arab Airlines with a similar title. It was after all both a dictatorship and a tribal state. Whether his membership was from choice or circumstance is neither here nor there. The job meant membership and membership meant the job. Even when he left the airline job he retained the accreditation and no doubt the security service post. He had close links and personal friendships with senior officers and also with Abdullah Senussi, who was head of operations at that time for the JSO.

A member he undoubtedly was and given his important job, a relatively senior one. He had after all been identified by Edwin Bollier as being at test explosions of the timers in Libya. He had also been involved in the purchase of radio receivers for the military from MEBO the year before. Also, he'd been involved in the procurement of an antenna for the head of the JSO. That had taken place after he'd left his role with the Airline in January 1987 and when Megrahi himself suggests his links with the JSO had ceased. Yet, the evidence shows that the antennas were ordered in November 1987 and it was Megrahi who conducted the transaction with MEBO for the security service. Indeed, on several occasions, MEBO staff were specifically directed to him. He was the conduit for much of the trade between MEBO and the JSO; much of it was commercial and nothing to do with the Lockerbie bombing or any other atrocity. However, it was done on behalf of the military and security services and shows a level of trust and involvement that would not be afforded a simple middle-man. His offices and roles were of interest and benefit to the regime.

His job allowed him to travel freely and access both countries and areas that would otherwise be restricted or arouse suspicion. Megrahi suggests that his membership was related more to com-mercial links than operational intelligence roles. Using his ability to travel relatively unhindered to carry out transactions for the regime, avoiding sanctions and not covert espionage or terrorism. That's no doubt so. But, he was still an agent and he would obey orders when instructed whatever they were. And so it was to be.

Megrahi flew in to Malta with the suitcase that was to transport the bomb. He travelled on a false passport that he only used once that year; and which he'd never use again. He had used it in 1987 for a trip to Nigeria where on one leg of the trip he had been on the same plane as another senior JSO official, Nassr Ashur, who had also been present at the testing of air detonation bombs. Though the use of such passports was not uncommon in Libya to avoid sanctions, their use was restricted. Moreover, he was unable to give any explanation for his journey. Whilst a court of law does not oblige an accused to testify, the court of public opinion most certainly does. Even in his own biography professing his innocence he simply says he can't recall why he went. It seems entirely incredible that anyone would fly to a foreign country for one night only, using a false passport and have no idea or recollection why they had done so. Finally, and no doubt the reason he chose not to give evidence, he had lied in previous public comments on his actions. In an interview with the TV reporter Pierre Salinger in November 1991 he had denied being involved with Libyan intelligence, which he clearly was; refuted suggestions that he knew or was involved in the acquisition of timers, which he had been; and in particular denied being in Malta on 20 and 21 December under a false passport, during which time he had been staying at the Holiday Inn Hotel, which he did. All quite damning. But, there was more.

The suitcase was a Samsonite model, sold heavily in the Middle East market. Megrahi had been to Malta the month before, which was probably preparatory for the scheme and involved discussions on the logistics of clothes, the suitcase and the bomb equipment. He may even have brought the timers in with him. He would meet with others in the embassy to discuss and build on plans already developed by the PFLP-GC – hence the interlining with a flight through Frankfurt in Germany. Though Megrahi had been involved in the acquisition of timers, and even witnessed their use in tests in Libya, he would not be the bomb maker. That would have been prepared in the Libyan People's Bureau as appears to have occurred in other terrorist incidents, such as the La Belle bombing in Berlin. It's a complex operation that takes experience and knowledge; otherwise it takes the life of the bomber, not the intended victims. However, prepared it was, and, similar to the PFLP-GC ones in some, but not all ways, since it contained two speakers not one.

The Libyan People's Bureau was close not just to Gauci's shop, but also to the hotel Megrahi was staying in that night. He had arrived at Luqa Airport on 20 December at about 5.30 p.m. accompanied by Fhimah, who had only gone back to Tripoli from Malta on 18 December to be briefed; and, as the Crown suggested at the trial, to assist Megrahi back through security at the airport. Fhimah's familiarity with the airport as well as contacts would be crucial. Having deposited the case that night at the Bureau, Megrahi would get it back loaded with both the clothes and the bomb secreted in the Toshiba radio cassette. Megrahi claims that he visited a Maltese man called Vassalo, who ran a travel agency, along with Fhimah that evening. The suggestion being that it shows the innocence of his trip. More likely, it was just filling in time whilst the suitcase was prepared and the bomb was primed.

The evidence of the super grass Abdul Majid referred to Fhimah as well as Megrahi. His entire evidence was discounted by the judges as being tainted. That's understandable in a court of law. He was driven by a desire to defect and obtain financial and other rewards. Much of his testimony appeared to be overblown and subject to hyperbole. It also appears that most of the information relating to Megrahi and Fhimah came out several years later and not at the time. However, that does not mean that everything he said was necessarily untrue – simply that great caution needs to be applied to what he said. A situation similar to the witness Gauci.

After all, Majid had been the assistant manager for LAA at Luqa Airport at the time assisting Fhimah. He was also a Libyan agent. He stated that he'd seen both Megrahi and Fhimah arrive at the airport from a Tripoli flight. He added that they'd been accompanied by two others, one of whom was another Libyan agent, Abu Agila Mas'ud, described as a technician. They'd been driven off in Fhimah's new car, which he'd only recently obtained on 14 December, though who the driver was remains in dispute. Moreover, he said that Fhimah uplifted a brown Samsonite case from the carousel. Megrahi and Fhimah flew in together and no doubt brought the case. Majid is clearly tainted, but some of his evidence still has the ring of truth about it. Megrahi came in with the Samsonite suitcase and Fhimah accompanied him to escort him through the airport.

The technician, Abu Agila Mas'ud, remains a mysterious individual who was clearly a JSO agent. But, he was never allowed to be interviewed by the defence. Requests were made to meet with and interview him but he had been spirited back to Libya and kept out of sight. Similar requests by police and prosecution, who were aware of him, had also been refused. He was one of a number of individuals they had viewed as being implicated in the events. However, when in 1999 investigators had gone to Libya to 'question government ministers, the officials refused to confirm or deny that Mas'ud existed'.[86] He was, therefore, neither interviewed, nor gave evidence

86   Keefe, 'The Avenger', *New Yorker*, 28 September 2015

about his roles and the events. But was he, perhaps, the bomb maker? A technician indeed.

There was good reason for the early suspicions of the investigators that point to Mas'ud as the man who primed the bomb that was placed on board Pan Am flight 103. Research shows him as being implicated in the La Belle bombing in Berlin in 1986. He had gone to the city and stayed in a nearby hotel. He had travelled on the same passport later used by him to go to Malta with Megrahi a few years later when the Lockerbie bomb was placed. According to a German prosecutor, a Libyan convicted of the bombing, Musbah Eter, stated that Mas'ud 'had brought the La Belle bomb to the Libyan embassy in East Berlin and instructed him how to arm it'. The convicted Libyan terrorist also subsequently told US investigators that 'Mas'ud and Megrahi were involved in Lockerbie, and that he heard Mas'ud speak of travelling to Malta to prepare the attack'.[87]

He remained out of sight for many years and through the trials, appeals and ultimate release of Megrahi. However, he has since surfaced and further information provided leads to the conclusion that the initial thoughts of the investigators were correct. As the Gaddafi regime fell, the protected became the pursued. Information on Mas'ud surfaced through diligent research by an American filmmaker and investigations by Human Rights Watch. They located him languishing in a Libyan prison cell and awaiting trial for bomb making. Not, though, for a trial about the devastation wrecked on Pan Am 103 or the town of Lockerbie, but 'of using remote-detonated

---

87 Ibid.

explosive devices to booby-trap the cars of Libyan opposition members in 2011, after revolution broke out'.[88] He has since been sentenced to ten years' imprisonment and is incarcerated in the cells once inhabited by Gaddafi and his henchmen's victims.

So, the bomb was prepared and primed, but it still needed to be placed on board the Air Malta flight. The following morning, Megrahi phoned Fhimah just after 7 a.m. to arrange a lift to the airport. Megrahi states he called but someone other than Fhimah answered. As a result, he said he took a taxi to the airport. He suggests that Fhimah later said he'd overslept, but the number called appeared correct and the call was made. Whether the call was to arrange a lift, notify of his departure or was answered, however, is irrelevant. It may have suited them to suggest they were separate to limit suspicions of collusion. What is certain is that they both arrived at the airport.

Megrahi arrived at the time of the loading of the Air Malta flight to Frankfurt. His flight to Tripoli saw check-in open at 8.50 a.m. and close at 9.50 a.m. The Air Malta fight to Frankfurt opened at 8.15 a.m. and closed at 9.15 a.m. Megrahi was checked in early by a lady at an Air Malta desk dealing with flights to Cairo. It was an adjacent desk to the LAA ones. That check-in had opened at 8.35 a.m. and was due to close at 9.35 a.m. Megrahi was checked on to the LAA flight sixth. According to the airline clerk, that would have been early on. That assistance at different airline counters was normal and was simply done to ease congestion. However, in particular,

88 Ibid.

it was for passengers travelling without luggage. Megrahi was going back without any suitcase, which was why she checked him in. That, also, was never clarified by him. Not only was the purpose of his trip never answered but why he landed with a bag and travelled back without one remained unexplained. But, he had firstly visited the LAA offices. There he met Fhimah and the suitcase was handed over. The case Megrahi had brought with him was not going back with him, but was being placed on board the Air Malta flight bound for Frankfurt, primed with the bomb that would detonate aboard the JFK flight from Heathrow. Megrahi's work was done; it was now for others to take over.

How was the bomb placed aboard? The case Megrahi brought with him would be tagged and placed for loading but not on the flight he was going on. Luggage labels for Air Malta were available. Fhimah, after all, had made a note to obtain them. His diary, that had been referred to in court, had noted on the page for 15 December to 'take tags from Air Malta'. It had also been subsequently marked 'ok' but in a different colour. It had also narrated, 'take/collect tags from the airport (Abdulbaset/Abdussalam)'. 'Tags' had been written in English and the rest in Arabic. The court accepted that but felt unable to draw the inference that it was to allow for an interlined bag to be placed on board; and accordingly that there was sufficient evidence for a conviction of Fhimah. However, they were certainly highly suspicious actions and led to the conclusion that Megrahi took the case to the airport, but it was Fhimah who would get it airside and beyond security. After all, he had flown out to Libya to accompany Megrahi back with the case and had made notes to prepare for that, including obtaining Air Malta tags. He had security passes, but more importantly a detailed knowledge of the airport and its layout which Megrahi did not have.

It was labelled for Air Malta, to be routed onto Pan Am through Frankfurt and Heathrow and to New York with the tags Fhimah's diary had referred to. The bag was placed in the system going airside without going through the formal check-in desks. Evidence was led at the trial that when the airport was extremely busy, airline representatives, including Fhimah, would help passengers and assist in placing luggage on the conveyor belt. Fhimah was familiar both with the procedures and to the staff who worked there. Placing a bag behind and into the system was a relatively simple task given the accreditation and access Fhimah had. The bag was tagged and en route to loading, but there were still significant other checks to overcome.

Behind the check-in desks was a conveyor belt similar to most other modern airports. Beyond that was a solid wall separating that space from the airside area. Doors connected the two areas but they were secure and kept locked as well as being guarded by the army. Behind the security walls, bags underwent sniffer checks and were held pending loading onto the particular flight. The checks at the final loading on to the plane correlated the numbers with those shown on the computer-recorded register for boarding. The numbers were meant to include both interline and rush bags. If there was a discrepancy, there was supposed to be a reconciliation check carried out.

How that was circumvented remains the great mystery of the Lockerbie affair. The sniffer test would have been relatively simple to overcome as semtex has no smell and the X-ray procedures may even have been circumvented by Fhimah. It may simply have been luck and the bag was miscounted. It may have been corruption or collusion with other airport officials, though that was never raised at the trial or FAI. It is possible that there were additional agents or sleepers involved in circumventing the tight military security at the airport and the checking of the manifest with bags at the hold. There were, after all, suggestions of security documentation going missing for the 20th and 21st.

The prosecution suggested at the trial that if there were fewer than five items out in a count, then reconciliation was dispensed with. That was denied by both the airport and Air Malta. There didn't appear to be any specific evidence to support that at the time but it does appear perfectly understandable. It may have been frowned on by management but equally may have become custom and practice. That's, after all, why the Crown referred to it. Counting must have been fraught at a busy airport, with many flights embarking and arriving. Disembarking an entire flight with the consequent inconvenience to passengers, airline and airport would have been significant. It would only have been done sparingly. The likelihood of some slight human error would have been high and balancing that with speed and embarkation perfectly understandable at those times. Passengers being disembarked for a reconciliation would have been a rare as well as unwelcome event. The airport still thought it unlikely that a case would get through, but conceded it was possible. They, though, had a vested interest in denying any slackness or culpability. Pan Am, after all, had paid the price in the courts for slack procedures but seemed to simply do the same checks as many others.

It will probably never be known just how the security measures were breached, but no doubt that was why the plot involved those with accreditation, access and knowledge of the airport. If anyone would know how to do it, then Fhimah would. The bag that Megrahi had brought in was placed on to the Air Malta flight to be transferred at Frankfurt for the fateful rendezvous in Heathrow. The records show that an unaccompanied bag was unloaded at Frankfurt from the Air Malta flight, yet the records from Luqa do not disclose that piece of unaccompanied luggage being loaded. There is no suggestion, though, that the Frankfurt airport authorities are mistaken. It was accepted by both the FAI and the court at Camp Zeist that it had been on that flight from Malta. It was thereafter routed with other unaccompanied baggage to be placed in a container; and thus on board Pan Am 103.

As it was an interlined bag, it was subject only to X-ray rather than a physical check; nor would there be an administrative match to a passenger before being loaded and going straight through airport procedures. It, thereafter, went through the system all the way to Heathrow and onto the JFK-bound flight. At Heathrow the Frankfurt bags were placed on a container that was the seat of the bomb. That container AVE 4041 had the interlined bags, including the Samsonite suitcase and others from Frankfurt. The links were clearly there. Pan Am 103 was doomed and the bomb that would be detonated over Lockerbie had been primed and placed aboard in Malta.

As mentioned before, there are aspects of the bombing that remain a mystery to this day. Given the nature of those involved and the passage of time, that's understandable. Moreover, given the death of many and the lying low of others, it's probable it will remain that way for ever. There are also aspects of the case that could not be sustained in a court of law with the high standard of proof beyond reasonable doubt required and specific rules on evidence needed. There are equally aspects of the case that may not have seen a criminal conviction sustained on appeal. But, this account of how the bombing was carried out and by whom is based on information gathered meticulously by police and prosecutors from the US, Scotland and elsewhere. It's also founded on intelligence and sources not available for a court or that have only come to light thereafter. Finally, it's also predicated on the words of the leader of Libya himself, Muammar Gaddafi, and those who replaced him when the regime fell. The suggestions of conspiracies by others known or unknown are fanciful.

The protestations of innocence by Megrahi are equally so, though his role was a very limited one. He was but a cog in a very much larger wheel, acting under orders from those far more senior than him. The triumvirate of Gaddafi, Senussi and Koussa were all involved, as would have been others in senior positions in the Libyan regime. This, after all, went right to the heart of the state, not simply to a JSO agent carrying a suitcase with a bomb.

Libya did it, Megrahi was part of it and other states and terrorist organisations also played their part. It was in revenge for the downing of the Iran Air flight by a US naval ship. It was, therefore, a coalition of the willing that brought down Pan Am 103.

WHAT HAPPENED NEXT?

When the dust settled after the return of Megrahi, the US and UK hoped that the relationship that they had been cultivating with Gaddafi would flourish. Certainly, commercial links boomed both for investment in Libyan natural resources and the sale of armaments to the Gaddafi regime. BP was to benefit, as had Anglo Shell before it and many multinationals from all parts of the globe. Equally, the sale of armaments to the regime mushroomed along with the training of defence forces. Even the US got in on the act, if somewhat belatedly compared with others. Armoured vehicles and personnel carriers had or were in the process of being sold when the regime fell. Discussions were also ongoing about the training of Libyan officers in counter-terrorism training similar to what the UK had been doing.[89]

---

89 Chorin, *Exit the Colonel*, p. 281

However, whilst the UK and US were nurturing the Libyan regime with one hand, they were equally preparing to destroy it with the other. Hopes that Gaddafi could be restrained and perhaps even the country democratised proved groundless. Even before the Arab Spring, it was realised that his behaviour remained unstable and his actions erratic. The issue over the arrest of Bulgarian medical staff accused of infecting Libyan children with HIV had run on from 1999 but remained a running sore. Other actions equally bemused and infuriated the West, notwithstanding the arms and ammunition they were happy to sell him. Similarly, he had had few friends in the Arab world and change was in the air. The enemies he had created over all those years were to prove his final undoing.

Trouble had been brewing in Libya before the commencement of the Arab Spring. The east of the country around Benghazi was always fraught for the regime. A different tribe from those in Gaddafi's inner circles, they had been and still felt different. Moreover, added to that was the spectre of Islamic insurgency against the Libyan state, again much concentrated in that part of the country.

So, when the Arab Spring commenced in Tunisia in December 2010, Libya would not be far behind. Demonstrations were held in Benghazi and other towns in the months following and the regime began to totter. The Gaddafi regime oscillated between repression and conciliation as it struggled to maintain a grip of events convulsing much of the Arab world at that time. Bigger forces than even Gaddafi and his henchmen were now at play. They included not just the Western powers and the UK and US in particular, but also the infectious revolution garnering not just the young and the religious, but many others simply desiring change after forty years of brutal rule. However, the regime was not without its supporters. The tribal loyalties ran deep and many had much to lose by the fall of the regime. Libya was heading for a civil war.

Demonstrations grew into open insurgency and the battleground spread out from Benghazi across most of the country. Open warfare was now taking place and those seeking to depose the regime sought the help and assistance of the West. Many, especially in the military in the US, were reluctant to be brought into yet another conflict. Iraq and Afghanistan were already stretching personnel and another field of conflict could result in it reaching breaking point. Political calculations, though, overruled the military doubts.[90]

The Obama administration and other Western governments had waxed lyrically about the Arab Spring and the winds of change blowing through North Africa and beyond. In March 2009, President Obama himself had made his Cairo declaration, stating unequivocally:

> Born, as we are, out of a revolution, by those who longed to
> be free, we welcome the fact that history is on the move in the
> Middle East and North Africa, and that young people are lead-
> ing the way. Because wherever people long to be free, they will
> find a friend in the United States.[91]

Libya began to be isolated and cut loose after years of the US and the West seeking to bring them back into the fold. The UN voted

---

90 Ibid.
91 Ibid., p. 209–10

for a no-fly zone supported by the majority of the Arab League on 17 March 2011. They condemned the action of the Gaddafi regime; though similar statements could be made about other regimes before and since in that part of the world. But, whilst that offered some respite, it was evident it would be insufficient to stop Gaddafi punishing and in all likelihood destroying the opposition with his heavier weaponry and garnering supporters including foreign mercenaries. Much of the armoury, ironically, was provided by the West when cultivating Gaddafi. Now, they were to be used against those seeking his removal. The cries for humanitarian aid were becoming loud and pitiful as the regime fought bitterly to hang on to power. Atrocities were being perpetrated on all sides but the danger was that Gaddafi would crush the opposition and be strengthened in power. Military action was therefore needed to tip the balance in the favour of the rebel forces or Gaddafi might win.

What seemed to tip the balance for intervention in Libya as narrated by one well-placed commentator was that 'the US had freedom to act without upending long-standing and economically valuable relationships'.[92] Gaddafi was odious, that was for sure, and his actions reprehensible. But, that could equally apply to many leaders or regimes in those parts. The Arab Spring and the winds of change would be welcomed in some parts and some regimes but not in others. Some were too important in their trade or political importance to seek to remove; others, though, were expendable. And so it was to prove for Gaddafi. Saudi Arabia and Bahrain amongst others could

---

92 Ibid., p. 282

be despotic and barbaric but act with impunity from the West. The Libyan leader was not to be so favoured. And so it remains to this day – some despots have gone but others have stayed. It's all been dependent on their relationship and strategic importance to the West, both trade and militarily.

The NATO bombing started in March 2011 and the Gaddafi empire was soon to fall. The intervention turned the tables on the regime, which had possessed heavier firepower and equipment. The Libyan Army and Gaddafi supporters were rolled back and began to fragment and flee. Peace and democracy has not, though, come to Libya and instead it appears torn by warlordism and factionalism. The troubles and afflictions imposed upon them by forty years of dictatorial rule have now been compounded by the collapse of civil order in many parts. Now, it is the base for refugees seeking to flee to Europe. A most distressful country for a long-suffering people.

Megrahi had died whilst the regime was crumbling. Gaddafi himself was slain by revolutionaries in October of that year. Moussa Koussa defected to the West early on 31 March. Ostensibly going on holiday to Tunisia, he was in fact spirited to London by MI6 to be debriefed.[93] Ironic in many ways given that he had been expelled from the UK in 1980 when working at the Libyan embassy in London for making threats against Libyan émigrés. He now lives in a luxury hotel in Qatar; by whom this is paid for is unknown. Abdullah Senussi fled to Mauritania. He was extradited back to Libya where he has been sentenced to death, along with Saif Gaddafi, for crimes carried out by

---

93   Ibid., p. 229

the regime. Those primarily responsible for the Lockerbie bombing are therefore either dead, dying or have gone to ground. Some of the mystery over what happened on 21 December still remains and with those involved no longer around to tell will remain unsolved for ever.

As for me, it was a privilege to serve as Justice Secretary for Scotland. I neither anticipated it nor any involvement with Lockerbie. In many ways, though, it has come to define my tenure in office. The interest in my decision was not just national but international, and though it has not been without consequence for me, I stand by what I did. It was stressful in many ways but I was ably supported by those who worked for me. Others pursued vested commercial interests or covert security agendas and were prepared, if not conspiring, to impugn the Scottish government. However, I believe I followed the rules and applied the values we live by in Scotland. I stepped down from Parliament to pursue other interests, but it was a privilege to serve and I departed with my head held high.

Like the assassination of John F. Kennedy or even the landing of a man on the moon conspiracy, theories will run for time eternal. That will no doubt be the case with Lockerbie. But, the evidence shows who did it, why they did it and how they did it. It also shows that the Lockerbie bombing did not happen in isolation but as part of a battle being waged by and against terrorism. Moreover, that both it and the Scottish legal processes that followed were but a small part of a much wider picture driven by international commercial and security pressures. Scotland and Megrahi were small cogs in a much bigger wheel.

ACKNOWLEDGEMENTS

I am grateful to all those countless individuals in both government and agencies who supported me during my involvement with Lockerbie. They include my private office and Scottish government justice officials, the Scottish Prison Service, law officers and Police Scotland. Their support was invaluable and their care much appreciated.

I'm also indebted to the many people who contacted me simply to wish me well. Some were friends and family but many more were strangers who just got in touch. Their kindness was greatly appreciated.

In writing this book, I am indebted to Linda Hamilton for her constructive comments at a time when she had both a demanding job and a young family. To Linda Pollock, Alistair Duff, Tom Halpin, David Strang and Tom Fox, who were generous with their time and insight. To Rosemary Goring for her helpful and considerate advice at the outset. To Caroline Michel and her team at PFD for their support. To Victoria Godden, my editor, for her patience and diligence under severe time pressures.